The
BIG BOOK
of
ANGEL
STORIES

ALSO BY JENNY SMEDLEY:

Past Life Angels

Past Life (meditation CD)

Souls Don't Lie

The Tree That Talked

How to Be Happy

Forever Faithful

Supernaturally True

Pets Have Souls Too

Angel Whispers

Soul Angels

Everyday Angels

Pets Are Forever

Angels Please Hear Me

A Year with the Angels

My Angel Diary 2012

An Angel by Your Side

Soul Mates

My Angel Diary 2013

My Angel Diary 2014

My Angel Diary 2015

Angelic Healing

My Angel Diary 2017

The
BIG BOOK
of
ANGEL
STORIES

JENNY SMEDLEY

HAY HOUSE

Carlsbad, California • New York City • London
Sydney •Johannesburg • Vancouver • New Delhi

First published and distributed in the United Kingdom by:
Hay House UK Ltd, Astley House, 33 Notting Hill Gate, London W11 3JQ
Tel: +44 (0)20 3675 2450; Fax: +44 (0)20 3675 2451
www.hayhouse.co.uk

Published and distributed in the United States of America by:
Hay House Inc., PO Box 5100, Carlsbad, CA 92018-5100
Tel: (1) 760 431 7695 or (800) 654 5126; Fax: (1) 760 431 6948 or (800) 650 5115
www.hayhouse.com

Published and distributed in Australia by:
Hay House Australia Ltd, 18/36 Ralph St, Alexandria NSW 2015
Tel: (61) 2 9669 4299; Fax: (61) 2 9669 4144
www.hayhouse.com.au

Published and distributed in the Republic of South Africa by:
Hay House SA (Pty) Ltd, PO Box 990, Witkoppen 2068
info@hayhouse.co.za; www.hayhouse.co.za

Published and distributed in India by:
Hay House Publishers India, Muskaan Complex, Plot No.3, B-2,
Vasant Kunj, New Delhi 110 070
Tel: (91) 11 4176 1620; Fax: (91) 11 4176 1630
www.hayhouse.co.in

Distributed in Canada by:
Raincoast Books, 2440 Viking Way, Richmond, B.C. V6V 1N2
Tel: (1) 604 448 7100; Fax: (1) 604 270 7161; www.raincoast.com

A catalogue record for this book is available from the British Library.

ISBN: 978-1-78180-853-5

Interior images: 1, 25, 59, 115, 125, 181, 211, 223, 237, 251, 303 123RF/Ekaterina Glazkova

CONTENTS

Introduction   vii

Chapter 1: Angels Answering Cries for Help ... or Not?   1

Chapter 2: Angels Bringing Past-life Knowledge   25

Chapter 3: Angels Who Help Us When We Lose Loved Ones   59

Chapter 4: The Baby Angel   115

Chapter 5: Angels Who Use Animals to Help Us   125

Chapter 6: Angel Rescuers   181

Chapter 7: Angels Who Help Us to Heal Animals   211

Chapter 8: Angels Who Heal the Body   223

Chapter 9: Angels Who Heal the Mind   237

Chapter 10: Angels Who Show Themselves in Strange Ways   251

Angels in the News   303

Resources   309

About the Author   311

INTRODUCTION

Now that I think back, there was never a time when I really didn't believe in angels. Certainly I went through phases of my adult life when I wondered if mine had gone on strike, or abandoned me, but deep inside I always knew the amazing truth, which was forever trembling to break free. Even when I was a small child I had an inner knowledge (as all children do), that I rubbed shoulders with these beings every day of my life, and that this seemed quite natural and not extraordinary in any way. It was only as I grew up and struggled (as all children do) to fit in with society and its latest fashionable belief or non-belief that I came to see a connection with angels as some mystical, unattainable, imaginary dream, and one that only the foolish among us admitted to. The 'middle' time of our spiritual growth that most of us have to endure is so sad. But with me, as it is for everyone, even if only in the final second of life, there came a time at last when a blinding flash burst forth and revealed that losing my childlike faith was what had made me foolish!

Now when I look back and visualize a map of my life, I can see when and where angels stepped in to help me, guide me, save me and bring me to my full potential, even if I gave them no credit for it at the time. Such is the way of angels: they *never* go on strike, no matter how frustrating our behaviour is; they *never* abandon us and they believe in us even if we stop believing in them for a while.

My real awakening came at the age of 45, when angels came to me at my darkest moment and showed me the truth of who I really was, what my history had been and how to walk forward with an unshakeable faith in them that has not been, and will never be, broken.

Since then, in the angel-led second half of my life, I have been immersed in angels: hosting a TV show, guesting on TV and radio, writing songs and books, learning to be guided to paint angels digitally and altogether having a wonderful time. Through this I have met, interviewed and written about hundreds of people who have been helped by angels, had their moment of unquestionable truth and never doubted the angels' presence again. In this book I have brought together some of their emotionally charged and indisputably angelic stories to share with you.

Chapter 1

ANGELS ANSWERING CRIES FOR HELP ... OR NOT?

People often ask me if angels 'always' help you when you ask them. And yes, the answer is always unequivocally that they *do* help us. Because angels always give you what you need. The problem we have as humans is that what we need is not always the same as what we want. I know that might sound clichéd, but this doesn't mean it isn't true. Many times in my life I've wanted something desperately and it's not been granted. Like most people I'd become transfixed with the story I thought should happen, and didn't think about what other outcomes there could be.

Humans tend to want to travel straight from A to B in the shortest time possible and I'm no different. It's only after we face the disappointment of things not happening as we expected them to, and yet find that we've still reached the other side of the rainbow, that we look back and see how much wiser than us angels are and how their apparent roundabout and tedious route has taken us to exactly where we wanted to go, but in such a non-linear way that we barely noticed it happening. We also often realize then that the way *we* had hoped things would happen would have been a big mistake if they had unfolded that way.

The following stories show both answered prayers and prayers that were apparently not answered. I am really grateful for these contributors sharing their personal stories with me, in order to help other people find the peace they long for.

One story in this chapter is about a lost lilo. Now it may seem that a lost lilo is a pretty trivial thing for an angel to help out with. In fact, I even had someone criticize me for telling people to ask their angels for help with things such as finding lost handbags, saying that angel energy surely shouldn't be wasted on something so meaningless. But in cases like this, it isn't so much the act, but the sign. The person who sent this story was in the right frame of energy at the time and her angel saw a good opportunity to prove their existence to her. That is why I will continue to tell people to start by asking their angel for help with small requests, and a lost lilo fits perfectly under that heading.

I once met a man – I'll call him George for the sake of his privacy – who told me that he'd been a heroin addict for quite a few years. All he wanted in life was enough cash to 'score' whenever he wanted to, to buy a fast car and to attract a girlfriend who would take care of him and get high with him. He got the cash, the car and the girl, but these were all things he wanted, not needed, and his angel knew better. Inside, his soul was crying out. He hated how his parents broke down and cried when they saw his addiction, but he didn't know how to stop. He hated the way people looked at him with condemnation in their eyes. He hated the deep hunger he felt, but didn't know how to appease it. He hated the scars on his arms that were caused by collapsed veins and showed everyone what he was, and he often thought of getting a tattoo to cover them. Finally, in desperation, he asked his angels to help him find a way out of his life.

A few days later he was involved in a terrible car crash while under the influence of drugs. He broke his pelvis very badly. While he was hospitalized and drifting in and out of consciousness, he saw his angel reaching out a hand to him and he took it. From that day the doctors agreed to help him fight his addiction, and his parents were reconciled with him because they saw the change in him. He fought his way back one day at a time to a good life. He still struggles because he knows his addiction is for life, but he also knows for sure that his angels will help him be who he really needs to be. He knows this because his angel told him that the tell-tale scars from the collapsed veins would disappear without the need for a tattoo. When he had his bandages removed from his lacerated arms, the heroin needle marks were gone, replaced by bumpy, but clean, white skin. George thought he wanted money, but bizarrely what he actually needed was to be injured in a car crash.

 *Gordon's story*

The freezer warehouse was the biggest shop I've ever seen. We're going back a few years now to when I was a stripling – a mere 80 years old. I'm 97 now. In those days freezers were, I believe, heavier than they are now. I was watching this young boy running riot through the place, opening and slamming lids on freezers and taking no notice of his mum's shouting or the salespeople's dirty looks. I was thinking about buying a small freezer – not one of the mammoth ones, no point with there just being me at home. Anyway, it seems that the kid's parents finally made a choice and were ushered away into the office to sign the papers or whatever. The kid, me and one salesgirl down the other end were the only ones left. I guess the parents thought their child couldn't do much harm to all these boxes – he was only about four years old anyway – and maybe they relished his being out of their way for a bit in the what, to him, was a huge playground.

Next thing I knew I heard a loud and terrified yell from the salesgirl. I turned and looked and she was pointing about halfway down the store. I don't know how it happened but it seems a stand had given way on one corner, and the precariously balanced chest freezer on it had toppled over. The boy was trapped underneath it. I ran for it. I hadn't run in years, but now I did, sprinting down the aisle and beating the girl there. The little lad was pinned on his back with the freezer across his tummy. I could hear voices, as I think the parents were shouting something, asking what was wrong, but they couldn't see from where they were. I reached down with both hands and hauled at the freezer. It wouldn't budge, of course. I looked heavenwards and yelled, 'Help me!' I grabbed the freezer again and, to my constant and everlasting amazement, the freezer seemed to suddenly weigh just a few pounds. I lifted it up and off the boy and stood it on the floor.

Then I fell over. I sat there panting as the lad jumped up, unharmed, just in time for a rollicking from his mum and dad. The salesgirl stood there, mouth open in astonishment at what she'd seen me do, but really everyone else was thinking about the boy. I'm guessing the parents were wondering if they were going to have to pay for the freezer, and the manager, who by then had heard the screams and come running, was wondering if he was going to be sued.

Me? I was just wondering what exactly had given me that temporary strength…

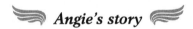 *Angie's story*

My faith in angels is strong, and I'm happy to say that my son has inherited that connection and trust, and isn't shy of admitting it. One day he was desperate to win a raffle prize and told me he would ask his angels to help him. He sat quietly asking and heard a lady nearby say, 'I am going to be so sad if you don't win now.'

He told her 'My angels always help me,' and with that they pulled the first ticket and it was his. He was so thrilled, the lady and I were choking back tears, and I felt that my son winning was a clear message to her, as it was a Stand Against Violence event and she needed to hear that angels are real so that she would ask for their help.

Concetta's story

From an early age I was visited by an angel who told me I'd never have children of my own. As I grew up I wanted the things that most young girls want – to get married and have a family of my own. But I always remembered what the angel had told me when I was a child. It wasn't until I met and married my husband, John, that I really started to worry about her message.

I'd only been married a short time when I had a tubular pregnancy that involved surgery. I was devastated, to say the least. But again I was visited by angels, this time telling me everything would be all right. I was told that I had a special mission in this life, which I didn't understand at the time.

As the first couple of years of my marriage passed by I began to wonder if I really was never going to have children. When I'd been younger, the same angels who told me I wouldn't, also told me that I'd have something to do with raising children. So I was confused. When I married John, who has two children from his first marriage, it truly didn't dawn on me that these were the two children I was to be involved with raising. And I continued to be visited by angels who were trying to help me let go of my goal, encouraging me to look ahead to a future without children of my own. This was very, very hard for me to do. I couldn't fathom what else could possibly fill my life, what else I could do that would contribute something positive to life. But all along I was being visited by many angels – spirits I had never known in this life, but who I knew loved me. I was also having difficulty with my husband's family, who never had taken to me. Knowing that they would all be happy if I couldn't have children made this experience all the more painful to deal with. I just couldn't give up. By then I was investing in in-vitro treatment, my last resort. But, nothing happened.

And still angels were present in my life: walking with me, consoling me, loving me, telling me it was going to be all right. They continued to reassure me that there was something I would be able to contribute, something I'd be able to give to life, to others' lives. You might think with all this heavenly reassurance I would be certain about the way things were meant to be and that I would be at peace with that. But I had no notion of the role I was to play. To say that I was angry and disillusioned with life would be to put it mildly. I was so unhappy. I felt betrayed by God. I felt useless as a woman.

But through all of this, I was visited by angels telling me to trust God because everything would work out. And slowly – very slowly – I made a choice to believe what they were telling me. I made a choice to trust God. And slowly I began to see the light. I began my work with the Other Side. I got older and wiser and began to realize the importance of the work I was doing, that this was my contribution. That, even without having children, I *do* make a difference to many children in this life here on Earth. I have a stepdaughter who is also 'my' daughter. She loves me and is one of my best friends. I have grandchildren, I receive Mother's Day cards. What the angels told me is true: without having children of my own, I'm still a mother.

I never thought I could be happy without my own children, but I'm pretty close to complete peace with that. I don't have to worry about every moment they are not in my sight. I don't think of myself as ever being alone because I have made lifelong friends, who are as close as family to my husband and me. And doing my work and living my life as I have has shown me that children are not always what young girls' fairy tales tell us they're going to be. In short, the angels were right, it's all OK.

I know how lucky I am to be able to hear the angels who surround me. But even if you can't hear them they are there.

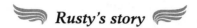 ## *Rusty's story*

Out the front of my mother's gift store in Florida was a clear view of a sidewalk, a massive parking lot and a major four-lane road. She'd been praying for some information on how to be an effective witness to people of the Jewish faith without being offensive to them.

One afternoon, the door opened and a tall, handsome young man with a backpack came in. Mother looked up surprised and asked, 'I didn't see you come across the sidewalk or the parking lot, how did you get here?'

In answer he just laid his backpack on the counter, took out a file of papers and handed it to her saying, 'I was told you needed this.'

My mother saw that it was the information she'd prayed about. She was amazed and said, 'Yes, I do need this. Thank you.'

The young man replied, 'Well, now you have it.'

Mother invited him to church with us the next day, Sunday, and he agreed to meet us there. He turned to leave as the telephone rang. Mother picked it up. When she looked back up the man had vanished. She went outside to find him so she could thank him for the literature and he was nowhere in sight of the centre, the parking lot or the road.

On Sunday at church, Mother looked over her shoulder and on the very last pew was the young man, and he'd brought a female friend with him. Mother went back and spoke to them, shook their hands and welcomed them to the service, and invited them to join us at home for lunch. She told my dad they were in the rear of the church, and he turned and looked at them. He waved and they waved back. At the end of the service people started leaving and the pastor shook everyone's hand as they passed. My mother asked the pastor if the couple had come out. He said he'd seen them sitting in the pew and they hadn't come out, but still they were gone. The mystery was discussed among our family for years as Mother thought they were angels.

Later I returned to Florida and to that same church and pastor. One night the pastor, his wife and I were dining together. I brought up my mom's angel story. The pastor looked at me, amazed. He said, 'Now, let me tell you the rest of the story that your parents didn't know. Sometime after you moved away, I was preaching on a Sunday night. I looked in the back of the church and there sat a young man I thought I'd seen before, but I wasn't sure. At the end I asked that anyone who wished to accept Christ as their Saviour come down and be baptized, and the young man did. We went to the baptismal room to change clothes.'

The small baptismal room was adjacent to the altar. Two ushers would join you, hand you a blue robe to put on and hold a sheet up while you removed your clothes and put on the robe. Then you'd walk upstairs and across the landing to the edge of the baptismal pool. The young man changed into the blue robe, ascended the stairs, walked into the water and was baptized, and then he walked out.

The pastor continued, 'After I baptized a young lady, I left the water and went down the stairs where the two ushers were. I then asked them where the young man was. And they looked at me as if I was joking. I asked, "What's wrong?"'

'The ushers replied, "Preacher, the young man is still up there, right? 'Cause he didn't come down the stairs."'

'I said, "Sure he did, I baptized him and he came down here."'

'They then said, "He never came down the stairs." At that point I remembered where I'd seen him before. It was when your mother had invited him to church – the same man. I'd just baptized an angel!'

My mother passed away a few weeks ago – I wonder what she thought if she saw that same young man in his angelic form inside the celestial city of God.

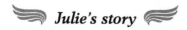 *Julie's story*

At a really low point in my life my husband and I camped out on a beach in Wales. We were sleeping on inflatable lilos inside the tent at night and using them in the sea by day. One day the wind got up and I let go of my lilo, and in seconds it had flipped out to sea. There was no chance of me getting it back. We couldn't even see it! I felt doomed at the prospect of sleeping on the floor the next night, so I said out loud, 'Well, if there is an angel of lilos, please can I have mine back?'

Nothing happened, so we carried on swimming and generally messing around with the remaining one. About five minutes later a guy on a jet ski turned up with the lilo tucked under his arm. He handed it back to me and didn't even say anything! How on Earth did he know it was mine when there were so many others on the beach? And where had he come from anyway? I have no idea because we hadn't even seen any jet-skiers that day! Strange but true!

Also, a lot of people ask me, 'What is the name of my guardian angel?'

And I reply, 'The very first name that comes into your head.' I did a meditation once to meet my guardian angel and the name I got was Henry. I was floored – everyone else had Raphael or Serena and all other kinds of fancy names. And I got Henry. I could see him very clearly, like a guy from the 1960s with a side parting – and a white robe. I said, 'OK, if your name is Henry I need confirmation three times in the next three weeks, please.'

That day I saw Lenny Henry, Henry Cooper and a Henry Hoover in three different locations!

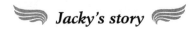 *Jacky's story*

When I was 18 years old and very impressionable, I fell in love with a boy called Kevin. Of course I thought the sun rose in his eyes, but after a while he betrayed me and dumped me. I was so upset I thought I'd die. As far as I was concerned, love was over for me. I thought I'd never find anyone else to love me. But I used every ounce of my strength, told my angels that I trusted them and tried to throw myself into my life. Just a couple of days later I was standing outside a shop in the mall when someone touched my shoulder very lightly. I turned around to see a strange-looking young man, dressed quite raggedly and looking pretty dirty. My impulse was to pull back, but something in his eyes made me stay close to him.

He said, 'Stop worrying so much, dear heart' (a strange and old-fashioned thing to call me!). 'Your life will come back on track and one day you'll even have a son. You'll call him Arthur.' I had to smile because I couldn't ever imagine calling a son by such a dated name. The young man turned and walked away and he moved very strangely, too, almost like his feet were a couple of inches off the ground.

Just two years later I met Gary and it was love at first sight. We had a son two years after that and I did call him Arthur, but not because I'd come to love the name or because of what I'd been told, but because, as it turned out, Gary's dad, grandad and great-grandad were all called Arthur.

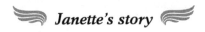 *Janette's story*

Last summer my partner, Andrew, bought me a pack of angel cards. I loved them and started reading everything about angels I could find. Very shortly thereafter I began feeling very peaceful about myself and started meditating, and asked the angels for a sign that they did indeed exist. Three days later Andrew and I visited a very old church and decided to take some photos. Andrew wanted one of me, so I walked about 30 feet away so he could take it.

As I stood there I heard a laugh and turned to see a lovely old man sitting on a bench to my right, smiling at me, and he said, 'Ha ha! I am going to be in your photo now!'

I laughingly said back, 'Well, I don't mind at all.'

We downloaded the photos on getting home and there was nobody sitting on the bench. I believe the old man was an angel sent to reassure me that angels were indeed real, and to tell me that I was on the right path.

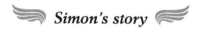

Simon's story

I'm a long-distance HGV driver for a small company and I started when I was about 22 years old. My parents were always worried about me and insisted that I called them whenever I arrived where I was going, so that they'd know I was all right. They hated all the miles I did on motorways in particular, as these roads are notoriously dangerous. However, when danger did come it was on a country road. My nanna used to smile when Mum and Dad voiced their worries, and say, 'He'll be all right, can't you see that light of angels around him?' Since when though do people listen to their parents? Mum and Dad still worried. Nanna would chat to me and encourage me in 'nonsense' as my parents called it. But I loved her stories of angels helping people and I liked to think I did have an angel.

This night I was heading towards home and the truck was empty, which was a good thing! It was a dark country road with no street lighting a few miles from the M6, which I was heading for. I don't like driving in lanes at night in my car because the glare of approaching lights can be awful, but in the truck I was higher up and it wasn't so much of a problem. Because of that I was able to see what the driver coming the other way couldn't. There was a stag standing in the road. It was a big red deer, and I knew that when the driver of the oncoming car saw it, he'd swerve, because if he hit it, it would destroy his car. It might seem stupid that he'd come at me in my several-ton truck instead, but that's human nature for you. We tend to react to the immediate.

Sure enough the car swerved onto my side of the road. I was already braking in anticipation, but it wasn't going to stop the inevitable collision. I had to turn the wheel left towards the hedge, because at least I'd give the car driver and maybe the passengers, if he had any, some chance of survival. The truck wheels went into a ditch I hadn't seen though, and it was my vehicle that went off the road and tumbled into a field. The car apparently missed the truck by inches.

As I realized that the field was really a hill and that my truck was going to somersault down it, I was scared for a moment, but then I heard Nanna's words in my head and for the first time I actually saw and felt the white light around me. It was as if I was in a bubble. The noise of the truck as it hurtled towards its doom, as inevitable as a dying dinosaur, was horrendous, but I wasn't afraid. I felt my body being catapulted around the cab, but I didn't feel any pain. When the noise and the motion finally stopped, all I could hear was the hissing of hot water from the radiator and, outside, only silence. There had been four people in the car and they all came running, not a scratch on them, expecting, judging by their voices, to find a dead body smashed to pieces. They dragged open the driver's door and stopped dead, as if they'd seen a ghost, when I looked calmly back at them.

Afterwards when I looked at my trashed truck from outside, I could see why they were so amazed to find me not only alive, but unhurt. There was no way I should have walked away from that crash. After that day my parents didn't laugh at Nanna any more.

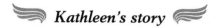

Kathleen's story

I was stranded on the side of a road in a rural area with no one in sight and my husband had gone walking for help (this was before cell phones). After he'd gone it felt very lonely out there on the highway, and I started viewing every occasional passing car with suspicion. I locked myself inside our car. Sure enough, a very scary man stopped and offered to drive me for help. I declined and stayed locked in the car, praying that he'd go away, and eventually he did. I got out of the car to look up the road to see if my husband was coming back, all the while praying to God for help, but there was no sign of him.

Then, suddenly, I turned around and there was a man in a white jeep pulling up. I hadn't even seen the vehicle approaching, but for some unfathomable reason I didn't feel at all uneasy. The man seemed to know exactly what we needed and he had water in his jeep to put in the radiator. I told him that it was amazing that he was there with water and all, and he said something I thought was a little odd: 'That's just something we do.' The word 'we' made me wonder. And if he was just a man out helping people with car trouble, why was he dressed all in white? That didn't seem logical. His jeep wasn't like the Jeep Cherokee-style SUV types; it was the old open-top military-style jeep (except that it was all white, which in itself was odd!). It reminded me of the promise of an army of angels to protect us.

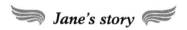

Jane's story

Of all the places to lose a gold necklace, a field of freshly cut hay has to be one of the worst. Not a needle in a haystack, but pretty close! I'd known the catch on the locket, which had once belonged to my mum, was a bit dodgy, but I felt so close to it that I guess I never thought I'd lose it. It was almost part of me. Besides, I felt naked without it and so I didn't want to leave it at home. Now I wished I had.

I'd been helping a friend and fellow 'horse nut' cut her field of hay. It had been great fun. We'd all taken turns on the tractor and the dogs had rushed around all day like maniacs, chasing (but not catching) all the mice and rabbits that had fled the grass as it toppled into rows on the ground. We were all exhausted, all looking forward to a sit-down in front of my friend's Aga and a nice cup of tea, or glass of wine if we were lucky. We'd been about to walk back to the welcoming farmhouse when I realized my locket was gone. It was all I could do not to just break down and cry. I was tired, and now I was also very upset. Through my mind ran thoughts of getting metal detectors to come and scan the field, or gold dowsers or something, because I couldn't imagine ever finding the thin gold chain and the rose gold locket strung on it in all this hay.

My friend is very big on angels and it was her idea that we should ask for help and then walk up and down the field seeking guidance as to where the locket was lying. I felt a bit silly, but my friend closed her eyes and asked for help. We set off – I was a little sceptical still – idly walking along, eyes glued to the ground and looking for a tell-tale twinkle of gold from the too-fast setting sun. It was hopeless, wasn't it? On top of the fact that we had ten acres to search, it was also slowly but surely growing dark. It was literally only maybe half a minute before my friend called to me from her side of the field. 'Is this what you're looking for?' her smiling voice asked. I couldn't believe it – she'd virtually walked straight to it. A coincidence? Possibly, but I don't think so!

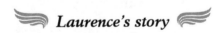

Laurence's story

This is the true story of what happened to me one morning when I thought I was going to die on the streets. It turned my life around. The road to homelessness is surprisingly short. One week you skip your rent in order to pay debts, or you get too drunk and blow all your pay, and before you realize what you've done, the eviction notices start arriving at the door. When you end up homeless, it seems like there is no way out, but sometimes you get the chance to hear a different message.

The lights of the city sparkled off the dark harbour looming below. I wondered what it would feel like to jump off into its dark waters beneath me. Would anyone miss me? How long, if at all, would it take until my corpse washed up on some wharf or jetty? Or would I just be consumed by a giant shark, never to be seen again? These thoughts crossed my mind.

The power of the city ground its success into to my face as the corporate logos illuminated the night sky; I was reminded of who I was and what I had become. A gentle zephyr caressed my face, as if to comfort me. I plodded along regardless. I made my way down towards George Street until I got to Central railway station. It must have been around 4 a.m. The city was silent. I made my way into the tunnel that links Broadway to Liverpool Street. There was not a soul to be seen. Only the giant rats that lived in the underground walkway were awake, and they scurried away from me into the drains that line either side of the tunnel. My footsteps echoed through the silence interrupted only by the sound of the rats.

'Laurence!' a female voice called out of the silence. The only way to describe her tone of voice is caring. Like when somebody who really loves you is trying to wake you up from a deep, deep sleep, so as not to frighten you.

I stopped and turned around to see who was behind me. There was nobody there, not even the rats! They'd all scurried off in fear of unexpected human intrusion. I checked myself. I must have been imagining things. I continued to walk as if nothing had happened.

'Laurence!' This time the voice was closer, louder and a little more serious, but still loving; as if to say, 'Wake up!' That's it.

I turned around again – still nobody in sight. 'Who is it? Stop playing games! If you want something just ask!' My voice reverberated through the tunnel. No other sight or sound of another person could be seen or heard. I started to walk cautiously, expecting someone to jump me. I listened very attentively to my own footsteps and waited for the sound of somebody else's as I continuously looked over my shoulder, hoping to surprise my attacker.

'Laurence.' This time the voice was right next to me. There was no one there, just the warm and comforting voice of what sounded like a beautiful woman: an angel.

This was my turning point. After being homeless for six years, I started the long haul back into society, and now I'm making the world my oyster.

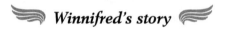 *Winnifred's story*

I'm certain I saw an angel once. I was going through a difficult time and was praying and crying. All at once I felt a power physically close my eyes. It was terrifying. I knew it was God wanting to show me something. I felt so insignificant, so small compared to this world and all the other worlds. What I grasped was this is a very, very short time (this life) and I felt we were like children playing in the sandbox at recess. This is a time for us to enjoy life.

I was in a room – I was not just shown a room – I was really there. It was full of women and children. I was afraid to look around because I thought they would know I was a stranger. The fear was very real. However, the women and children didn't notice me. Their clothes were very colourful, without seams, and they were happy. It was a place of transition.

Then a man appeared in the room. He was tall with grey hair and striking blue eyes. He was walking towards me and, as he approached, he read the question in my mind and answered, 'Yes, I'm an angel. Do you want to touch me?' I was very afraid and somehow communicated, 'No.'

When I was crying and praying earlier I had been asking for an answer to a difficult question. The angel asked me 'What was your question?' The feeling I got instantly was about how insignificant my problems really were. I had an impression that the angel was an extremely busy being. He was in many, many different places and times. I felt so honoured and insignificant. When he leaned towards me, because he was very tall, he shielded his bright blue eyes and they sort of glazed over. I knew those eyes were more powerful than I could take. I asked my question (it was personal). He gave me an answer and the most outstanding advice I could've ever imagined. I wish I could have been strong enough to take it. This problem remains my nemesis. I'm weak spiritually.

After he'd answered my question, I had so many others, but was afraid to ask them because I felt too small and he was so powerful. I knew he was leaving. He asked me if there was anything else. I said, 'Yes, can I touch you?' I grabbed his arm and it was so warm and real. I instantly opened my eyes and I was back at home with my arm outstretched. I knew I was given the biggest gift ever. I was on cloud nine for months, but being a weak person I shrank back into superficiality.

The clincher to this is that the angel was wearing blue jeans, cowboy boots and a belt with a big buckle. I wasn't on acid or under the influence of anything. I wasn't asleep. Anytime I've told someone, their response has been sceptical. This was 14 years ago but very real. I know it happened. And I would love for it to happen again.

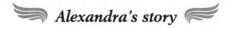

Alexandra's story

I have always believed in angels. My mum – who is a Catholic, but also very spiritual and psychic – used to help me pray to them for protection and guidance when I was very little. I've always felt protected and watched over, and when I was young I knew that if I prayed hard enough I could manifest the things that I needed. In my teenage years I became really interested in all manner of spiritual subjects – I dabbled in Wicca and Tarot and developed a huge love of working with crystals, which I still use today in my crystal layout work.

When I first moved to the UK at the age of just 21, I went through a terribly difficult time. I was in an unhappy relationship, far from home, my career as a journalist stalled and, as an Aussie, I really struggled with the cold weather and darker days and nights. I battled depression off and on for a good few years and totally turned my back on my spiritual side – mainly to please my controlling boyfriend, but also because I just couldn't see any light at the end of the tunnel.

I now know that if you choose to see it, it's certainly there. My reawakening came on my first visit home to Australia after living in the UK for two years, when my mum gave me Diana Cooper's book, *Angel Inspiration*. As soon as I started reading the book, I began to see incredible signs that the angels were with me. White feathers would appear as if from nowhere and I would see the word 'angel' written on signs, T-shirts – everywhere I looked. It was as if they were shouting out, 'We're still here! We haven't forgotten you.'

That's when I started asking them for help again and, miraculously, life changed for the better. I left my boyfriend, my magazine career got back on track and I really started to fall in love with living in England. I managed to get some freelance work with *Spirit & Destiny* magazine and decided that I'd love to do more of that type of thing. Although I took a full-time job at *NOW*, a celebrity magazine, I still did some freelance writing for a few of the spiritual magazines.

In the meantime, I decided to work on my inner self to combat my depression and also get to the bottom of why my romantic relationships never seemed to work out. After trying counselling and hypnotherapy, about two years ago I stumbled across a healing technique called Theta Healing. One of the exercises on the Theta Healing course was learning to do angel readings. Let's just say, I took to it like a duck to water! I was doing a reading for another woman in the class, who asked to see which angel was with her and helping her at that moment. Suddenly, an immense golden angel materialized right behind her. He was sparkling and glowing in bright golden light and he was so big I couldn't get a handle on his actual size – but he seemed out of this world. I asked him his name and heard a booming voice say, 'Metatron'. I had heard of this angel before, but didn't know much about him. He reminded me of a giant Transformer, like in the film, as he seemed very angular. But then I realized he seemed to be made of sacred geometric shapes and he showed me a cube, which he passed through this woman's chakras one by one to balance and cleanse them. When I told her what I was seeing, she confirmed that she, too, felt that Metatron was with her. This was my very first experience of channelling these magnificent beings.

A fellow Theta Healer, Sabi Hilmi, who was assisting on the course, had been standing on the opposite side of the room and when I began my angel reading she leaped up from what she was doing and ran over to me. She told me later that she saw the whole thing and had to tell me how much the angels want to work with me. She told me I especially needed to develop my writing. We are now great friends!

I had a lot of angelic help on my quest to follow my path! The angels are with me every step of the way – every single day.

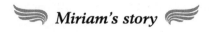 Miriam's story

I was a bad mother. I used to slap my kids and scream at them. I'd drink to take away my misery and take out on the kids the fact that their father had left us. One New Year's Eve I was sitting, the worse for drink as usual, crying, moaning that everyone was out celebrating and there was I on my own. I didn't remember much about my own parents. They'd handed me over to Social Services when I was about seven, I think. After that I'd lived a life in care, had no one who ever loved me, and now I was trapped with three kids. So, who was going to take me on? Talk about a pity party. I bathed in misery and gloom.

Then I fell asleep on the sofa and I had an awful dream. I dreamed that I was choking. I was gasping for air and trying to gag up something stuck in my throat. There were people all around me, but they took no notice. I was going to die. Just at that point in the dream when I thought I was a goner, I suddenly woke up as I was turned over and the stuff that was choking me (I'm sure you can guess that it was booze) spurted out of my mouth and I could breathe. Standing, cradling me, were my three little girls. Two of them were holding my arms, supporting me, while the other banged me on the back. I was mortified that they'd seen me like that, and that they loved me enough to help me when all I ever did was shout at them. They were all crying with relief that I was awake and breathing.

Then they told me something that changed my life. They said that a beautiful lady had come to them. They'd been able to hear me gagging and were scared, but the lady told them not to be afraid and to go downstairs. The kids said she told them what to do to help me. My skin pimpled into goose bumps and I felt dizzy with a thrill that maybe life really could be different.

I'm not saying I never shout any more. I am human! But I try not to unless I have to, and I've stopped drinking, except for a glass of wine on special occasions. I started a new job and I have faith that things are getting better. After all, I must have been worth saving for something, mustn't I? And even though the angel came to help my girls really, rather than me, it still means I'm worth something to them.

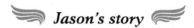 *Jason's story*

I was homeless, scared, broke and alone. I didn't really know what to do in the night, when the city shut down, and I spent my days anywhere I could be comfortable for free, like parks and libraries, and McDonald's if I felt like splurging. At night it got more difficult. And by this time it had been going on for months. One day I sat alone, homeless in Queen's Park, clipping my nails and trying to feel like a dignified, worthwhile human being. I'd only eaten a single muffin and a single croissant in three days. I felt pretty broken, beaten up by life.

I had big dreams, big ambitions, and here I was miles away from them all with no one I felt I could turn to. I was letting my thoughts run away with me when suddenly an old man approached me, and in a thick accent he said, 'Are you homeless?'

Tenaciously holding on to any shred of dignity I could, I said, 'No, I'm just chillin'.'

He looked at me briefly, cocked his head and then said, 'Well, my friend over there…' He gestured to an even older man sitting on a bench '…wants you to have this.' He then handed me a plastic Ambrose's Organics bag. (Ambrose's is a natural food store.)

What else could I do but take it? I opened it and glanced in quickly. Inside was a piping hot loaf of freshly baked bread, an unpeeled banana and a new, unopened bottle of water. I thanked the man and he wandered off. The whole experience was absolutely surreal and I could feel some electric, magnetic charge in the air as it all went down. That food kept me full for about two days. I never saw the men again. Did I suddenly feel blessed, cared for by life and that I was worth something to someone, somewhere? Yes, I did.

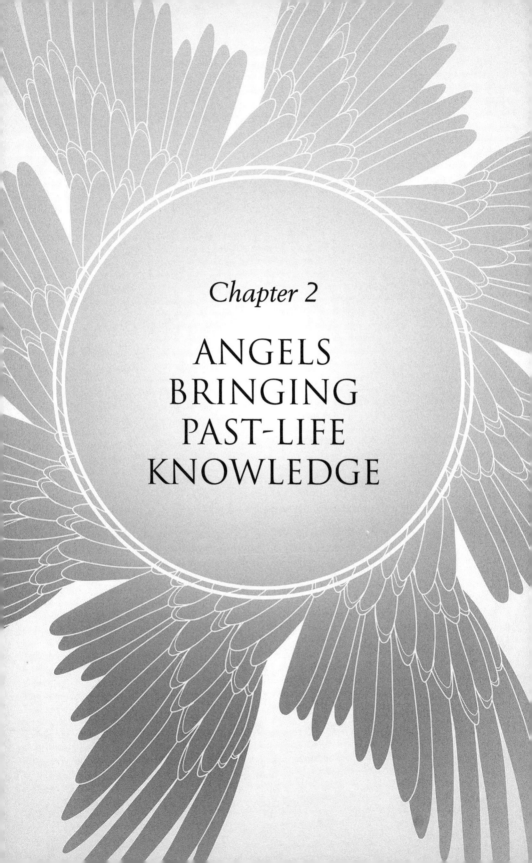

Chapter 2

ANGELS BRINGING PAST-LIFE KNOWLEDGE

A lot of my most successful books have been about previous or past lives. My own transformational angel experience revealed a past life to me. So, I really do have to connect the two subjects of angels and past lives, as to me they are inextricably linked. Quite a few years ago I had an incredible revelation, which I totally believe to this day. It's been proven to me over and over again, and to me it answers every single question there's ever been about why we are here, what we're meant to do here and what happens to us afterwards.

This revelation showed me a new realm of angels, which I call Soul Angels. The full explanation of them is contained in my book, *Soul Angels*, but here is a shortened version.

These angels are *us*. What others have called our higher self is in fact our divine self. This divine part of us is more magical and more wonderful than people ever dreamed. This part of us is angelic. These angels are not ethereal messengers from God, unreachable and untouchable by us mere mortals. These angels are not in another league from us. These angels are not incomprehensible beings of pure energy, who we can only gaze at adoringly. *Each and every one of us is a facet of one of these angels.* We're only 'mere mortals' because our divine part, our soul, is housed in a mortal body while we're in this world, and our roots are not just spiritual, they are angelic.

Once I got over the shock of this revelation, I was shown how it all came about. Many, many thousands of years ago, it was decided by the universe, or God, or whatever you feel happiest calling the supreme power, that further evolution had to take place in particular within the angel realms. To this end it was decided that they needed a catalyst to push them into a new design. So some new fledgling angels were created and they could detach a part of themselves, which could then become a soul. This soul could reside in a physical body on a planet, whereas the angels themselves were made of pure energy. This was done in the same way that all matter was created: by turning some of their energy into light.

These souls – fragments of the Soul Angels – would live many lives on Earth (and possibly on other planets too). They were encapsulated in body after body, learning and experiencing what they couldn't learn or experience as immortals. One day we'll all return to our angelic roots, whole and evolved to the highest level an angel can aspire to.

It is these Soul Angels who constantly nudge us with past-life memories, whether through dreams, nightmares, phobias, déjà vu, mysterious illnesses or scars etc., because they need us to wake up to our souls and thereby allow them as angels to evolve. All they can give us are nudges, for our inability to recall past lives naturally is the challenge both they and we accepted before we came here.

So because the Soul Angels' futures depend on ours, and their progress on ours, they tend to push us, and sometimes where they push us to is not a comfortable place to be. But equally sometimes – and I don't know if this is just a compassionate gesture on their part, like those you read about in some stories – the Souls Angels will send a past loved pet back to us to help us on our paths. I also believe that Soul Angels find animal souls very easy to work with and they'll stay with us, nudging us to our awakening, no matter what body we're inhabiting.

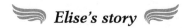 *Elise's story*

My story begins with a dream I had at four years old. My mother would put me to bed, and as I lay curled up on my side looking at a painting on the wall, I imagined all the creatures from the picture going about their daily business. There were foxes, rabbits, squirrels, badgers, mice and birds in a woodland scene with all the characters dressed up and going shopping, riding bicycles, cleaning windows and living like little people in their tiny village made of trees. Then I would look up at a hole in the ceiling where a pipe ran into the loft and, in my imagination, a fox would come running down the pipe.

At this point I began to hear footsteps and my heart would beat with fear. 'Don't make me go, Mummy, please don't make me go with him. The Sandman's coming, Mummy, please don't make me go,' I'd plead. But she told me that I had to. There was no choice in the matter. I'd hear the boots, black boots… thump, thump. And, terrified, I'd be put in a cart and taken away. Then I was in some kind of bath house where all was a kind of sepia colour. There were many women in the same room and none of us had clothes on. I was about eight years old and aware that my auntie and one of my sisters were also there. Then I would wake up, still terrified.

The dream was recurrent for a long time until eventually I stopped dreaming about the Sandman, the cart and all the naked women in the bath house. The memory of it all, however, stayed with me for life.

I was born in 1957, the middle daughter of three female siblings to Jewish parents, neither of whom had any direct experience of the Holocaust. My mother recalls her own mother taking in a Jewish refugee in Manchester during the Second World War, and eventually learning about the horrors of the Holocaust through the media. My father joined the Royal Air Force and spent time as a radio engineer in Egypt and the Middle East, but had no connection with what was going on in wartime Europe. As children, we were overprotected to the point of being smothered and shielded from anything to do with the attempt to obliterate an entire race, my own race. At four years old, I knew nothing about the Holocaust, and yet it seemed as though my dream was triggered by an inexplicable memory of something terrifying and horrific.

A shy and nervous child, I was terrified by school. Uniforms made me very uncomfortable. During my adolescence, the showers at school were an experience I had to avoid at all costs, as the mere thought of having to take off my clothes in front of others scared me 'to death'. Desperately unhappy in a rigidly controlled academic institution, I was asked to leave my grammar school at 14 due to my work not being up to standard. The reason was the fact that the school environment, to me, felt like some kind of prison camp, the teachers like Gestapo officers, and I was bullied and called a 'fat Jew girl'. I recall an incident when I was 13 and my mother took me to have my hair cut. The hairdresser cut it too short for my liking and I screamed with horror, demanding my mother should buy me a wig to cover up the short hair. I wore the wig until my hair had grown back to what I considered to be an acceptable length. On another occasion, at the dentist, I began to scream with terror as he pulled a tooth, my reaction prompted by a vision of some other world or lifetime.

By the time I reached 15, as a misfit and a victim I had taken my first overdose. The second followed in my early twenties during my first marriage. My career was unstable until my second marriage, motherhood and an opportunity to enter an open-ended period of psychotherapy. When my son started school, I resumed a Counselling Diploma that I had started years previously but had been unable to continue due to adverse financial circumstances.

Five years' intensive study, following years of spiritual searching, inner exploration and working with alternative therapists looking at the possibility of past lives led to a Master's degree in Psychotherapy and

Healing at the age of 52. A big achievement for someone who had left school with two 'O' levels! My dissertation was based upon my own spiritual journey and the research I had undertaken into past-life therapy and the question of the transmission of memory for second- and third- generation Holocaust survivors.

As part of my research I undertook various forms of regression therapy. In every regression I found myself, after being captured by the Nazis, standing in a line of naked women. There were piles of suitcases on the ground, reading glasses, hair from where heads had been shaved, and clothes. Screams could be heard where teeth were being pulled out. And then there were the showers. But they weren't showers at all and I screamed as the gas was turned on and I knew that I was going to die. But I was only eight years old. I knew nothing of death. Surrounded by terrified women, I was nevertheless completely alone. During one regression session on a weekend workshop with Dr Roger Woolger (author of *Other Lives, Other Selves*), after 're-experiencing' the death and while in trance, I found myself travelling through layers of grey fog until colours changed and became lighter. A short transcript of part of the session follows.

'Suffocating, no breathing. It's over? [Where are you?] I don't know. [Can you see your body?] It's on the ground, still in the room, I'm not dead yet. My body is huddled on the floor, there are other bodies around and above. I don't know what's happened. Where's Mummy? I left my doll. They all look lost. It's all grey. Why's it all grey? It's cold, so cold. I don't understand life is over. I don't know what happens after people die. Why did Mummy go? Why did she leave me? Crying. Holding the crying in, can't let it out now.

I can see down. Piles of clothes. The smell, burning, big fires. It's not me, it used to be. I stay a long time looking for Mummy. Can't find anyone now. Floating above it. Just cold, still looking for Mummy. It's like we're all lost, we're in a mass of grey hovering over, all confused. Bodies are being thrown into a furnace. I see my body being thrown in.

It's getting lighter. The colours change, different colours. Still cold, shivering and trembling. I see what's happening still. More people going in, and smoke, and screaming. They're pulling teeth out. Coughing, changing colour, orange, green, pink, gold. All changing everywhere.

There's something at the end of the tunnel, a gold figure, an angel? Arms outstretched. I can come, it's OK. Will Mummy be there? He says it's OK. Embraces me, bit warmer. "I'll take you." He's taking me to Mummy. Crying. Is it all right now? It's not cold any more. An energy... [ask why she left]... they took her away, that's why she sent me away, she hoped I'd escape. She holds me for a long time.'

The most profound part of that session and the most healing (termed in therapeutic language – 'healing in the Bardo' the Tibetan Buddhist term for the realm to which we go after we have passed) was meeting the most amazing light being, a golden figure of pure loving energy; what I felt must surely be some kind of angel.

The following year we were travelling in Egypt and spending a week in Aswan. While relaxing by the hotel swimming pool, I noticed an attractive older woman moving her hands around one of the guests who lay with her eyes closed on a sunbed in the shade. She was dressed modestly in the style of a smart Muslim woman, complete with headscarf, although she was a white woman and not Egyptian. Being familiar with many types of spiritual healing, this was nothing new for me but I was intrigued to speak to her and approached her when she had completed the healing process she had been working with.

Over the course of the next few days I came to know Ingrid Hartmann/ Fatima as a friend, healer and profound mystic (married to a younger Egyptian man, she had taken the Muslim faith as her own, hence the traditional dress). I arranged a healing session with her for the following day and we agreed to meet in the hotel lobby. As I went to greet her at the arranged time, she immediately took something from her handbag and said to me, 'A healer friend of mine gave this to me and said that it was yours – it is a picture of the angel Uriel,' and handed me what looked like a photograph. It was the identical figure that I had seen/met during my regression session – an angel of golden light.

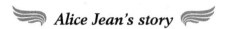

Alice Jean's story

My friend, Renee, e-mailed several people on her list to say that her friend, Gigi, had to find a home for two cats her mother couldn't take to the nursing home. (Gigi and her husband are trying to move out of state with their dog and two cats.) There was a photo included but I didn't look at it. I didn't even look because I was saying in my head 'No. We don't need two more cats.' They were a neutered male and a spayed female that had been together all their lives and were about 10 years old. Both were black and white. She'll be OK and find them a home, I told myself. Then hubby came home from work and asked me if I got the e-mail from Renee and did I look at the photos. He pulled them up on his computer to show me, and I couldn't take my eyes off a photo of one of the cats especially. He looked familiar to me but I didn't want to think about it. I did e-mail this concern to Gigi and told her not to worry – I would also ask around and if it came down to it I'd foster them at least. Then it all began! Gigi and I e-mailed each other and couldn't get over the synchronicities in our lives. I wish I could send you all those e-mails, they're unbelievable!

Then, I said we'd come to get the kitties as the month was running out and they'd had no other offers. My knees were really hurting that day so I sat downstairs while hubby went up with Gigi and John to put the two cats in the carriers, so I didn't see their faces till they were put in the car. Before I got in the car I peeked in on them and when I looked into the eyes of the male, for some reason I found myself asking him, 'Is that you?' He answered me with a one-syllable meow. I almost started to cry right there. I just knew he was my big male black-and-white,

Smudgie, who had died many years before. I had loved him so much and he had loved me too. He was so big, and such a happy guy till the day he got sick. The vet did all kinds of blood work, etc. in an effort to save Smudgie but to no avail, and he was sure he had gotten some kind of poison.

I figured that in a few days I'd know for sure if the new cat was the one I'd lost. I needed a good sign. It only took a day. I was about to open my eyes the first morning they were there when I felt a cat jump on the bed. A 22-pound cat! I kept my eyes closed as I felt him making his way up towards the pillows. I was on my right side, with my arm and hand on the middle pillow, as I felt him hoist his weight just right to where he wanted to settle. Then I got my sign... he put his head in my hand! Total déjà vu! It surprised me so much I didn't move a muscle. I just opened my eyes to see that he had his head tilted up so that I could see that faint black smudge under his chin. My kitty that had died of kidney failure many years ago had had this smudge (not a patch of black fur) slightly larger in the same place, and got named Smudgie the day he was born. Oh, and Gigi's mother had named him Angel Kitty.

The female, who is not his litter-mate, is Abigail and so sweet! She acts as if she knows me too and I'm trying to figure her out. She came to my side of the bed the first night they were here, meowing and rubbing on the bed. I got up and picked her up and she purred, so I put her on the bed and she stayed.

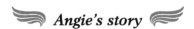 *Angie's story*

My grandad always used to tell us he would come back as a cat when he died, and we'd all smile and laugh and think nothing more of it. Then, when grandad died suddenly in his early sixties, it came as a dreadful shock to us all. I was only eight at the time, and apart from having lost a rabbit and a guinea pig, this was my first proper experience of death.

It was a few months later that a cat appeared in my nanna's garden and adopted her. This beautiful long-haired tortoiseshell was called Fluffy and Nanna was forever telling us this was Grandad come back. There were plenty of other cats that came into the garden, but none stayed like Fluffy. Nanna had that cat for years before it sadly passed away.

Now we jump to the mid-1990s. I've always adored Persian cats. I know they're bred very cruelly to make them look the way they do, and would never consider buying one from a breeder for that reason. Rescuing one, however, is a totally different story. Again, a cat appeared in Nanna's back garden. Because she'd had so many cats come and go, I thought nothing of it and didn't see it until the day someone said the magic word: Persian! I was round there like a shot, having decided no matter what, this cat was coming home with me! I went with my sister to Nanna's, and there in an old ramshackle chicken shed, huddled tightly in a corner, was this poor tatty cat with the biggest orange amber eyes you've ever seen, looking petrified. My sister pulled her from her hiding place and placed her in the cat carrier I was holding and we promptly took her home.

Once home, I opened the carrier and let her survey her new surroundings, and she had us all in hysterics when she made her way to a large potted plant on the floor because she needed to wee! From that day on, though, there was no doubt in anyone's mind whose cat she was, because she rarely left my side. I called her Pudding. The moment I got in from work, Pud met me at the front door, even knowing the sound of my car when I pulled up outside. She always wanted cuddles or a lap, and it had to be me if I was in. Other people were only good enough if I wasn't there.

In 1997 she got a new friend. Little did I know how close they would become, and how their friendship would blossom, but these two became real soulmates. Chester was a long-haired Peruvian guinea pig who had health problems, and he went blind within a year, but he knew how to play and live! The two of them adored each other and would sit together, and sometimes Pud would steal Chester's dried food when I wasn't paying attention. But sadly Chester died in January 2000, and Pudding never really got over losing him. I did get some more guinea pigs after him, but she never took to them at all. They weren't the same and she simply didn't want to know.

It was in the May of 2000 that I discovered that Pud had kidney cancer. I was absolutely beside myself. I noticed she'd not been well and her behaviour had changed in that she was distancing herself from me. It was as though she was preparing me for the parting that was shortly to follow. The vet said we could prolong her life by giving her injections once every three weeks, but by the second one it was obvious she'd had enough. So, cuddling up together, it was as though we decided together, somehow, that next time she went it wouldn't be for a life-prolonging injection but a final one to let her go and be in peace.

Those last days went way too quickly and I was a total wreck the night I took her and said goodbye. She passed away peacefully on my lap, and the sense, almost of euphoria, of peace and knowing I had done the right thing by her, was overwhelming. But there was one last strange thing she had to show me before she finally left. When I got home I showed her to my family before she was laid to rest next to her beloved Chester in the garden. I went into the kitchen and opened the back door, and as I did so, I saw my beautiful little Pudding run out past me and into the back garden she had loved so much, so I knew she was free and happy and out of pain.

I believe Grandad came back twice as a cat, once for Nanna and once for me. I have a photo of Pudding following one of Grandad's favourite habits – reading the paper! She was a beautiful, playful and most loving animal, and I didn't have her with me long enough, but I will never ever forget her or the friendship we had. She was a very special little lady and I miss her so much. Her last day with us was 14 July 2000, but I know she is happy where she is now, and when it's my turn to leave this mortal coil, the first faces I want to see are hers and little Chester pig's.

After both Chester and Pud had died, I had a film developed from an old camera. I don't recall taking the photo I discovered. It almost had me in tears in the shop where I had the pictures developed, but there in front of me was the most beautiful photo of Chester and Pudding lying side by side. I think it was their little gift to me.

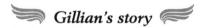

Gillian's story

I was working at a dog shelter when on one particular occasion a very old and unhappy-looking Jack Russell was sharing his run with the puppies. It was very cold and windy and the dog had a snuffly, runny nose, and was wearing a jacket to keep him warm. He kept disappearing and hiding behind the bushes, and he looked so thoroughly miserable that my heart went out to him. After quite a bit of thought I decided to take him home with me. The name the animal shelter had given him was Mr Grumpy.

I'll never forget the soulful look he gave me as he was driven to my house. He had huge eyes with great depth to them. He was a bit on the stocky side and got his name because if any attempt was made to pick him up he would growl fiercely and look as though he was going to bite, even though he didn't have many teeth.

Early in his stay with me I decided to give him a bone, and he immediately got it stuck on one of his remaining back teeth. The vet who removed it thought that Mr Grumpy was wrongly named and that, going by the state of his teeth, he'd probably never had a bone before in his life. I decided to rename him Tenby, which seemed to suit him. His growling was quite fearsome, so when we had occasion to get him into the car, we devised a method of coaxing him onto a blanket and then hoisting him, blanket and all, onto the back seat.

He'd been living with me for about six months, and seemed to be settling in, when I went on holiday and left him in the care of a friend, who managed to lose him. I was heartbroken and scoured the district looking for him, asking all the neighbours and contacting the local animal shelters, but he was never found.

Around this time, in my daily meditation, I attempted to tune in with him mentally and I asked him to show me where he was, so that I could find him and bring him home. As I asked the question my candle blew out, though there was no wind or draught or movement of any kind in the room. I couldn't accept it then, but later I came to acknowledge that this was a communication from Tenby, telling me that he had moved into spirit. Three or four months after this event, as I was driving along very near to the spot where he'd gone missing, I saw a kitten at the edge of the road. I stopped the car and picked her up. She was bleeding from a gaping head wound, so I rushed her to the vet to get her stitched up. I was delighted to see that her colouring was ginger, black and white. She and I became very close and I called her Sparkles because she washed herself so much.

It's my theory that Tenby reincarnated as the injured kitten to be with me again. The timing was just right, and who is to say whether this is possible, or true or not? Whatever the case may be, it made me so much happier to believe that Tenby had returned to me as Sparkles, and the hole in my heart was healed by her presence in my life.

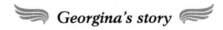

Georgina's story

Ever since my early teens I'd regularly suffered from severe migraine attacks. The pain usually started on the left side of my head, just behind my eye, and then it spread all around to the back of my head. I'd always assumed that these migraines were the result of physical battering I'd had from my mother – who I now know was emotionally unstable. But that's a whole other story! These migraines were debilitating in the extreme. The warning signal always came from my stomach, a churning sense of fear that moved up my body within seconds, and then exploded into extreme pain, dizziness and nausea. Sometimes I was out of commission for two or three days – not helpful for school studies or my work track record.

As I got older and moved away from home and started exploring a different world, I decided to find alternative ways to deal with the migraines. I went for vitamin therapy and for a while the headaches subsided, but they never completely went away. I tried aromatherapy, colour therapy, meditation, pure willpower and pain medications. Each solution worked partially for a while but then the headaches would become unbearably severe again. I saw many doctors, specialists and healers. Nothing seemed to work.

I grew up in England and, for me, believing in the supernatural is a given. I believe there are fairies at the bottom of the garden and ghosts at Hampton Court Palace. I understand that we can talk to or communicate with the other side. And I also know that, real or not, as long as there's a healing or closure, that's all that really matters.

In 1997 I chose to give up the corporate world and become a hypnotherapist – a practitioner and teacher – opening a clinic and a school. It was a no-brainer to move on to working with past-life regression, the 'interlife' and spirit and entity-release work.

One day in class, a past-life regression led me into the life of a woman in what looked and felt like medieval England. I could see a small village nestled in a circle between hills. The village was surrounded by farmers' fields and seemed to be very primitive. Although I could see the village, I didn't feel part of it, and on further exploration discovered that I lived by myself in a cave on the side of a hill, as a witch or crone.

It was hard to tell my age. Close to starving, I depended on the villagers for food. I was so dirty I could smell myself! My hair was filthy and matted. Very much an outcast, I was lonely and lived in fear. The women of the village would leave me bits of food from time to time so that I'd live and help them with their births and illnesses.

My role, my job, was to help women give birth and also to give abortions. I spent my time collecting herbs and making potions to encourage easy births or painless abortions. From time to time men would visit me secretly at night and ask for some herbal cure for their impotence. But always I was treated with distain and made to feel less than the animals in the fields.

One day I was called into the village to help a woman give birth. It was a difficult one, and nothing I did would stop the bleeding. The child – a baby girl – was healthy, but the woman died in childbirth. Not an unusual experience in those days. That night, under cover of darkness, her husband came into my cave. He was obviously drunk. He was yelling and throwing stones at me. I moved to the back of the cave, crouched down in fear, trying to protect myself. He picked up a large rock and smashed at the left side of my skull with that rock until I died.

As my soul left that body, I was encouraged to forgive the man, remembering he behaved the only way he knew how, and leave the pain of that life behind.

Since that past-life journey, I have never had another migraine.

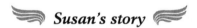 ## Susan's story

I'm surrounded by a beautiful violet light and there's a being inside the light. I can't see any details, but I feel loved and peaceful and serene. I'm going into the light and I can hear the being's voice. It's gentle, tinkling, sort of how I'd expect a benevolent alien to sound, like silver bells. The being is welcoming me back into spirit and inviting me to review the events of my previous life. I'm encouraged to comment and state my feelings. My body has vaporized and I feel incredibly light. I'm almost floating and as I am drawn into conversation with the being, I am also gradually becoming one with it.

It's very strange, this feeling of having a conversation with myself, and after a few moments it's like we're speaking with one voice, not even out loud. I think it's just thought forms being exchanged. I see how my family thought of me in that past life. I had thought I was a caring, loving parent, always worrying about my children, but only in a natural way. I see that in a lifetime many lives ago, before I had my current problems, I lost all of my children to a house fire. Further back I lost my children to an attack on our village. Now that I can recall those times, I come to understand why I have been perhaps overprotective of my children.

I'm shown the children to come in my present life, and myself acting the same way as I have before. Suddenly I see the truth. My previous children and my children to come don't/won't see me as I do. They don't see love and concern, they see controlling behaviour and overbearing criticism. They don't see a parent who loves them above all else, they see a parent trying to live through them, trying to dictate their lives to them.

I'm devastated as I realize at last that I have been repeating this behaviour life after life, terrified that I would lose my children again, and in the end creating that loss by driving them away. I understand, though, that this time it's not too late. There's still time for me to change the way I am. With this new wisdom I can help myself.

Jacqueline's story

I arrive in what looks like a temple, with polished marble floors. I am a young boy of eight. I am struggling with my studies as I learn to be a priest. My mother was a priestess. She was tall, beautiful, very distant and wore long gowns made of gold and silk. There was a protocol that I had to adhere to with her: I was her son, but only by birth; I was a child of the state. I belonged to the priesthood and was heir to leadership that the priesthood carried in that world. I did not like being in this position. I privately wanted to experience God. I felt a tragic personal failure that I had not found Him as yet.

(My therapist has me go back earlier in that life to another significant event.) I am three. I feel myself trying to show love to my mother, but she punishes me when I exhibit any such feelings. The world we are in teaches us all to utilize and develop only our minds and to deny our feelings. As I feel this punishment as rejection by my mother, I begin to shut down emotionally and seek to conform to the development of mental powers. In that I might be accepted.

(Then my therapist has me regress back further, to experience myself within my mother's womb.) Here too, I feel the void of connection with my mother. She has shut down emotionally and cannot relate to me. There is no love, no welcoming. I feel very lonely, and frightened. This leaves a major imprint upon my life.

(Then I am led to other significant events in that life.) As a young adult I continue my studies but any memories of feelings or yearnings for God have long since been buried. I've learned to move stone with my thoughts, to control the minds of others and to rule with what seems a total control over my environment and the physical world. There are also many deep initiations and rituals that are passed on to me in order to provide for the people and the country. I become a priest.

Later in life, as a high priest, I have great responsibility but have grown arrogant about my powers. I am fully ingrained in my position and in charge of all. While we have felt the earth quake and rumble over some years, I've stubbornly believed I could handle (control) any physical disruption.

One afternoon, without warning, the earth begins to move violently. Walls begin to fall and the marble temples begin to crumble. Fires come up from below, people are falling from buildings into what looks like hell, and they are all dying. I am beside myself. After so many years under the illusion that I have total control of the environment and the world,

I do not seem to have control now. I dig deep within my powers but to no avail. I bellow with every ounce of my power. I stand on top of a hill overlooking my city, watching its total destruction. Then I too die in the destruction of the trembling and fire. But I do not leave the earth plane for some time. I cannot comprehend that my world has been devoured by the very elements I once had the power to control. Soon I realize I am no longer in my physical body and I become full of despair. I wander about the destruction for what seems like a long time: dead tree trunks, smouldering earth, a total devastation of everything I have known. I feel I have completely failed… as a priest, as a leader, as a man and as a soul.

An angel finally appears and takes me. Yet I feel I am unreachable. I am in total collapse. I later find myself in the place where one discusses and reviews one's life. I cannot speak to the celestial being that has been sent to help me. I am stubbornly inconsolable. I am finally taken away to where one has time to heal.

Then, continuing in this 'interlife' and with my therapist's suggestion, I slowly find myself opening to the presence of the light of God. The experience begins to soften my stubbornness and melt my self-pity. I see my own arrogance and how I had shut down emotionally in that life and how the false sense of power over my world had been created in me to replace the loss of love.

I stay in this presence as my heart continues to heal, and then upon my therapist's suggestion, we carry back the presence and the feeling of the light into the major experiences just visited in that lifetime, to watch and feel its impact.

First, in the womb, the presence of the light makes me feel loved from the inside out. While my mother is still distant, I no longer take it personally.

Growing up I feel and see how the presence of the light has an impact on every aspect of my life. I can feel the presence of God, and my development in the priesthood is more whole. I grow as a loving person, not one dominating everything with a misplaced sense of power. I feel humility in the presence of the earth and with others. When the earthquakes happen, I no longer feel the responsibility or the failure as before. Instead, I know warmth and inner glowing and a sense of the impermanence of things of this world, and how this reflects what is happening inside us.

I return to this life with a wonderful feeling of gratefulness in my heart. In my work, relationships begin to shift and take on a warmer quality. I find myself less arrogant and controlling and demanding of others. The business begins to take on a more vibrant quality. This session and further instances of regression therapy have shown me a whole different way of being connected inside and a growing awareness of God.

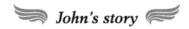 *John's story*

I've never believed in angels or psychics or past lives or any of that flaky stuff. I'm a journalist and have always stayed objective and shied away from anything vaguely supernatural. But I have to admit I was driven to seek help from this unlikely quarter due to a problem I couldn't get rid of. I wanted to be an actor. Rather than writing the words, I wanted to be acting them out. I was passionate and determined and yet, every time I went for an audition, I flopped. My knees would quake and I'd not be able to utter a word. I'd go bright red and end up running off the stage in a panic and very scared. I didn't tell anyone how I felt because I was so embarrassed, but of course word got around and I felt everyone was laughing at me. I gave up for a while. But it wouldn't let me be. I'd have dreams of being an actor. The weirdest thing was that I never, ever got nervous before the audition. It was just when I walked on stage and saw the few seats that were filled with producers and directors. They were all looking at me, and that was it, I was finished.

I'm not a shy person. I'll talk to anyone, interview anyone, so I didn't understand it at all. I went for all kinds of classes in self-confidence, etc., but I knew that wasn't the problem and I was right – they didn't make the slightest difference, just money and time down the drain. It was suggested that I go for hypnosis to cure the problem. I did, and it worked a little – enough for me to want to try again. It was on my second visit that something really odd happened. The hypnotherapist took me back through my life, searching for the cause of my problem, back and back, until suddenly, just like that, I found myself somewhere else – or should I say 'somewhen' else. I was a scruffy young man, aged about 17, I think. I was wearing a rough leather jerkin and some sort of hessian trousers. I had no shoes on. I was being roughly manhandled along a cobbled road. The hypnotherapist asked me what year it was and I said without hesitation '1794'. My brain was turning cartwheels by now, but I stuck with it.

The men dragging me were wearing some sort of military uniform, and by their rough words and hands, I figured I'd done something to upset the army. Next thing I knew I was forced to the ground in front of a wooden device, and my head and wrists were soon clamped and locked into holes. A crowd of onlookers stood around shouting gleefully, and I felt incredible humiliation as they jeered at me. Then it really started. They began throwing stuff at me: nasty, smelly rotten vegetables and any old rubbish they could lay their hands on. One man rushed out of a nearby house and threw the contents of a chamber pot in my face. It was filled with urine and faeces. I was hit and slapped, and all the time I felt trapped and helpless. They called me names and what they said made me writhe with shame as well as pain. Finally, I'd had enough and I asked the hypnotherapist to bring me out, which he did.

Now I understood why standing on a stage with people watching me and shouting directions at me made me feel so afraid and so humiliated. It all made sense, but was it real? I can't say for sure, but from that day forth I have been cast in three plays – only small parts, but I never thought in my wildest dreams that I'd ever get that far.

Do I believe in 'flaky' past lives? I'm not sure, and if you asked me in person I'd probably say no. But if I'm honest, here, where I'm not going to give you my real name, I'd have to say… probably.

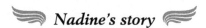 *Nadine's story*

I could barely walk, let alone think or imagine going out. My body's immune system had collapsed. I was living in hell. A meal would knock me out for hours; walking down a street caused my glands to enlarge in pain and my breathing to become asthmatic; crowds terrified me, travel the same. In dark moments – and there were many – filled with confusion, pushed down and grovelling on my hands and knees, I would sob over and over again, 'Mother, Father, Sister, Brother! Where are you?' Who is this imaginary family? What is happening to me? Why am I so terrified of trains, of crowds, of people?

A three-month hospitalization only confirmed my disabilities.

My regression. I'm a child running on a train platform. Crowds of people are being herded into boxcars. Chaos and panic permeate the air, which is pierced with sirens. The skyline, cold grey, is sheared with black smoke. I'm a five-year-old boy who has lost his mummy. I run backwards and forwards, jostled among the mass of bewildered people. I spot my mother's black hat with the peacock feathers. As I run towards her along the frostbitten platform, uniformed soldiers emerge out of the crowd. Menacingly they shout orders. I must get to my mother and her warm, protective body. Suddenly, I reel as searing cold steel glances across my temple. I feel sick and strange. A man scoops me up as he runs along the platform. All goes black. I'm on a train, swaying, jostling in dizziness, coldness, blackness. Then no clothes! Where are my clothes? Where is my mummy?

The stone floor is so cold. I'm shoved along, crowded together with others through a concrete underpass into a room – a shower room.

The door seals shut. The water taps with the warm water we've been promised don't work; that yellow mist coming down must be steam but everything is still cold. I cough! I choke!

During that past-life session in October 1991, every single symptom I'd become familiar with all through my life was triggered. The feeling of dying had been such a part of me, I had known no other way of being! From that day onwards my symptoms dropped away.

What is interesting is that I'd taken the lid off a scenario I'd feared but had never allowed myself to see. For almost a year, I was in amazing recovery mode: eating what I wanted, going on tube trains, unconcerned by busy crowds, no longer obsessed with loneliness, not even bothered by winter. The memory had been brought to light and released. The miracle I had hoped for had come.

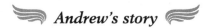 *Andrew's story*

First of all I found myself back in my current childhood, hearing again my mother's strident voice criticizing me and verbally abusing me for making mistakes. I was a sensitive child and her constant berating made me grow up into a perfectionist in an attempt to avoid further criticism. In some ways this paid off, as it made me excel in my work, but the burden of always trying to be perfect made it impossible for me to ever be truly content, because which one of us is really perfect all the time? Using guided imagery, my therapist helped me to speak my truth to my mother, which helped me to release the old painful feelings I had about those childhood memories. When I came out I felt better, but I still had feelings of guilt and some sadness, so she asked me to follow the sadness and guilt back in time, 'How far back can you go and still have the awareness of the sadness and guilt being there?' she asked me.

I responded, 'Even beyond birth.'

She suggested we try past-life regression. It's the time of the Second World War. I'm a young man living in a small village in Germany. I've been taken in by the speeches of Adolf Hitler. When the German troops come to my village, I admire them and desire their respect.

I've done something terrible. I've reported some of Jews who were hiding with our neighbours. The Jews have been shot and our friends hanged in the town square, to warn others who might 'betray' Germany. I thought I was doing the right thing, but when I see them killed I know that I've been mistaken. I've made a terrible mistake! My mother never forgives me and the townspeople shun me. My guilt and shame are immense. I go into the woods and die alone.

At this point in the session, I began to cry. I realized that I have the same mother in this life as I did in Germany. It's why she has been so hard and critical of me in this life. My therapist tells me to go to the time right after I died in the woods, when my soul left my body. She asks me what I have learned. 'I don't have the right to be happy after what I've done,' I respond. 'I've learned how precious life is. I've learned the value of loyalty and withholding judgement on others.'

She then helps me to let go, 'If wisdom erases karma, can you give yourself permission to release the guilt and sadness that you carried forth from that life?'

A year later, Andrew contacted his therapist to let her know that he had made peace with his mother and with himself. He had stopped working so hard, had found a girlfriend and had started volunteering at a charity in his community. 'Life is good,' he told her.

 *Madeleine's story*

I was called out to a livery yard and met a lovely horse called Seamus. He was a beautiful dappled grey and he stomped nervously, snorting through his flared nostrils as I gently tried to reassure him that I was there to help. He had some fears about being loaded into a horsebox, and some confidence issues with his ridden work. However, I discovered that although these issues were very real to him, there was a much deeper reason for his behaviour: he was indeed fearful, but also very worried about a chestnut horse that really needed my help.

I checked this piece of information with his owner and she said she thought he might be referring to her daughter's horse, Raj. However, her daughter Mary and Raj were away at this time but Raj was becoming increasingly unpredictable and she was worried for her daughter's safety at times. We discussed the emotional healing that I would perform for Seamus and perhaps some remedies that my veterinary friend could prescribe, and agreed that when Raj and Mary came home I would visit and see if I could help.

I subsequently got a call a few weeks later. I entered the barn where the horses were stabled. I was greeted by Seamus who, I swear, winked at me and pointed with his head in the direction of a large chestnut horse at the end of the barn and said, clear as day in my head, 'For goodness sake, sort them out! They've got real issues.' I thanked Seamus for his help and said telepathically that I would do my best.

I was eyed a little suspiciously by Raj as I neared his box. He was a very large and powerful horse and Mary looked rather diminutive next to him as she held his halter rope. Mary described some of the problems she had been having with Raj, how he had lost his confidence and that he seemed to have a real issue with turning to the left. When I questioned Raj in my mind, connecting telepathically with him, he said that he needed Mary to be more confident in herself, so that she could be a stronger leader for him. If she believed in him, he could then believe in himself. I then noticed a large splash of much darker fur on his right shoulder, surrounded by a white outline. When I asked Mary about it, she said that she had been told that he had been born with the large mark and that there had been no injury to his shoulder as far as she was aware.

I felt there were bells going off in my head and I tuned in to the energy of the shoulder. I asked Raj to show me what was going on and if this was the cause of his concerns. In the past I have been asked to remove energetic 'foreign objects' from a past-life wound, and in that moment I was 'shown' pieces of shrapnel-like metal, embedded as a memory within Raj's shoulder. I wondered how I was going to explain this to Mary and her mother, who were watching my strange actions as I visualized removing energetic pieces of metal. They must have wondered what on Earth I was doing as I physically plucked what looked like thin air out of Raj's shoulder, and then I visualized filling the area with healing light. Mary then started to feel a stabbing pain in her left shoulder.

I described as gently as I could the video-like clip that Raj was running through my mind. I was being shown a past life in a Napoleonic battle. I could see Raj as a powerful grey horse and Mary as a soldier on his back, charging through a battlefield amid cannon fire. Mary, as a man, had her sabre raised, but unfortunately they were hit broadside as a cannon exploded next to them and metal flew into Raj's shoulder, throwing them sideways onto their left sides. Sadly the wounds were too serious for Raj to survive, and Mary, though crushed beneath the dying horse, somehow managed to survive the battle. She sustained severe injuries that left her with a withered arm and a much-weakened left side.

Mary was a little perplexed at the increasing pain she was feeling in her arm and her mother probably thought that I was deranged and was surely wondering what had possessed her to call me out in the first place! I worked to remove the negative memory in Mary's arm and I asked her if she could imagine the scene that Raj had shown me – to her amazement she was able to describe every detail of her uniform and how they both looked in that lifetime. Mary's mother was also astonished and, I expect, still wondering where this was all leading. I knew that Mary was really feeling the past-life trauma in her body, and could feel tingling as though something was changing in her arm. She then disclosed that she had always been very weak in her left arm, and in fact her whole left side was much the same way and that she had experienced difficulty in steering and controlling Raj because of the weakness in the left side of her body. I felt this contributed to his difficulty in turning to the left.

She said that she felt that, somehow, the renewed energy in her arm had become a little blocked at the elbow, so I asked Raj to help me to clear it. He had become very quiet and totally focused on the proceedings, and was working so hard to support Mary through the process, it was almost as though he was fixing her with his gaze, willing her to continue in order to finally release their trauma. I was guided to ask Mary to visualize little taps at the ends of her fingers, which we could open to allow the old blocked energy to be released. I pretended to turn imaginary taps on each finger and asked Mary's permission to hold her hand between mine so that I could facilitate the release of the old stuck energy. I visualized dark, treacle-like energy coming out, and asked Mary what she would like to transmute it into.

Amazingly, she said that she could imagine little daisies floating skyward, taking all the trauma away. She also visualized the pain in her shoulder leaving and turning into daisies, which carried away the pain. She also felt a block in her head, which she released by blowing daisies out of her mouth. I thought this was very interesting, as the homeopathic remedy for deep tissue trauma can be *Bellis perennis*, which comes from the daisy plant. I then asked Mary to visualize changing the outcome of the battle so that this time they could dodge the cannon fire and gallop to safety. This she did with the help of Raj as she described the fear, but also the relief at escaping, unscathed, from the battle. Suddenly Mary went white as a sheet and she exclaimed that she felt very sick. She looked as though she was about to pass out, so I suggested that she sit down. She slid down the stable wall and sat in a heap, looking alarmingly pale. With that Raj gave a huge sigh and almost collapsed onto the straw. His eyes were tightly closed and his muzzle was pressed on the floor as he snorted and groaned. I was rather alarmed, as I had never experienced quite such a dramatic response from either horse or owner before. However, I knew that it was just a huge energetic shift in their cell memories taking place and that they merely needed time to adjust to their new way of being.

I guided Mary to take some deep breaths and to allow herself to rest. We visualized the new tingly energy filling her whole left arm and when it reached her fingertips we imagined turning off the taps to seal in all the new healing energy. Eventually the colour started to return to Mary's cheeks and she felt strong enough to stand. Raj was still out for the count and breathing heavily. I felt he had worked so hard to help Mary and himself release the past, that he, too, had needed to just 'flop' in order to recover and adjust to his new energy. I felt that Mary needed to get back to the house and have a warm drink. Her mother and I gently led her up the yard to the house and, amazingly, Mary began to smile. She almost shouted that her whole left side felt different – stronger somehow, much to her mother's amazement. When she was handed a mug of tea once inside the warm kitchen, there was more commotion. She shouted in amazement that she could actually squeeze her mug. She had never been able to make a strong fist with her left hand. Her mother was incredulous, but the evidence was there in front of us. Mary proudly demonstrated her tight fist that she was now able to make, and practised several times as if to convince herself at the amazing change in her physical ability. I was so thrilled, but still a little concerned about Raj, so we tiptoed down into the barn to make sure he was OK. As we passed Seamus, he said, in my head, 'Thank goodness, about time!'

There at the end of the barn, nonchalantly leaning over his stable door was Raj, cool as a cucumber, looking as though nothing had happened. His eyes were calm and he seemed really happy and relaxed, which was very different to when I had arrived. I finally felt confident to leave them both, as I felt they were settling into their new personas, having released all the past that was so limiting to them both. I advised Mary to rest herself and Raj as much as possible over the next couple of days and to let me know how they were feeling and give feedback on their progress. I had several other calls to make with horses in the area, and wondered what I would be confronted with next on my day's adventures. The other cases were all interesting and rewarding, but the case of Mary and Raj had been so dramatic with instant results. I was totally blown away by the chain of events that had led me to working with them both. I felt that Seamus, in his wisdom, had decided to get this sorted once and for all so had possibly exaggerated his behaviour so that I might be called to rectify it and then the really pressing issue of Mary and Raj could finally be healed.

The feedback was fantastic. Seamus was loading beautifully and was a very happy 'bunny'. Mary and Raj were literally going from strength to strength, giving each other so much confidence that they were finally able to bond completely as a team for their combined equestrian endeavours.

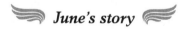

June's story

I knew that I needed to look into my past life with my cat, Jessie, because every Christmas without fail Jessie would become sick. I know what you're thinking – that it was food treats that caused the problem – but it wasn't. She'd be very ill, vomiting so much that I thought she would die and one year I was so worried that I took her off to a holiday cottage where there'd be just the two of us, and – I know it sounds mad – we just didn't do Christmas. Still, there she was on Boxing Day, as sick as the proverbial parrot. After it was over she'd sleep for hours, unmoving. I lost count of the emergency vet call-outs I had to pay for, but all to no avail: they could never find anything wrong – no fur balls, no fish bones, no infections, no parasites – nothing.

When I followed advice and sat with Jessie to see if I could figure out what was going on, I found our past life came through easily. It took place in the 1600s. Jessie showed me that back then she was a sandy-coloured mongrel dog named Charlie, the best friend of a young boy named Nicholas (me!). This made some sense, as Jessie had always got along surprisingly well with dogs of all kinds and none ever chased her. Anyway, it was the time of the Great Plague, and in London where we lived the disease was rife. People were shut up in their houses and left to die if they were thought to be infected. The main symptom was uncontrollable vomiting. It happened to my family one 25 December, and the men came to hammer planks over the doors so that we wouldn't spread the plague. I was terrified that my dog Charlie would die with us. I didn't know if dogs could get the disease or not, but I knew he'd die if he was shut in with us, so at the last second I bundled him out of the door and he was barricaded outside. I thought he'd wander off and find a new home, but it was a huge mistake. He sat outside and cried and howled. It was worse than dying, hearing his distress. Eventually, all my family died, except me, and when I staggered out into the light three weeks later, having been released, I was greeted by the awful sight of poor Charlie's pathetic little body lying on the doorstep. People told me he'd never moved from that spot. Some kind souls said they tried to feed him, but the poor little chap growled when they came near. I expect he thought he was defending me. Of course, by the time he was too weak to keep doing that, it was too late to save him. My Jessie was now being sick in an attempt to remind me of our past together and the fact that it needed healing.

I was instructed in how to rewrite this sad tale, so that I could change the past without harming anyone else's, because I knew that Nicholas never got the plague. I sat and made a 'video' in my head of the day the door was locked shut, only this time I squeezed out and ran off with Charlie, so the two of us were never parted. People might say this is just imagination, but placebos don't work on animals and from that day onwards Jessie was never sick again, so make what you will of that!

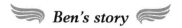 *Ben's story*

I've always been scared of cats – well, not just scared, terrified! People laughed at me when I was young and I would cross the road just to avoid one, and I didn't even like walking next to a fence in case a cat leaped up just as I was passing. The idea of suddenly being confronted eye to eye with my nemesis was really frightening. My girlfriend, Kate, who's always been into New Age stuff, said that maybe I used to be Egyptian in a past life and had been killed because I'd accidentally hurt a sacred cat. Maybe she's right. I've never hurt a cat in this life, I just don't want to be near one, and I especially don't like the idea of looking one in the eye. They have that slit thing going on with their pupils, and I really don't like that.

No, I was a 'dog man' through and through. Dogs were cool; dogs didn't stare at me the way cats did. I had a Staffie called Ringo, and I really loved that dog. Ringo had a great sense of humour. He'd like to hide and then jump out on me, laughing all over his little fat face. He'd put things in my bed, like wet bones or soggy toys, and laugh about that, too, when I'd shriek and jump out of bed. We had a great time together for ten years and I always felt fine when I was out with him, because I'm ashamed to say I taught him to chase cats. That one word, cats, would have him whipping himself up into a frenzy, looking all around for the offending cat. He never caught one and of course I'd never have let him, but I felt safer knowing the neighbourhood cats would always keep their distance when I was with Ringo. So, of course, I was always with Ringo. That's why, when he died, I was so devastated. He'd been my buddy and my protector, so we'd been very close. Without him I felt naked and defenceless again, just like I used to when I was a kid.

From that day it was as if the local cats were getting their own back on me. Everywhere I went there they were, skulking under cars and hedges, peering out at me with their slitty eyes, especially at night when their eyes would glow. Kate got fed up with it and so she hatched a plan. She really did think she'd come up with the plan all by herself, but I know different.

One night she was waiting for me in the flat with a little cardboard box with air holes in it. I was thinking that if it was a puppy in there it had to be a really small puppy. I was horrified when I peeled the lid back and there was a cat! I recoiled and then peered fearfully over the lid. It wasn't so much a cat as a tiny, bedraggled kitten. It was wet and shivering, and I have to admit I felt sorry for it but, 'Take it back! Right now!' I demanded.

Kate told me she couldn't. She said it had been thrown in the canal and she'd rescued it. I wasn't sure I believed her. It seemed far too convenient a sob story to me, but she wouldn't budge. She said she'd take it to the RSPCA in the morning, but it was late, they were closed and it would die if I chucked it out that night. So I told her that, so long as I didn't have to touch it or go near it, I'd let her look after it just for the night. She got it out of the box and dried it, then she gave it a tin of tuna and settled it in a big fluffy towel on her lap.

In the end I went and sat next to her, because the kitten had gone to sleep. All I could see was the top of its head where it poked out between the folds of the towel. Kate insisted on taking it into the bedroom with us, and in the morning when I woke up it was snuggled up against my neck. I nearly freaked out, but even my fear wouldn't allow me to hurt the little thing. Kate had vanished from the room, and so for the next half-hour I lay there, frozen, with the furry bundle up against my neck. It woke up and didn't move, but started to purr. I'd never felt a cat purr before, and it was kind of a nice feeling. To cut a long story short, you've guessed it, that kitten got into my heart and we kept it. But I wasn't cured. It was only that cat I liked. When I was out I still avoided other cats like the plague.

A few weeks later, Priscilla, as Kate had called the little black kitten, was ready to venture into the outside world. Kate and I intended to go out into the garden with her and keep an eye on her the first few times, but there were no real fences and so we were worried that she might run off and get run over before she got 'street wise'. I had a brainwave and suggested we put Ringo's collar and lead on her. It was one of those collars where the spike of the buckle just punches a hole in the strap, wherever it fitted, so it wasn't such a crazy idea. The crazy thing was that when I got it out of the cupboard, Cilla sat up immediately, looking right at the lead and waiting for me to put it on, just like Ringo used to do! Cats don't do that! Anyway, it seemed to be working, so out we went, and she walked as nice as pie on the lead as if she'd always done it. It got weirder. Over the next few days I decided to take her out for a walk on the lead around the streets, and when I did it was almost like old times with Ringo.

Of course, eventually it happened. Another cat appeared in the garden the other side of a low wall from me and I froze. With that Cilla leapt up on the wall, growling and spitting and all her coat standing on end. The other cat legged it, vanishing around the side of the house in a flash! It was really strange and to this day Cilla still won't tolerate another cat near me, whether she's on the lead or not.

Then Kate and I started to realize that Cilla plays with Ringo's old squeaky toys and lies down everywhere he used to lie. I have a feeling my old boy, with his great sense of humour, thought it would be hilarious to come back as one of my arch-enemies! He could also have done it as a test of my love for him. Would I still accept him in the body of a cat?

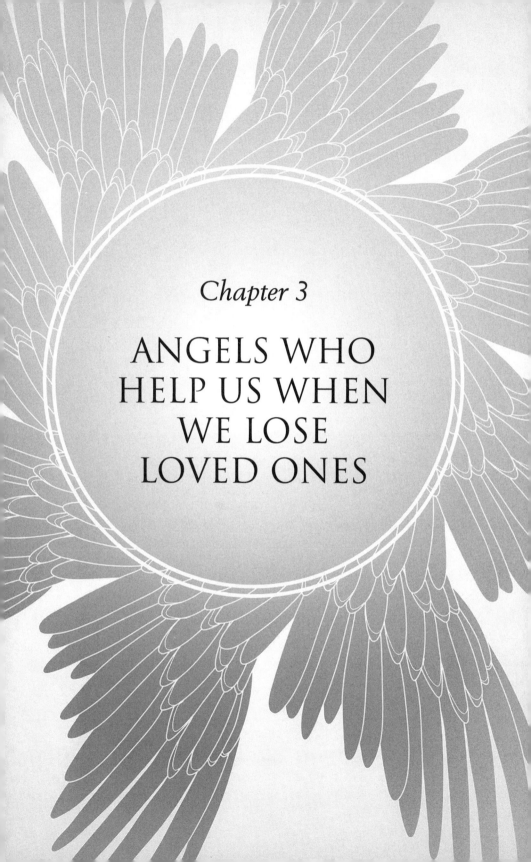

Chapter 3

ANGELS WHO HELP US WHEN WE LOSE LOVED ONES

Although angels don't really understand our grief when we lose a loved one, because there is no difference between 'down' here or 'up' there to them, in either state the person still exists unquestionably, so they don't consider the soul as 'lost'. To them it's just like the person stepped into another room and is still as accessible as they always were. But of course angels deal in the energetic body, not the physical one. They don't really understand why we would miss a hug from someone. They do, however, understand that we are sad and upset, and they don't like to see that.

They will help us connect to the departed one in ways to either soothe the sense of communication or the sense of energy. In fact it's quite difficult for passed-over souls to reconnect with loved ones on their own. If it were easy, spirits would be appearing all over the place and possibly even making speeches! So, when a loved one wants to reach through to the ones that feel they have been left behind, they often need the help of an angel to 'tune themselves' back in to the Earth plane. Even to bring through a message in the form of, for instance, a butterfly, or in 'coincidental' events using numbers or song lyrics, they will need angelic help.

If you read the stories below and feel sad that your loved one hasn't managed to get through yet, please don't. Just remember it *is* very hard for them to do, and if your own energy is in too much of a state of grief, it can be like trying to tune in the radio as it used to be when a very noisy motorbike was in the vicinity. Turbulent emotions, like grief, can interfere with the signal and cause 'static'. So, in time and with patient faith, I'm sure you will get the contact you've longed for.

On their own, without the urging of a passed-over spirit, angels will comfort us when we're in pain of any sort, and the pain of losing someone we love is the most painful feeling of all. So, although at the time many might dismiss it, a huge number of people, when pressed, will say they did feel a gentle touch as their loved one passed.

It might surprise you as you read these stories that spirits often revisit people they weren't related to or in love with, as well as those they were closest to in life. In some cases this might be because the closest people were too grief-stricken to accept the gift of their visit. Perhaps their energy was too turbulent and dark for the angel to bring them through to the 'right' person. If this was the case with you, and you feel you missed out on the actual connection with someone you loved, don't feel bad, because their message and their visit were still for you. They just needed a third party as a 'transformer' to push the energy through.

If you feel this chapter has as many – if not more – stories about the loss of a pet than a person, it makes sense to me because losing an animal that we've lived with daily for many years can be as bad, or even worse, than losing a person. This is because animals often help us through a crisis where a person never could, and they ask nothing from us in return, except love. They love us even if we have no one else. So sometimes, as in many of the stories that follow, animals come back in spirit form to help us because angels ask them to, and sometimes angels themselves help us when we lose an animal, in the same ways they do when we lose a person.

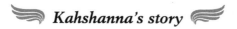

Kahshanna's story

My angel experience took about seven years to process from what I saw on September 11th. I saw the second tower crumble from inside Chelsea Piers, and then I hitchhiked up to Harlem. Some very generous Dominican people were kind enough to tote me and anyone else who would fit in the small, chugging vehicle. I still feel deeply compassionate at their gesture of not wanting any monetary gain. They just wanted to help and understood that everyone wanted to get home.

In the years that followed I researched healing and wellness, much of which entailed retreats to cultivate and experience some of the traditions and healing techniques I'd later offer to clients. In that time I was able to name and access my own intuitive and healing gifts and remove energy blocks. Receiving a healing session, or an illumination session as it is called, seven years after 9/11, I lay down, fully clothed, and began the breathing portion of the session, which a seasoned wellness practitioner was offering me. I had been feeling off; small things upset me but the emotion seemed out of reach, even for all of the work I had done on wellness, Reiki, yoga and meditation... this one I could not do alone. So I asked for help.

I found myself taken back to 9/11... I was witnessing it again but there was a difference. I heard a voice direct me, in this waking dream state, and the next image I saw was a light so beautiful, so radiant and softly glowing. And the people who had died didn't know what had happened and were walking into the light where they were greeted by angels. It was so incredible. I saw people I'd never met look confused and then be greeted by the angels I had only read about in school books.

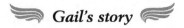 *Gail's story*

An uncle, whom I thought the world of, passed away really unexpectedly and suddenly, leaving us all in shock. A difficult situation meant I couldn't attend his funeral and not being able to say goodbye made me feel so sad, but I knew I could do so in my own way. On the day of the funeral I put up a photo of my uncle in the lounge next to the stereo and I said, 'I'm going to play you an Elvis song, as I know how much you like his music.' I got the CD out of the cupboard and sat on the floor, took the disc out of the case and placed the case on the floor while I put the disc into the stereo. As I reached down to pick up the case to choose a song to play, I saw that a beautiful white feather lay on top of it. It hadn't been there before. I instantly burst into tears and felt a huge surge of comfort envelop me. I truly feel an angel helped me that day.

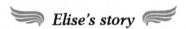 *Elise's story*

My father, then in his early eighties, was ageing quickly and was frequently in and out of hospital. I was visiting one weekend when he awoke from sleeping in his armchair with a huge start, looking shocked and afraid.

'Who was that man?' he asked us sharply (several family members were in the living room at the time).

'There was no one there, Dad,' I said to him.

'A man, dressed all in black. He was stood there,' he replied, pointing to the floor in front of him.

He was obviously very shaken and disturbed, and perhaps on some inner level he had an idea who the man in black really was. I had no doubts that this was no dream, so I kept silent. My father had been ill for some time, but as a stubborn, articulate man, whose brain remained totally intact until the day he passed, he refused to give in to something he feared with every fibre of his being. I knew then that he might not last another year, and accepted silently the fact that he would move on to the next part of his journey in the not-too-distant future.

In my own spiritual journeying I had come to have an understanding of 'the man in black' visiting the old ones or the sick, or even those whose death may be imminent from some other cause. The 'Angel of Death' appears in many forms, this being one of them. It brings a warning or sometimes even an invitation that the time is coming to move on.

When Dad had forgotten the incident a couple of weeks later, we were chatting about this, that and the other in an amiable kind of way.

'Will you make me a promise, Dad?' I asked him.

'Well, if I knew what it was, then maybe,' he replied.

'Will you promise me that, after you die, you'll come back and prove to me that I'm right, that there is no death?'

He laughed, but he made me that promise! My father, who was Jewish and a founding member of our local synagogue, had no belief in God, although he was a Humanist, a true humanitarian and a caring man who practised his belief in his love of humanity in the many and varied charitable works that he did, until shortly before he passed over. He was terrified of dying and his fear of the unknown prompted his refusal to give in to the many signposts leading him to the next stage of his journey.

In May the following year my mother, my older sister and her husband took their last holiday with my father to one of their favourite destinations in Spain. On their return it seemed painfully obvious that Dad was nearing the end. He became very ill, then was admitted to hospital, where he remained after one brief visit home, until he was deemed well enough to be transferred to a Jewish nursing home in Clapham, London.

Nightingale's was a home he had specifically chosen himself even though it was at least an hour's drive for any of the family, so none of them would be able to get there in a hurry. The dreaded call came early on 17 August 2007. I'd just completed an assessment for a new client at the doctor's surgery where I worked as a counsellor, and so I didn't get the message on my mobile until after 11 a.m. My younger sister had texted me to ask me to call immediately I received the text. It was time, and a family friend was driving my mother and older sister to the nursing home – they would collect me on the way. I packed my things and drove home as fast as I was able and waited for our dear friend to arrive, which he did about ten minutes later.

I often wonder if my father chose the place where he would pass deliberately knowing that it might not be possible for any family member to be able to get there in time to be with him when he moved on. He was a proud man; perhaps he preferred that we remember him the way he used to be: a strong, handsome and capable husband, father and friend to so many. On our arrival, we were greeted by the manager and quietly told that we would be unable to see my father just at that moment. He led us into an office where he informed us that Dad had died peacefully a short while before our arrival.

'Was anyone with him when he died?' I asked.

'Yes… a nurse,' he answered vaguely, which told me that no one had been with my dad at the time of his passing. Something outside of my control then seemed to take me over as we entered my father's room.

I hadn't been fully trained in healing practice, but I was in the middle of completing my Master's in Psychotherapy and Healing, and also I'd experienced many forms of spiritual healing myself as a client. It was as if I went into automatic pilot while my mother and sisters sat crying in the bedroom. I stood at the foot of the bed, arms outstretched, quietly asking for divine guidance to assist in the release of my dad's spirit and help him to pass over and move on into the light. I have no idea how long I stood there and then at some point moved on and around the body, working with some unseen energy field, eventually moving towards his head. At that point I moved closer and 'worked' with my hands around the top of his body. Eventually it was as though some unseen voice said, 'It is enough, it is done,' and I moved away and held my mother and my sisters to comfort them.

The funeral took place a few days later (in the Jewish faith the funeral is as close to the time of death as possible) where, again, I instinctively moved towards the coffin, saying whatever prayers came to me and moving my hands around the coffin asking for further divine guidance should any of his energy or spirit still remain and need assistance moving on. I offered a eulogy afterwards, despite the Rabbi warning me that I might not be able to speak and might break down, but I did not. I adored my father. He was like an unreachable God to me (very Freudian, very Electra!) and in reality we were never as close as I would have wished; nevertheless I loved him with a passion.

Later in the week I went to visit a friend's esoteric shop in Teddington, called 'As It Is', wanting to find something to give my younger sister for her birthday, which fell exactly one week after Dad had died, on 24 August. I wandered round the shop and found a beautiful photograph frame, carved with the forms of angels, and felt I had to buy it and put in a photograph of my father. The energy in the shop is amazing. It's very calm and peaceful, a warm energy that makes you feel like you could stay there for a long, long time. On this particular day it was stronger than ever and I struggled with tears (as I am while writing this!). As I looked at different things, something pulled me across the shop to a shelf on which were various carvings, statuettes, boxes and so forth. I nearly fell over backwards as a piece virtually jumped off the shelf and fell into my hands. It was a pair of clasped white alabaster hands holding a tiny baby and I heard the words, 'I am with God now.

I am safe.' As I paid for it along with the frame, the lovely woman in the shop said that she also felt there was an undoubtedly stronger-than-usual energy there that day and, interestingly, at that particular time the usually busy shop was empty except for me and the woman at the counter.

That night I had a dream. I was standing in my kitchen with the back door open and my father walked in through the door holding three trays of food. They were large trays, one laden with flat bread, one with meat and one with fish. It was a huge amount of food for two people, and far too much meat for my father, who had had diabetes and high cholesterol and had suffered heart problems.

I questioned him, asking, 'Dad, how can you eat like this? But I suppose now you're in spirit you're able to eat whatever you like?' and I placed the trays of food in the oven.

We sat down at the table looking at each other without any words being spoken, as we communicated by thought and energy and I asked him, 'Dad, how are we able to talk like this now, as we never could while you were alive?'

And he answered, 'Because you saved my life.'

In meditation a few days later, I felt the presence of an energy and began to sense the appearance of something in my room. I heard the words, 'I am your father,' and initially thought *Oh, wow, I must be having a serious religious experience here*, until I began to see the faint outline of a man. It was a man who strongly resembled my own father as he had been in his forties. He was very handsome, dark and with a moustache. He came towards me.

'Well', he said 'have you heard me yet? I kept my promise!'

'Oh yes, Dad, I've heard you loud and clear – every time. Thank you – but I don't want you to become too tired – if you must move on now then so be it – I love you, Dad. I will always love you.'

After that, I believe he did move on and, although I long to speak with him again (and maybe one day I will), that was the last time I really 'heard' him.

 *Elizabeth's story*

My dear late mother had cancer for over ten years. She was my best friend and a real inspiration because she bore her illness with such acceptance and fortitude. When she passed away, although I was overjoyed she was free from suffering, I was also very sad because she had always been there for us and to be truthful was a light in the family. A day or so after she passed over, I went to bed as usual. I'd not been sleeping too well, but that night I seemed to be overcome with weariness and I fell into a deep slumber. The strange thing was I was also awake because I felt enclosed by what I can only describe as warm, enfolding wings. I felt peace and love such as I'd never felt before and I knew it was an angel nursing me.

The next morning when I awoke I felt better than I had for ages and I knew that it was my angel who had brought me comfort, as well as the will to look after my father, who was also grieving. Although he had not acknowledged such experiences before, Dad believed my account and said it was an angel sent by my mother to help us.

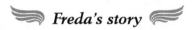 *Freda's story*

Tragedy scarred my mom's soul, and yet she clung to Jesus with childlike faith. The day that gnawed at her heart had happened two years before I was born when my brother died in a huge fire that burned their three-storey house. Mom was able to get my sister out and break the fall of my aunt, who was seven months pregnant and had jumped from a second-storey window. The firefighters had had to hold my mother back from going back into the flames to save her son.

Only a few years after that devastating tragedy, my sister was severely burned in an electric heater accident and was in the hospital for more than a month. My mother almost lost another child to fire. I think that God protected her by giving her that childlike faith. My mom taught me so much. For instance, she taught me the immense value of friendship by her lifelong commitment to helping an elderly lady who was blind and almost deaf, and a family who had no car and needed help with shopping. Mother's attitude to life was truly remarkable and she blessed many people as she demonstrated selfless love.

Later a very rare complication of surgery occurred and Mom had a major stroke. Our world as young adults turned upside down. Over the next few months, every tiny step of healing came as a miracle, borne of prayer and our deep love for her. She was in a coma for several months and then slowly she awakened and began to focus upon us. We appreciated the smallest moments of fun with her. Her body was left partially paralysed from the stroke, but God brought brightness to her life, as if she was still a five-year-old child sitting on the Lord's lap. She was always happy, though she suffered much physically.

We were given several more years to enjoy my mother's company, to take in the love she had given us and return it to her. Then, all too soon, she became severely ill. Within just days, we knew Mom was dying. I stayed with her overnight at the hospital. I held her hand, prayed with her, sang to her and talked softly to her. I dozed and awoke to find her breathing was more laboured. Then her breathing became less frequent. I prayed again, releasing her to God's hands. When I opened my eyes, I sensed there were several angels in the room. I could not see them, but felt the presence of beings on a divine mission. When my dear mother's last breath was released and no other came, I felt her spirit was lifted from her body and escorted by these wondrous beings to God's presence. Immediately, the temperature in the room fell by about 30 degrees. It was the frozen breath of death.

I had to leave. I scooped up my things, went to the nurses' station, reported that she had died and then broke down and wept. It was most profound and beautiful, yet it was also the most difficult thing I have ever experienced.

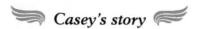

Casey's story

I was at my son's funeral and it was the worst day of my life. He was only 28 years old when he died suddenly of a brain aneurism. I always blamed myself, as every mom would do. He hadn't answered his phone on the day that he'd died and I had worried, but hadn't taken any action. He'd told me off so many times for being overprotective, so I'd given myself a good talking-to and left him alone. Of course the medics told me that it wouldn't have made any difference, that there was nothing anyone could have done, but still I wondered.

So, I stood at the open grave and watched as they lowered my darling son's body into the cold ground. Any mother can understand what I was going through. I just wanted him back. I wanted him warm and alive. My knees felt weak and I honestly thought for a moment that I was going to fall into the hole. My husband, Barney, grabbed me and held me up.

I found myself thinking of something my son had said to me one day. He was quite religious and he believed that we all had a Guardian Angel. I had wanted so much to believe but I hadn't been able to at the time. My son had said, 'One day, Mom, when you really need it, your angel will give you a hug and then you'll believe.'

So, as Barney held me I started saying to my angel in my mind, 'If you are real, then give me that hug right now. I'm ready to believe.'

Right at the very second I felt something fold around both my husband and me. It was warm and soft and, when Barney and I exchanged notes later, we both agreed it felt like a pair of wings more than anything. The feeling was so real that we both leaned into the support we got from the hug. Other people at the service said they saw a bright white light surrounding us.

From that moment I knew my son was right, and I took a lot of comfort from that. During the next five years or so, as grief slowly softened to a quiet pain deep in my heart, I often thought of those wings in my darkest moments.

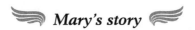 *Mary's story*

My father passed away on 27 August 1967 in Spencer, New York, and was buried in Evergreen Cemetery the day before my nineteenth birthday. I'd just graduated from business school in Syracuse, NY, two weeks before. I'd had an apartment all lined up to share with several of my housemates; I'd had an interview for a good job at Syracuse Medical Centre all set up. My life was just beginning. Then Dad told me he wanted me to come home because my mother needed me. I adored my father, so his wish was my command, even though I could not understand his request.

My mother and I didn't see eye to eye very well (she had always been extremely controlling) and I just didn't see her needing me, but I did as my father asked. I got my very first job at Cornell University working in the Equine Research facility, which was just being built. I'd been there a week when my father passed away, leaving me to cope with our farm, my mother, my new job and the insanity of it all. I finally understood why he'd said my mother needed me.

During the next nine months, I sold off the farm animals and most of the farm equipment. My mother had major surgery, followed by a nervous breakdown. I managed to hang on to my job and I grieved the loss of my father. I could hardly bear to go through each day without his strength and his support. I missed him terribly, and because of his death, my life changed 180 per cent. I had to grow up fast. I became the person on whom my mother depended. She went back to being the control freak she had been before and I hated it. It had all happened so quickly – in the flash of an eye.

One day in the spring of 1968, I was standing at the window at the top of the staircase looking out across the back yard at the empty barns and the unplanted gardens, crying, still mourning the loss of my father. Suddenly, he appeared to me in 3D. He was wearing his coveralls and his boots and was walking across the back yard towards the cow barn. My collie dog, Smokey (also deceased), was walking along beside him just as he had done when he was alive and I wasn't around.

My dad got directly across from the open window and stopped. He looked up at me and smiled, looking directly into my eyes. Then he turned and continued on towards the barn, he and my dog fading into the daylight.

I was stunned. Then suddenly I felt a sense of peace and comfort rush through my body, while a warm feeling of love flushed from my head to my toes, like the buzz from a gentle electrical current. It was euphoric. [At this moment I believe Mary felt her Guardian Angel reassuring her.]

Then it all went away as quickly as it had come. In its stead, it left a sensation, a feeling, the 'knowledge' if you will, that my father was happy where he was and that I should stop grieving for him. From that day forward, I knew he was only a heartbeat away from me, he would always be with me and my life would be just fine.

My dad and my angels have been with me all of my life. My father came back to escort my mother home in January 2005. One day I will see them both again.

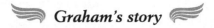

Graham's story

I had a bad back so one evening a spiritual healer came to my house to work on it for me. We were in the dining room and I was sitting at the table with the chair round the wrong way and my head resting on my hands on the back of it. With me being so relaxed and the healer tuning in the way he was, some amazing energy was building up and I think that must have allowed my angel to come through with a very special gift for me, because suddenly the room was empty, the table and chairs and the healer all gone and I was standing up.

Then the French windows opened and my mother, who had passed away previously, walked in. She came across the room towards me, held out her arms and embraced me and then her eyes met mine as if to say, 'Everything is all right.'

It was so real and vivid. We hugged and then, as quickly as she had come, she was gone and the room was back to normal, with my friend totally unaware of what had happened. It was such a wonderful experience and I will never forget it.

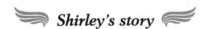

Shirley's story

I was 11 years old when my father died and I had little understanding of what was happening to him at the time. I know now that he had bowel cancer and suffered terribly, my mother nursing him to the end.

Around this time, I recall two occasions when I was lying on my bed, my mother having tucked me in for the night. Both times I glanced at the wall beside me and I was aware of a huge yellow pulsating light beamed onto the wall. I looked around the room to see where it was coming from but couldn't identify the source. I wasn't frightened, but I was bewildered, so the second time it happened I asked my mother what it was, as she was still in the room with me at the time. She had no idea what I was talking about, and although I was pointing to the light and showing her where it was, she couldn't see it, so it appeared to be for my eyes only! It was really only in later years that I began to ponder on the experience. Was it my father coming to say goodbye or was it an angel watching over me? I'd love to know which.

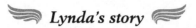 *Lynda's story*

My grandmother (mum's mother) passed away in January 2005. Since her passing I've experienced rock crystals thrown at me and landing at my feet, a shampoo bottle spinning and even my iPod coming on by itself. I'm not worried about these things happening as I believe they are my angel sending me signs from my grandmother.

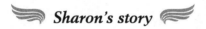 *Sharon's story*

My little brother, William, had an experience none of us could ever explain when he was about two years old. I've been taught that children have a natural close connection to angels. I've also been told that there are angels who will play with children sometimes, and bring through passed-over loved ones for a visit, but I never thought it would happen to one of my family.

Willy, as I called him then, wasn't very well. He was a bit grizzly and, as I had to sleep in the same room as him, I was a bit grumpy about it. Being an older sister wasn't all it was cracked up to be as far as I was concerned then, but after this incident I started to see him in a different light! He had his cot filled with toys and yet he was demanding his Polo Bear, which was all the way on the other side of the room. He called it 'Polo Bear' because it was white and wore a woolly hat and scarf. He couldn't say 'polar'. He couldn't get it himself because he still had the sides of his cot up at night at that time. As well as being tired, I was feeling a bit sad, as our great-granny had just died. Willy had never met her as she lived in France, but I had, just once. Her house had a pool and I'd been hoping to go there again. I thought Willy was being a cry-baby, when really, people had died! I was a bit of a prima donna, I think. I was all of seven years old at the time, and thought I was grown-up.

Anyway, I told Willy to be glad he was alive and to go to sleep – a silly thing to say to a two-year-old, I know. Eventually he did go to sleep and in the morning I was totally staggered to see he was cuddling Polo Bear. Then I realized, of course Mum must have come to check on him and given it to him. But he'd been asleep, I was sure, so how would she have known he wanted it? When Willy woke up I asked him if Mummy had given Polo to him. 'No,' he replied, 'Ganmar came.' I was sure he'd never known that's what Mum had called Great-granny. She had done so since she was a child. When Mum showed Willy a photo of Ganmar, which she kept tucked away in her dressing-table drawer, Willy said that was the lady who gave him Polo Bear.

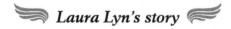

Laura Lyn's story

During one summer night, my papa took me to a Memorial Day celebration near a large lake. He prepared me in advance for all the noise and ruckus from the fireworks. He told me that each boom and beautiful colour represented an angel, and the bigger the boom, the closer the angel. Together we counted the booms, and soon lost count. The noise continued and I was mesmerized by the bursts of light against the dark sky and the reflection of the bright lights against the lake.

In my mind there was an angel for each splendid display in the sky, and another one for its reflection in the lake. After the grand finale, Papa hugged me and said, 'There are over 10,000 angels by your side, who will always be with you.'

The first time I saw my guardian angel I was lying in bed next to my sister. I remember basking in the contentment of the previous several days, when I'd spent time with my grandparents. I was looking up at the ceiling and a purplish glow in the right-hand corner caught my eye. I felt instant comfort and peace and quickly realized this was my angel. I soaked up as much of the energy as I could muster. I hummed, and heard a sharp-pitched vibration resonate back towards me. I felt we were in loving communication with each other.

I looked nightly for this wonderful glow, and felt certain disappointment if I did not achieve the vision. One night the glow grew brighter and brighter and revealed itself to me, growing very large and luminous. The angel had on what appeared to be, in my childish eyes, a luminous wedding dress, surrounded with hues of purple, blue and lavender. I watched in amazement as the glow transformed into an angel and filled up the entire bedroom. I felt very comforted, as if I were wrapped cosily in a large overstuffed blanket. As the angel revealed herself I could not see her face, but she had two beautiful crystal blue eyes, from which rays of light shone.

The angel had a sombre message and informed me that my grandfather would soon be going away. I nodded and accepted the message. To me, 'going away' meant going on a trip. The angel promised she would always be with me. Two weeks later my grandfather died, and from that day on my life changed for ever.

My angels have helped me all my life, bringing messages to others. I am grateful towards my papa for bringing their light to me.

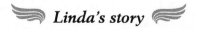 *Linda's story*

I'd come down from Norfolk to visit my parents in their home in Maidenhead. I was alone in the house with my baby son, Simon. It was a bright, normal day and I was busy changing his nappy when the front doorbell rang. My hands were full and I couldn't leave my son alone on the table in case he rolled off, so I called out to my visitor to ask if they could please wait a few moments. I then pinned the fresh nappy on my son, put him safely in his pram and went to see who was ringing the bell. I went to the front door and opened it, just in time to see the unmistakable figure of my father-in-law turn the corner at the end of the gravel drive and disappear behind a tall hedge. I was about to call out his name and run after him, when I stopped cold. The complete improbability and impossibility of the situation struck me.

My father-in-law, Jack Hutchinson, was a genial, open-hearted ex-policeman, and was in many ways the complete opposite of his brooding son, my then-husband Daniel. Jack and I had grown very close during my marriage to his son (which ultimately failed), and I was very fond of him.

The reason I'd stopped, shocked, at the front door that day instead of calling out and running after Jack, was because I knew that he was in Norfolk suffering from terminal lung cancer, with Dan by his side. There was no way Jack could have been in Maidenhead, 200 miles away.

Shortly afterwards Dan phoned to say that his father had passed away and I knew that dear Jack had been brought by an angel to come to say goodbye to me.

 *Michael's story*

A certain day in 2005 was particularly fateful for me. After a few months of worsening dementia along with lung fibrosis, my mother had to be taken to hospital for care, as she could no longer be looked after properly at home. After initially resisting, she complied and spent the afternoon and evening in the hospital undergoing various checks and tests. At one point, I had to physically restrain her from removing the tubes that were in her body, while she stated calmly, 'What do you have to do to die around here?' This was a symptom of the dementia; not her normal outlook. Eventually, a doctor suggested I go home as there was nothing else I could do there.

So I got the bus home and was walking the few minutes from the stop to my place when I saw Isis, one of my two cats, lying on the footpath, not moving. He (yes, he) had obviously been hit by a car, probably in the previous day or two. He liked to wander off, so not seeing him for that long had not been unusual. He didn't seem to have suffered any major physical damage but he was not breathing and had certainly left us by that stage. A dramatic and horrible day? Yes, you could say that.

One of my psychic friends picked up that there was an undiagnosed small tumour in Isis' head, which would only have got worse. Since cats are one of the few creatures that can choose their time of passing, he said Isis chose to spare me the upset, tears and expense of seeing that happen and trying to get it treated. Given his caring disposition, that doesn't surprise me.

There may have been an added dimension to this as well because, not long afterwards, my mother started seeing a cat in her visions (many of which were odd by the very nature of the dementia, but the experiences of dementia patients must have the same spiritual basis everything else does, by my estimation). This cat was apparently great fun and loved to dance to entertain people. It wasn't the large long-haired, grey tabby that Isis was, so maybe it was another animal or another incarnation of him. I just find the timing of this second cat's sudden appearance quite a coincidence.

It was also interesting to walk through a couple of different shopping centres in the weeks afterwards and twice notice the in-store music playing the song Mr Bojangles. This has the lines 'The dog up and died/After 20 years he still grieves', which made it very clear to me

– even more so when it happened the second time – that it was a musical embodiment of my own grieving for Isis. Another psychic friend also suggested that this might be a way of conveying Isis' message to me from the Other Side about how he was feeling, too.

This was made even more apparent when, not long after Isis' passing, I just sent a general thought to him saying, "You'd better be waiting for me when it's my turn to go.'

As clearly as I've ever heard anything, I got the immediate reply, 'I promise.'

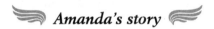 *Amanda's story*

I've seen nearly all my cats – Tigger, the ginger-and-white moggy; Whiska, my little black huntress; and Spooky, my grey girl – after they've died. They were cats we had when I was growing up and I'd see glimpses of them around our old house every now and then. I think it was after Whiska died – she was run over – that I was lying in bed one night and I felt her jump up onto the bed and curl up on my chest. We didn't have any cats at that time so there was no logical explanation for that.

I also had a black kitten, Raphael, when I was about 12, who 'told' me telepathically that he was very sick and was going to die soon. I told my parents but they didn't believe me and we went on holiday for a week (I had to be dragged away, crying) while my grandparents came to cat-sit. When I came back, he had died. I think it was from leukaemia, but I know the vet was sufficiently worried it might be too dangerous a virus to perform an autopsy. I saw Raphael about for a bit after he passed, too.

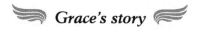 *Grace's story*

As with a lot of people and their pets, Jericho, my dog, was my baby. He meant the world to me. Also, like most people, I lived in dread of something happening to him, and me being helpless to do anything about it. My main fear as he got older was how I'd cope with the aftermath of his passing, even though I did believe in life after death, even for animals. He was one of those dogs that always wanted to be with his owner, and I was afraid I was going to constantly wonder if he was OK and had found his way to wherever he was supposed to go, or if he'd be wandering round in spirit, looking for me. I'd experienced losing my mum some years before, and I knew how awful I'd felt for months and months, wondering if she was all right, and never, ever, getting a sign to reassure me.

Jericho was a blue merle Border collie, with very unusual markings. Everyone commented on the lovely mixed colours in his coat. He was 11 years old when my fears came to pass. One morning I called him to come and get in the car. I was a district nurse at the time, and he always went with me. If the patients wanted me to I'd bring him into their homes and they'd love petting him nearly as much as he enjoyed being petted. We lived on the Yorkshire Moors, so Jericho got enough glorious runs for ten dogs throughout the day. He loved going with me, and that was why a cold hand clutched at my heart when he didn't come running as usual. When he did appear he was obviously in pain. I won't go into the details of his illness, because it is too painful to relive it.

Suffice to say that on a cold, grey day in March, Jericho and I took our last drive together in the car. Afterwards, I drove back to the farm, where I lived with Dad, alone, crying and inconsolable. The empty seat beside me was like a cold, dark space. Jericho's body was wrapped in a plastic sack in the boot. When I got home we buried him in the yard, just where he'd have wanted to be.

That night I couldn't sleep, of course. I thought, here we go; this will be my life for the next few years. Then I thought I heard a bark down in the yard outside my bedroom window. It sounded like Jericho, but there were three other dogs on the farm.

I heard the bark again. It really did sound like him, and I told myself I should go and check, whichever dog was barking. There might be something wrong.

I peered out of the kitchen door and, as I did, the security light came on. That in itself was odd because any previous movement in the yard, whether by a dog or an intruder, should have already triggered the light. I was blinded to the area for a minute and, as I walked forward clutching my dressing gown around me, I thought I could see a light on in my car.

It was very odd. At first I thought maybe I'd left one of the car doors slightly open, but the light had a strange luminescent quality I'd never seen before. I moved closer, peering into the car. Then suddenly there was a loud bang off to my left, and I jumped, startled. This was getting quite scary. I honestly thought about high-tailing it back indoors without even looking to see what the bang had been. When I did pluck up the courage to look, it wasn't anything I could have ever imagined. There was a sort of portal, an opening, surrounded by a corona of white light. The white light went back, slowly fading, into a tunnel. The thing it reminded me of was the white light and tunnel that I'd heard people who've experienced NDEs (near death experiences) describe.

What happened next was something I will never, ever forget. A figure appeared in the distance, in the tunnel. As it came forward I could see it was a woman. Then my attention was switched back to the car, because I heard the door swing open. Revealed, enveloped in the unworldly white light, was… Jericho! He was sitting in the passenger seat, just like he always had done, just glowing.

A voice speaking to me dragged my eyes back to the tunnel. 'Gracie ...' It was my mum's voice! And there she was, see-through and flickering, but standing in the entrance to the tunnel, unmistakably my mum.

'Oh God,' I muttered. Mum held up a hand as if to ward me off.

'Don't come over here,' she said, 'It's not your time, but is it Jericho's.' She pointed to the car. 'I don't want him to be stuck on Earth, following you round aimlessly. Tell him to come to me, Gracie.'

Shaking, absolutely enervated, I looked back. Jericho was sitting, staring studiously out through the windscreen, determinedly ignoring what was going on. I gaped.

'Gracie!' said Mum, 'Send him to me, before it's too late.'

Totally spaced out with emotion, I did as she asked. 'Jericho!' He looked at me guiltily, and tears filled my eyes, 'Come on, baby,' I said more gently, 'Come on, boy.'

Jericho slid out of the car and stood trembling on the ground, the white light having accompanied him. I wanted so much to go and hug him, to go and hug my mum, to do something other than stand there like an idiot while miracles were unfolding around me.

Mum must have read my mind. 'Gracie!' she said in much the same tone I'd used on Jericho, 'Now, Gracie. There's no time!'

Not wanting my baby to be trapped on Earth, alone, I told him, 'Go to her, Jericho. You'll be safe with my mum.' I choked back tears as he walked slowly past me and over to the tunnel. My mum reached out and patted his head. My dog looked back at me one last time, and my mum, incredibly, waved, smiling. They turned and walked together into the light, into the tunnel. Then, with a softer, yet still startling snapping sound (a bit like an elastic band being stretched and then let go), the tunnel vanished and there was just the cool empty night air, leaving me feeling like I'd just been sleepwalking. But I hadn't been.

 *Pauline's story*

Way back in 1978 I went to the RSPCA kennels in Coventry to adopt a puppy. There were four small black bitches that had just been taken from their mother, and all were asleep. I put my hand into the box and chose the puppy that licked my fingers sleepily. I named her Pongo. She was six weeks old and a Labrador cross greyhound. Pongo was a very intelligent girl who used to tug the hem of my skirt whenever my baby cried, just to let me know.

When Pongo was seven, we moved to Tamworth. I took my child to his new school on the first day and I didn't know anybody there at all, but suddenly Pongo pulled with all her might, dragging me over to a lady who stood by the gate. Pongo made a fuss of this lady, who told me that the previous day her old dog had died. It was almost as if Pongo knew and wanted to comfort her.

After Pongo died I was heartbroken. She was 16 years old by then and had been my best mate for all that time. My husband and older son took her to the vet for what, unbeknown to me, was to be the last time. I was sitting on the sofa alone when I suddenly saw Pongo running across the room towards me, looking very young and happy, but she disappeared just before she reached me. I looked at the clock to see it was 5:30 p.m. When my husband and son came back with just a lead and collar, I knew. He said Pongo had been put to sleep at exactly 5:30p.m., so I believed she'd come to say goodbye to me.

I cried solidly for three weeks, but after that time we decided we should adopt another unwanted dog. We chose Misty. It was 16 February, and I asked Pongo to please send me some snow if she approved of our choice. Ten minutes later snow began to fall, although none had been forecast. Pongo used to sleep in her favourite spot under the stairs, so that was where we agreed to put Misty's bed. However, she wouldn't go under there at all but would just stare at the space with her ears up, whimpering.

I knew Pongo was reluctant to give up her bed, even in spirit, so I asked her to please let Misty into the bed, as she was only a puppy and needed comfort. Straight away, Misty walked to the bed and lay down.

Lots of people have seen Pongo around the house since she passed over. One evening I heard her running up the stairs and felt her leap onto me as I lay in bed. I could feel her licking my face, but couldn't move as she had pinned my arms down under the duvet. I asked her to get off, which she did. The dogs were never allowed upstairs in the bedrooms, but now she is in spirit she has no boundaries.

On another occasion I was having meat delivered by a butcher. It was a cold day and he stood with his back to the gas fire while he chatted. Next minute I was fascinated to see the tails of his white coat lift up. He shot around and said in a quivery voice, 'Now, tell me that was Misty,' but I said that Misty was asleep by the patio door. I knew it was Pongo. I don't know why but she found men's bottoms fascinating and would always have a sniff if she could. The butcher was pretty spooked, as he said he'd felt a dog's head lift up the hem of his jacket.

Misty's in spirit now, too, and like Pongo she frequently visits us. Misty has also jumped on the bed, which she used to do when she was younger, but she always used to lie at my feet, whereas Pongo would try to get as close to my face as she could. So I know which one is visiting me and I always move my legs over when I hear one of them run up the stairs, so that they have room to lie down.

Another story that happened while Pongo was still alive involves Pippa, a friend's beagle. Pippa used to come with her owner each Friday for a cup of coffee and a biscuit. Pippa got on really well with Pongo and the dogs would happily play together. One day my friend told me that Pippa had been diagnosed with leukaemia and couldn't walk too far any more. However, they still came to our house on a Friday, and Pongo would bring one of her chews and place it before her friend. Pippa couldn't manage to eat it – but the thought was there.

The following week my family and I went on our fortnight's holiday. When I got back I discovered that Pippa had died in our absence. On the Friday that she'd died, earlier in the day she'd disappeared. Her owner had searched everywhere, and eventually found her sitting outside my front door. My friend took her home and that night she passed away. We both believe that Pippa came to say goodbye to us all.

June-Elleni's story

Rocky was my gorgeous white boxer dog, my faithful friend for five years. Then one awful day when he was eight he was diagnosed with an inoperable tumour on his heart, and I knew it would be only a matter of time before I'd have to make the dreadful decision to let him go. I spoke to Rocky and explained that our time together had almost come to an end and that I'd do my very best to make his last few weeks or maybe months as pleasant as I could. I vowed that I wouldn't let him suffer and that when I felt his quality of life was no longer acceptable, I'd send him into the spirit world, where we could meet again when my time was over. I felt he knew, as if this was a decision we'd somehow agreed upon even before I'd adopted him as a rescue dog. He'd stayed with me through very vulnerable times in my life and now I was stronger, his job was almost done. We both knew, and on a deep level accepted, what had happened.

One morning I looked at him and I could 'see' his skull showing through his face. I knew it was time and that the dreaded day had arrived. The inner voice began its vocal accusations. I tormented myself with questions. Had I left it too long? Was he suffering too much? Was I being selfish? But then the inner knowing kicked in and assured me that I'd kept my end of the deal. That day was indeed the right time.

I fed him a steak and even let him have a slurp of wine, as it was the last meal he'd have in this dimension. I took him for one last walk in the park beside the vet's surgery, and when the appointed time was upon us, I gave him a big hug. Caught up in my own grief, I just told him we were going to the vet's and that he was going to go to sleep. He accepted calmly, as he always had done through all the examinations, injections and X-rays he'd been through before. As the vet administered the fatal injection, my heart broke and I screamed out in pain. I was left hugging Rocky's limp body until I couldn't cry any more. I left 30 minutes later, resolving that I would smile because of the time I'd been given with him, and not cry because it was over. I'd celebrate the time we had and be glad he was no longer in discomfort – but that was easier said than done! For the next week I felt him following me around, but put it down to my imagination. Even when I was in a restaurant having dinner, I thought I saw him waiting outside by the door. Again I put this down to wishful thinking on my part.

Then one night I was proved wrong. I woke up suddenly, thinking, *Oh my God, I can't breathe!*

I staggered out of bed, panicking, and rushed for the window as I felt my chest fighting to expand enough to draw in a breath. I felt dizzy as I struggled to open the window. With my head hanging outside and the cold night air blowing directly into my face, I still couldn't breathe deeply. It was horrible, as if my worst nightmare was continuing even though I was wide awake. Gradually the palpitations decreased, breath returned and I began to feel calmer.

What on Earth had happened?

I suddenly realized that Rocky was there. He didn't know what had happened to him, and he didn't want to leave me. I hadn't said goodbye to him properly. I'd picked up the symptoms of his heart problems as he'd jumped onto the bed and lay beside me in his spirit body that night.

That breathless encounter convinced me that Rocky was indeed still there, waiting for me to explain what had happened, and to say goodbye. Now I'd experienced for myself how uncomfortable it had been for him towards the end, but at least I knew for sure then that I'd made the right decision in letting him go. After I got my breath back and closed the window that night, I calmly explained to Rocky's spirit that I'd asked the vet to end his life in the body that was causing him such pain, and that I'd always love him. I told him that now he could move into another dimension, where he'd be free of discomfort. He could go to a place without the limitations of the physical plane, and somewhere I'd be with him again at the right time. And maybe, just maybe, part of me was already there, waiting for him.

He seemed to understand what I said, and a golden light began to fill the room. As it reached a peak and then slowly faded, I suddenly felt happy that the chapter was complete and that Rocky was free to move on. This was such proof for me that our pets do have spirit bodies and that their consciousness does survive the death of the physical body. I'm convinced Rocky and I are soulmates, and that we'll always have a loving connection.

Fausteen's story

Before our daughter was born, my husband came home one day with two ginger kittens and they were delightful. We named them Brownie and Goldie after the colour of the collars they wore. When they were about 18 months old, Brownie went missing. I received a call at work, a kind stranger (or an angel, maybe?) telling me they had removed Brownie's collar from the corpse they'd found on the roadside and were thus able to pass on the sad news that our cat had died. That evening Goldie and I were in the kitchen, both looking towards the window, when Goldie let out a sound I had never heard before or after, and turned his head to me with profound sadness.

Goldie remained with us for another ten years until, finally, he got sick. He spent a night at the vet's but I knew he was dying so I brought him home. He painfully made his way upstairs, calling out to our daughter and not finding her in her room, then settling down in the passage to wait. When she returned with her dad, Goldie was 'travelling', his breathing had the death rattle and he could barely move. We were having our bedroom remodelled and were sleeping in the lounge, but I remained with Goldie and our daughter in her room until the small hours. Eventually, I crept downstairs.

Some while later I awoke to music. Beautiful, indescribable music... Startled, I thought it was the radio-alarm clock above in our bedroom and I roused my husband and asked that he go check. He reported that the radio-alarm was unplugged; however, Goldie had passed. The music I had heard? It was the heavenly host of angels greeting our much, much loved pet home.

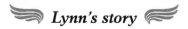 *Lynn's story*

When I was 17 years old, our pet American cocker spaniel, Sandy, had a heart attack. I was deeply upset about Sandy being ill, especially as earlier we'd left him alone in his basket and had all gone up to bed. I couldn't rest, though, as somehow I knew that he was going to be leaving us, and I lay in bed crying and listening to Spandau Ballet on my little cassette player.

As I lay there with tears streaming down my cheeks, soaking my pillow, I suddenly saw Rover and Royce, our old dogs, in my room, followed by Sandy. I knew then that he'd died, and went running into my mum's room saying I was very thirsty and needed a glass of water. I asked her if she would go and get me one. One look at my face told her that I knew Sandy had died, so she agreed to go into the kitchen to get my glass of water. She went downstairs and a minute later called up to me to get my eldest sister up. I went and got my sister, who went down to join my mother. I could hear them talking together and some movement before they came back upstairs. Sandy had indeed died in his sleep in the kitchen.

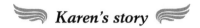 *Karen's story*

I've always been open to spirits, and seen more than a few inexplicable things in my life, but this one had me flummoxed. I was on my way to a party one evening, on foot as it was at a neighbour's house, when I suddenly realized that a little dog was tracking me along the other side of the road. It was a tiny little thing, a chocolate-coloured toy poodle, and I didn't really think it should have been out alone, but the housing estate was quiet at that time of day and the dog didn't seem to be in any distress, just trotting along, glancing across at me now and again as if to make sure I was still there. I stopped to talk to a friend outside her house and the dog carried on its way, as if it knew where it was going, so I forgot about it.

Minutes later, when I went around the next corner, I saw the same dog again. Just as if it had been waiting for me, it was sitting at the kerbside. When I got close, up it got and on it went again, always in the same direction as me. I went past a small shopping arcade and decided to pop into the off-licence for a bottle of wine to take with me to the party. When I came out the dog had gone again. I carried on and this time I was watching out for it, but I didn't see it. Then I reached the party address, and as I turned to walk up the garden path I caught a glimpse of movement out of the corner of my eye. I looked ahead, further up the road, and there was the same dog again. It was about 50 feet away and sitting staring across at me from the other side of the road. I decided to put an end to the mystery and go and have a proper look at the dog. To come out of the garden I had to pass behind a big buddleia bush, and when I got to the street the dog had gone again. I couldn't understand this, as there didn't seem to be anywhere it could have gone.

I shrugged and went in to the party. I started chatting to my host, and she told me that the whole family had almost decided to call off the party because they weren't in a celebratory mood. They'd only gone ahead because none of the family could bear the thought of trying to call all the guests and put them off. Besides, they thought a party would take their minds of what had happened. I asked what that was, of course. She went on to tell me that their little toy poodle, Fancy, had escaped from the garden that morning and had been hit by a car a few streets away – right along the route I'd taken to walk there. I was staggered. This was the first time I'd been to their house, and hadn't even known they had a dog. I was even more staggered when she went on to describe the dog, which matched exactly the one I'd seen.

I persuaded her to go outside with me, thinking she might see the dog, but there was no sign of it. I had no option really but to tell her what I'd seen. She burst into tears, luckily happy ones, and rushed me back in to tell the rest of the family. It was great, as I quickly became the hero of the party. But I'm still puzzled as to why the dog appeared to me instead of to its owners, as surely that would have been of more comfort to them?

Marshall's story

Bear and I grew up together. He was a black Labrador puppy, and when he arrived I was a baby. My parents told me that from the day I was born, Bear would lie by my crib while I slept, let them know when I was awake and oversee my baths, like some kind of canine nanny. As soon as I started moving under my own steam, scooting round the house on my hands and knees, Bear would be right behind me, trying his best to stop me getting hurt by grabbing my clothes and steering me away from anything dangerous. Bear was my best friend, and as we grew up we got ever closer. I had a tough time at school, being picked on because of my Christian upbringing. It was a rough area and I often came home from school bloodied and bruised. When I got home Bear would be waiting and he'd lick me and curl around me, trying to take the hurt away. One funny thing, though, my brother was born after me, but Bear didn't want anything to do with the new baby. He was just 'my dog' and that was all there was to it.

Life was so much better with my big buddy, and he made me feel special and needed, when I didn't ordinarily feel that way. When you're a kid it's hard to imagine people and animals getting sick and then dying and leaving you – maybe that's for the best. I had no premonition, but on my tenth birthday, right in the middle of my party, Bear started acting weirdly. He was puffing and panting, and foam gathered around his mouth, dripping to the floor. He was jerking around, too. Because I was only ten I didn't understand what was happening to my friend, although now I know that he was having serious convulsions. Of course my dad knew what was going on, so he told my mom to take the kids home and meet him at the vet's. Then he scooped Bear up and put him in the truck, and I went with him. I'm shaking now, recalling how I felt on that drive, when I looked down at my buddy's apparently lifeless body. His eyes were glazing over and I was very scared I was going to lose him.

The vet did some tests and some X-rays and told us we had to leave Bear with him overnight. It felt so wrong going home without him. The truck was silent and I thought that was one of the worst things about being just a kid – you didn't get to make decisions. I would have rather my dad had left me at the vet's with Bear. I would have slept better there just feeling his breathing body tucked up to mine. I didn't sleep at all in my bed.

First thing in the morning we rushed to the vet's to find out the news. They told my parents that poor Bear had a brain tumour and it was causing internal bleeding on his brain. They would, they said, do what they could to help him. They did do their best, but during the longest week of my life Bear deteriorated and the vet said he might as well go home. I wasn't told what was wrong with him, and all I knew was that Bear was coming home. I was totally stoked about it. Sure, I could see he was still sick, but I thought he'd be better at home with me to care for him. He lay in the yard on a blanket and I lay down next to him. I remember saying, 'No matter what happens, I'll always love you.' I was so happy that I was bonding with him again.

I went to bed that night feeling better than I had all week, but the next morning when I rushed down to see him, Bear's bed was empty. It was the worst day of my life. When my mom told me Dad had taken Bear to the vet's again, and tried to explain gently that my buddy was never coming home, I just collapsed. I'd thought I'd got him back, and now he'd been snatched away again. I couldn't believe it, but it was true. Dad brought home his ashes. That was all that was left of my best friend, just a pile of ashes. It was surreal. We buried them with his favourite bone, and planted a little tree there. I put a bunch of flowers on the grave.

I lay awake that night, crying. I was heartbroken, absolutely heartbroken. I got up and went down to the kitchen, supposedly to get a cup of water, but I was just looking, searching for something to cling to. When I turned on the light I didn't want to see Bear's empty bed, still where I'd last seen him alive, but I had to look, and I gasped, because there he was. Well, his spirit anyway. Bear had a bone in his mouth, the same bone we'd buried with his ashes. He was wagging his tail and looking really happy. I didn't know whether to laugh or cry. It was impossible, but it was true. Bear dropped the bone, but it fell silently, not making a sound as it hit the floor. He gave it a little shove with his nose, as if to say, 'Come on! Play with me, buddy!' I walked over and went to grab the bone, but then he and the bone disappeared. I fell to my knees and broke down, sobbing. My mom and dad heard me and came rushing into the kitchen to comfort me. They let me sleep in their room for the rest of the night.

Every once in a while, it doesn't matter which house I'm living in, I'll sometimes see Bear, just out of reach, wagging his tail, just telling me that he's still there and that we'll be reunited again one day. Writing this story down was really hard for me. It's hard losing a pet... especially when you've become so close.

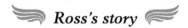 *Ross's story*

Oscar always liked men better than women, but he was a very shy cat with strangers. A black-and-white tuxedo-wearing cat (just like the cartoon cat, Felix), he had a very sweet nature and loved to show his affection to my late dad and me. I was devastated when Oscar got sick, aged about ten – young for a cat – and the very bad news was that he had an inoperable stomach tumour. The vet did his best, but could really only postpone the inevitable with painkillers.

Eventually the dreaded day came. I'd spent the night before with Oscar and he'd seemed quite serene, almost as if he knew and was quite happy about it. He was put on a drip at the vet's so he was in no pain and, happily for us both, he passed away peacefully during the next night. I really loved that cat, and although some people might say, he was 'just a cat', to me he was a gentleman and a very good friend. Oscar never judged me or fell out with me, and he was a faithful buddy.

A few months later, Oscar paid me a visit. It was as if he was proving to me that he had no hard feelings and was still faithful. I'd just woken up and was still lying in bed face down. I felt the mattress spring back slightly as if something fairly light jumped onto the bottom. Then I felt very slight, ethereal footfalls going up, all the way up and along my back, and then a weight settled down next to the pillow, right by my head. I felt something touch my head, which could have been a paw nudge, or a sniff or a huff of breath. Then the weight moved away and got off the bed, without making a sound. It struck me then that this was just what Oscar used to do, exactly what Oscar used to do in the mornings.

I threw back the covers and jumped out of bed to see if any of our other three cats were in the room, but the door was shut fast and there were no cats to be seen. I think this was Oscar, and I think he came to say goodbye, because that had been my only regret, that I hadn't been with him when he died. I believe that cats and all animals have souls, and it's just that science hasn't yet found a way to register them.

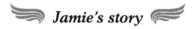 *Jamie's story*

Sam, a striking, all-black American shorthair, was our beloved cat for 21 years. After I grew up and moved out, he continued to live with my mom and dad, but whenever I visited Sam would come running, meowing to greet me and wanting me to pick him up and carry him around. He was closer still to my dad and watching them together it was almost more like a man and his dog than a man and his cat. Mom sometimes felt a bit left out because when we were in the room Sam's attention almost always turned to Dad and me. Yet in the afternoons when she came home from work to watch her soap operas and neither of us was around, Sam would always curl up next to her and gave the impression that he was watching TV, too.

Sam was a very healthy cat all his life and it wasn't until his final week that he started to slow down. Up until then, guests never believed he was an old cat, although it wasn't hard to tell that he was an old soul. When he got a bit doddery, we took him to the vet's for a check-up and it was right there, on the vet's table, that Sam had a stroke and, with the grace and dignity he'd always had, passed on. We were heartbroken and we missed him so much. Still, Mom was just a bit wistful to think that we'd had a closer connection to him than she'd had.

A few weeks after Sam's death, I had an amazing dream. I dreamed that I was in a mansion and my dad and Sam were there. Also there was Cherokee, Sam's sister cat who'd died about six years previously.

Cherokee looked the same as always, meowing and seeming very happy, but Sam had changed somehow. I realized that he was trying to speak words and he did just that, forming them very slowly as if his cat mouth and vocal cords were causing him a problem. 'Ask them,' he said to me, and I knew he meant my parents, 'why they're still hanging that hat over there.'

Dad, in the dream, replied, 'Tell him that's OK. We're sorting it out.'

Then Sam said, 'Tell her,' meaning my mom, 'I saw how she arranged the pictures of the children. She did a great job, and I'm so proud of her.'

After the dream I immediately called my parents and related the whole thing to them. My dad explained that my mom was dithering with changing her job and he figured that the reference to the hat meant they had to stop 'hanging their hat' on her old job. But it was my mom who really surprised me. She laughed and said, lightly, 'That's nice. When you come over, I'll show you the pictures of the children.'

'What pictures?' I asked. 'I don't know about any pictures.' Mom realized then that she'd never mentioned the pictures to me. Stunned, she told me that she'd been working hard each night on assembling photo albums of the children at the local school where she'd worked.

I was astounded and I told her 'You see, you always worried that you didn't have as close a connection to Sam as we did, and now you know you did. He went to all that trouble to prove it to you.'

I've no doubt that this really was Sam in the dream, because how else could I have dreamed accurately about something that I'd known nothing about?

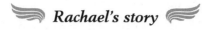

Rachael's story

One terrible day our cat, Floyd, was killed by a car, but I had no idea it had happened until later. Before I'd even noticed he was missing, my then five-year-old daughter came out to me looking very startled, saying that she'd seen Floyd walk right through the wall into the laundry room, and then she'd seen him jump through and into the washing machine. She was very upset and scared he would be 'washed' and hurt if we didn't get him out. I went into the laundry room but couldn't find him. It then occurred to me that I hadn't seen him all day and we went searching for him. We found poor Floyd lying dead on the side of the road.

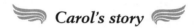

Carol's story

My gorgeous Arabian gelding, Ramsay, had a very unusual temperament for an Arab horse. He was very beautiful, with the traditional 'carved' head that made him look as if he was made of porcelain. He was chestnut with a blond mane and tail, and had tremendous 'presence'. But to ride he was a real sweetheart: calm, responsive and balanced, whereas some Arabians can be a bit 'high energy' for the average rider. I never felt a moment's fear when I was on him, even in heavy traffic. He wasn't even spooked by juggernauts. Sadly, I believe it was his lack of respect for traffic that was his downfall.

One night someone opened the gate to the field he was in, along with nine other horses, and they all got out. We pieced together the events of the night later. It seemed that the horses all meandered along the quiet lane the field opened onto, grazing the lush grass that they normally couldn't reach from the other side of the fence. It was a warm summer evening and I imagine they were all relaxed. Gradually their grazing nibbles took them down the lane towards open countryside beyond. They should have all been safe, and they were – all except for Ramsay.

It seems that while the others continued walking and grazing, something gave Ramsay a fright and he started off along the footpath at the bottom of the lane, in the opposite direction taken by the other horses, which were found safe and well in the morning. Ramsay must have galloped along the footpath until he came to a junction, and then, wanting to find his way home, he turned up towards the main road that ran along to the top of the stable's lane, thinking, I imagine, that this was the quickest way home. Poor Ramsay didn't stand a chance. He ran straight out into the road right in front of a speeding lorry. Another horse might have backed off when he heard the huge vehicle coming, but Ramsay wasn't afraid of them at all.

I was totally devastated when I was woken by the police coming to tell me what had happened. I went into total shock and the rest of what happened was, mercifully, a bit of a blur. Ramsay had already been removed by the time I reached the scene, but of course the lorry that killed him was still there. I felt sorry for the driver. It hadn't been his fault. One of my main concerns was to speak to the attending vet and make sure that Ramsay had been killed outright. Having not been there I was worried that he might have been in pain. The vet assured me that the catastrophic injuries had killed my horse instantly.

The next few weeks went by in a daze of anguish. I'd lost my rock and I wasn't sure I'd be able to continue riding, which I loved, without him. I knew for sure that I'd never have another horse like Ramsay. I tried, though. The hole left in my life was so big, I had to try and fill it somehow, because I really didn't want to give up. But luck wasn't on my side. I tried three horses over the next six months and every one had to be returned, as they were all totally unsuitable for me.

Then I thought I might have found the answer. It turned out that Ramsay had a full brother, and he was for sale. When I first saw him I couldn't breathe, because he was the exact double of my horse. There were differences, though, because this horse was skinny and his mane and tail were matted. His eyes were runny and his feet were long and untrimmed. He had a pot belly and was obviously riddled with worms. He wasn't as unflappable as Ramsay had been, either, but that was just down to training. When I rode him I felt confident that this horse could be the answer to my prayers. But I still couldn't commit to him. I think part of me worried that Ramsay might feel betrayed, that seeing another horse identical to him in the field would make it all feel wrong. I didn't want another disappointment. I went back to the yard, deep in thought, to be met by a friend, Jane, who said the weirdest thing to me.

'So, you found one then? He's totally gorgeous!'

'What?' I asked, totally dumbfounded.

'A Ramsay lookalike. It's nice seeing that beautiful type of horse again.'

It turned out that she'd just come back from getting her own horse in and had seen a new horse that looked exactly like Ramsay, cantering and generally showing off, up and down the bottom side of the field.

She saw the stunned and perplexed look on my face and we both rushed out to see this 'new' horse. There was nothing there. Three times we walked the field, counting and identifying all the horses, thinking we'd gone mad. There was no new horse. It had to have been Ramsay, telling me that he was happy with my choice, and that a horse like him did belong in that field. I bought the horse and called him Murad, which means 'wanted'. He's turned into a dream horse just like his brother, and he's now healthy and glossy and much loved. I can't believe I've been so lucky again.

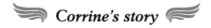 *Corrine's story*

I called my pony Jasper because his colouring was very like that precious stone. His coat was a rich red, and it wasn't until he was well into his twenties that the colour started to fade and turn grey. I bought him at an auction. Everyone else ignored him apart from the dealers who wanted a bargain, because he was dusty, ragged-looking and stood stubbornly with his ears back when the men tried to get him to run around the pen. If any of them came too close, armed with a stick or not, Jasper would bare his teeth and run away, and then turn with a nifty twist at the last second and ping his back feet towards them. He never actually kicked or bit anyone, though. He was skinny and his back legs bowed together at the hocks. So why did I buy him? It wasn't because I felt sorry for him, although I did. There was something in his eyes, a sort of spark that meant his spirit was still in there, underneath that musty coat.

Of course, I had a bit of trouble loading him onto to my trailer and had to be a bit nippy myself, dodging those teeth and feet, but I was canny. I had my elderly pony, Smokey, in the trailer and when Jasper saw him he became sweet enough and walked right in. When I got him home I turned him out in the paddock with Smokey and just left him for a few days to unwind. Then I took Smokey away (he would come to my call) and I went into the field with a bucket of feed, thinking Jasper (as I'd already named him) would be a pussycat for food. I was wrong! When I got to within 20 feet of him he came at me backwards, feet flying! I skipped smartly to one side and then whump, whacked him on the behind with the bucket. It wasn't done to hurt him. The bucket was only plastic. It was more the noise I wanted, just to shake him up a bit and let him know that I was the boss, not him!

That pony was incredibly intelligent. Right away he knuckled under, coming to me and looking very chastened. I found out later he'd been cared for by unattended children and had quickly learned to intimidate them to avoid their attentions, which was why he was so skinny and so scruffy. From that day on we never had a cross word. I'm lucky that I'm small, which means I can ride ponies rather than bigger horses. I prefer ponies because they are generally smarter, and Jasper was the best. Jasper really loved his hay, pretty much more than grass, which is unusual in a pony. His coat soon had a beautiful shine, a combination of good grooming and the right food. That was when I added the word 'King' to his name, and King Jasper was born.

I had him 32 years, which made him about 38 when he passed away – a good age. One morning I found him just lying in the field, stone dead. He'd passed away in the night. My only regret was that I'd never said goodbye, although during those last few years I always knew when I hung his hay-net each night that I might be saying goodbye when I left him. I kind of hoped that's the way it would go, because I sure didn't relish ever having to have him shot.

A few weeks later I was standing in the field shelter, right where King Jasper used to stand, hanging a hay-net for my new pony. He was a lovely creature, not as young as Jasper had been when I got him, because I was no spring chicken myself by then. The pony was still in the stall at this point because I wanted to hang the hay-net before I let him out. He was a bit fretful and I thought the food being there would settle him, rather than have him go chasing round the field in the near dark. I hung the net and stood back. Jasper was on my mind and I could almost see him waiting for me to step back so that he could get to his hay.

That was when the hay-net started to move. There was no wind and I watched, transfixed, wondering what on earth was making it sway. Then I realized what was happening. The net had taken on a characteristic movement – characteristic, that is, of when a live horse eats the hay. The net would sway gently, then stop, move sharply the other way (as if a horse were tugging at a mouthful of the hay), then commence swinging freely again, only to be stopped and snatched again. There was no doubt in my mind that King Jasper was there, eating that hay just as when he had been alive. I chuckled to myself, wondering don't they have hay in Heaven, boy? I watched that net for about five minutes, and then I came back to Earth with a thump as the new pony started yelling his head off for me to let him out. I glanced away, glanced back, and apart from a little residual movement, the hay-net hung still.

To this day I have never forgotten that Jasper came back to see me. It's given me a whole new perspective on life.

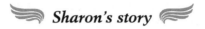 ## Sharon's story

The 12 months between 1996 and 1997 were the toughest of my life. This was the time when I lost not only my nan, whom I loved dearly, but also my precious dog, Tara. Then I got sick, too. My nan, who was my mum's mum, was called Doreen Page. She was a beautiful, statuesque lady with pure white hair. She was six feet tall, very graceful, and everyone said that she was a 'real lady'. She owned a racehorse once, and ran her own steel business until she left the UK to live in Spain. As youngsters, my sister and I used to stay some weekends with her in her apartment down by the sea front on Canvey Island in Essex. When she moved to Spain I used to fly out there for school holidays. My most abiding memory of her is her wonderful infectious laugh. In 1996 Nan was diagnosed with terminal cancer and we had just one short month to say goodbye to her.

My dog Tara was a cross-breed. As a puppy she had been one of the ugliest in the litter, which just made her all the more beautiful to me. She was about the size of a springer spaniel. She had a short, glossy coat, and a long tail with a white tuft on the end. Her main colour was black, with four tan-and-white legs, a tan-and-white chest, and her face was black and tan with a fox-like white nose and beautiful dark brown eyes. She always literally used to smile when her photo was taken. She sometimes used to sleep curved round my head on my pillow and I'd sleep with her nose poking in my ear.

Tara was the best kind of dog. She was faithful and gentle, and we adored each other. She would lie on the settee with me, pouring her long body into the space between me and the backrest. She'd rest her head on my shoulder and I'd feel her wet nose pressed against my neck. I'd feel so safe and secure with her. One of her less endearing habits, but just another reason I loved her, was to chew her marrow bone for a while and then take it out into the garden and bury it. She'd reappear, paws and muzzle all covered with mud, a big grin plastered on her face. The really yucky bit came later, when she'd go and find the bone again, often months later, when it was all slimy and covered in mould, and drag it all over the lounge carpet, leaving a trail of mud and unidentifiable gunge behind her. If she wasn't spotted and stopped, she'd then take it upstairs and place it tenderly on the floor next to my bed for me to find later.

Tara got sick that year, too. I looked after her night and day; nothing was too much trouble. She had to have radiotherapy, but it was unsuccessful at shrinking her brain tumour. Finally, and this I think was what made me ill, I had to make the hardest decision of my life and put Tara out of her misery. That was in June 1997.

After she passed away, my health got worse and I discovered I had ME. This is an awful illness and the worst of it is that some people won't even accept that you're ill. I suffered constant tiredness and aching joints. Sometimes it was so bad I couldn't face getting out of bed unless I could fall straight into a hot bath. I got more and more depressed and barely had the energy to walk my other dogs. It was only Tara I wanted.

Then one day after a walk I came back to find big, muddy blobs dotted right across the lounge carpet. I couldn't believe it. They certainly hadn't been there when I went out. I followed the dirt trail upstairs, already certain of what I would find. Sure enough, there beside my bed was a big, muddy bone, blue with mould. I was sure it was Tara who'd put it there. None of my other dogs ever buried their bones, and they certainly didn't dig them up again and put them by my bed. That was Tara's trick, and anyway the dogs had been out with me. A few days later I got confirmation that it had been Tara. I was in the bedroom and, out of the corner of my eye, I saw the tuft of a tail – her tail – just disappearing round the door. I ran out to look but there was nothing there.

My ME became more and more debilitating, and I felt miserable. I started to really think I couldn't take any more. I lay on my bed and all I wanted to do was go to sleep and never wake up. But I had a dream and the dream saved me – or Tara did. I dreamed I was in a grassy meadow. I could see all the colours so vividly, the rich green grass and the white picket fence that surrounded the meadow. There was a little path across the grass and it led down to a gate and out onto the hills beyond. My nan was there, standing right by the gate. And Tara was just a few feet away from me, the most natural place for her to be. She wagged her tail furiously and ran to me. I couldn't believe how wonderful she looked, so healthy, and I felt healthy at that moment too. I looked at my nan and she waved at me, smiling.

I hugged Tara and she licked my face, licked the tears of joy that were running down my cheeks. I could hardly speak, but I told her that I had missed her so much, and I said, 'Mummy loves you Tara, Mummy loves you so much.' It was wonderful. After a while, though, Tara started to walk away. She went a few steps and then looked over her shoulder at me. I didn't want her to go. I could hardly bear it. I begged her not to go, and after she kept walking further away, and turning to look, I started to hurry after her.

But I could hear my nan speaking. She was saying, 'No, Sharon, you can't come.' I understood. If I followed them, it really would be the end of my life, and I'd never be waking up back in my bed. Tara reached my nan, and Nan bent down to stroke Tara. Nan looked up and smiled at me, and Tara turned and wagged her tail one last time, then the two of them went through the gate and gradually disappeared from sight.

Next minute I was awake in my bed. I felt alone, but I also knew somehow that my life wasn't over after all and that I'd get on with it again. My nan and Tara came back to save me, to tell me that I still had a life and that I could beat the ME. I will do it, for them, because they saved my life that day.

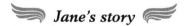

Jane's story

My poodle, Roxie, was the light of my life. From the day we picked her up as a sweet, chocolate ball of fluff, I lived in dread of the inevitable day when she'd leave me. We all know, don't we, even if we don't talk about it, that our beloved pets will leave us one day. Roxie was a toy poodle, so she was tiny – not exactly guard dog material – but that didn't matter to her. She was ultra-protective of me, fussing and worrying over me if I was upset or ill, and staunchly defending me against any perceived threat.

I suppose I was one of the lucky ones, because at 16 years of age Roxie just didn't wake up one day. When I awoke, there was her little body curled on the bottom of the bed, where she'd always slept. I waited expectantly for her to spring to her feet and come to give me a kiss, as usual, but she didn't move. My heart clamped up in my chest as I realized that Roxie had passed away. Life would never be the same again. The house was as empty as my life and I grieved as much as anyone would for a child or a husband. That's how much difference she'd made in my life. I never thought I'd see her again.

I'd always had poor eyesight and had to make sure I had regular check-ups at the optician to be able to keep seeing anything at all, but after Roxie died I just couldn't be bothered. I got to the point where I knew my eyesight was deteriorating, but didn't do anything about it. My eyes became red and sore. Then one evening I was flicking through TV channels, watching an ever-more blurry and ever-more boring succession of images. I hadn't even bothered to put my on specs because I wasn't really interested in anything the television had to offer. They were lying on the floor next to the beanbag I was sitting on. Suddenly something caught my attention, a dark shadow that seemed to be emerging from the wall. I instinctively reached for my glasses, but as my hand brushed them the 'shadow' leaped across the room and pounced on them. As it leaped the shadow materialized into a small brown poodle. While I gasped in astonishment, the poodle – my Roxie – grabbed at the glasses. Her mouth passed right through them and she pounced again, and I heard her excited little yap – the one she always did when she was desperately trying to make me understand something. Then she vanished.

I was totally ecstatic that Roxie was obviously still around and not entirely lost to me, and tears filled my eyes. The salty tears reminded me how sore my eyes had been getting of late as they stung, and that's when I understood what Roxie was trying to tell me. She wanted me to get my eyes checked. I went to the optician's the next day, to discover that I was developing glaucoma. The optician said he didn't know what had made me come after missing so many appointments, but whatever it was had saved my sight, because without treatment I would certainly have gone blind. Roxie always was my guardian… and she still is.

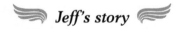

Jeff's story

My horse was THE horse, the best one that ever lived. He was really smart and I taught him all kinds of tricks. He could count, tell colours apart, shake hands, bow, almost anything a dog could do. He could even 'fetch' things. He played ball with a giant one, rolling it around with his feet. He lived until he was 25 years old. Of course I'd had him since he was a foal and we were really close. Chester trusted me and I trusted him. He was a quarter horse, which is an American breed and the best in my opinion, and he was the reddest mahogany bay you ever saw. We had a wonderful time together all through his life and I don't believe I ever once had a cross word for him.

When he had to be put down after breaking a leg, I was devastated. He was a good age, but he could have lived until he was 40 or more. I vowed never to have another horse. Chester was a one-off and I didn't want another. We didn't have any other horses on the property, so that kind of beauty vanished from our lives.

Then something very strange happened. One night last year I was in bed asleep when I was woken up by the sound of a horse whinnying. You know how it is when you get woken up by a noise – for a while you're not sure what it is. My wife, Jenny, said, 'What was that noise? It sounded like… well, it sounded like Chester.'

Of course, it couldn't have been, but she was right. When we heard it again it did sound like Chester. You might think one horse would sound just like another, but they have their different voices, same as us. The horse was doing Chester's 'hurry up' voice. It was shrill, impatient and maybe a little scared. It was coming from right under our bedroom window. I jumped out of bed and looked out the window. There was no horse. What terrified me more than an invisible horse at the time was the smoke coming from the barn. It was on fire!

We were lucky we weren't too far out of town and the fire was brought under control pretty quickly. It had been caused by an electrical fault. Once we had all calmed down and filled in the insurance forms, we had time to think. Jenny and I both believe that Chester came back to save us. Fire is something that all horses fear and that might have been enough to bring him back. He saved us both, and the house. The way the wind was blowing the whole place would have gone up if we hadn't woken up when we did.

I'm thinking now, maybe he wouldn't mind if I got another foal – especially if I called it Little Chester.

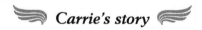 **Carrie's story**

We called our cat Lucky because we figured she was very fortunate we came along when we did, as she was the last of an unwanted litter of barn cats and was about to meet her Maker care of a bucket of water. It turned out we were the lucky ones.

We lived in a nice cottage-style house, which was a bit shabby but big and comfortable enough for us. Lucky grew up there, and she was a great cat. Jet black with a tiny white star on her nose, she was very pretty, and we'd been shocked that her owner had been going to kill her without giving her a chance in life. Anyway, she was really well behaved and she never wasted her time bringing us useless things like dead mice or even rats. Oh no, Lucky would go out across the fields and bring us rabbits – something we could eat that would supplement the family's food budget. It might seem mean, but I'd rather eat a wild rabbit than a pig that's known nothing but a tiny pen all its life.

When Lucky got ill 14 years later, we were very upset. She had a stroke and went totally blind. We tried so hard to keep her going, but it was terrible. She was never an indoor cat, and if you kept her in she would just cry and yowl to be let out. She was just miserable. If we let her out she'd be all right for a while and then she'd lose her bearings and we'd find her sitting out in the middle of the lane, a sitting target for any fast car that came along. Even a slow car could easily have hit her because she wouldn't have seen it coming or known which way to run.

It took me a while, but in the end I decided that she was trying to tell me that she wanted to go. I won't go as far as saying she wanted to kill herself and that when she sat in the road she knew exactly what she was doing, but sometimes it seemed that way.

I finally did the deed, holding her in my arms while the injection from the vet took effect and Lucky went limp. We buried her out in the woods, nice and deep so nothing would dig her up, and built a little stone cairn over her.

It was sad without her. I'd keep seeing her shape flitting around in the corner of my eye, but when I turned there was never anything there. I never got another cat.

We got older, the children left home and then it was just me and my husband Jeff. The house had got older, too, and we never did seem to have enough money to fix anything. A few weeks before the event I'm going to tell you about, during the dead of winter, I started to feel ill. I had a lot of headaches and I felt hungover all the time, but we rarely drank anything alcoholic because we hardly ever had the cash, so it wasn't that. I thought it was some kind of flu. Jeff didn't get so badly affected because, as we figured later, he wasn't in the house as much as me.

One night I'd gone to bed early because I felt so rough, and it wasn't long before I was in a really deep sleep. But something woke me up at about 3 a.m. I knew something was wrong because Jeff wasn't beside me, but I didn't seem to care. I couldn't get up. Then I heard a plaintive meow and it sounded just like Lucky. *Oh,* I thought, *you know where it's warm, don't you puss?* I reached out with my hand, sleepily, and my fingers found her soft fur. I snuggled up to her. Part of me was thinking, *Hang on, she's dead, Lucky's dead,* but the rest of me just wanted to sleep no matter what.

As I said, Lucky was a good cat, and she never ever scratched or bit anyone. So when I felt her fangs digging into my fingers, piercing the skin, I fairly leapt out of bed, grabbing at my hand to stem the blood. I was dizzy and I flicked on the light. There was no cat. There was no blood. I turned my hand over and over, thinking it must have been some dream! Then I realized how dizzy and sick I felt, and that Jeff hadn't come to bed. I staggered downstairs, barely keeping my feet, to find him out cold on the sofa. The gas boiler was roaring away and suddenly it hit me. Carbon monoxide poisoning! I grabbed Jeff and shook him. When that didn't work I slapped him as hard as I could.

That worked and we both staggered out into the frosty air. The fresh air in our lungs soon revived us, and I was able to go to a neighbour's and phone for an ambulance. Like I said at the beginning, we were the lucky ones.

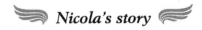 Nicola's story

My grandfather on my father's side was a wonderful man, a gentle soul who'd be the first in line to help anyone. Because he was an excellent mechanic, my other grandfather – my mother's father – had roped him in and asked for help with the maintenance of his ice-cream van. My grandfather worked on the van all day and evening, and when he'd finished he climbed into the driver's seat and started up the engine. The ice-cream van ran smoothly, so he felt able to return it back to the depot so that my mother's father wouldn't lose another day's work. He dropped off the van and got a lift back to his works to collect his car. Finally, he was able to set off for home.

It was a winter's night and black ice was hidden on the tarmac of the busy Liverpool roads. As he was approaching Hillfoot Avenue, my grandfather felt drawn to look to his right, in the direction of Allerton Cemetery. Having family members buried there, he said a small prayer for them as he continued to drive home. Then, turning back to the dual carriageway, he saw that there was a man standing there thumbing a lift. The man had an animal, a dog, standing next to him. It was past midnight and grandfather knew it was freezing, so he stopped for the man and his dog.

Pulling over to the side of the road, Grandfather wound down his window. He asked the hitchhiker where he wanted to go. Within a blink of an eye, the man disappeared. The hairs on the back of my grandfather's neck stood on end, and he felt an almighty chill go through his body. At the same time, the dog leaped up through the open window and sat on the passenger seat, giving my grandfather another fright because he hadn't realized that the dog was still there! Quickly winding the window back up, my grandfather drove away, feeling very nervous and shaky.

His mind raced with wonder as to where the man had gone and whether or not he was a spirit who'd appeared to make sure his dog was safe.

In any case the dog was real and couldn't be abandoned in the icy weather. When they got home, the dog followed my grandfather into the house, where they were greeted by my nan and great-grandmother. My dad, who at that time was a young teenager, was tucked up in bed fast asleep. While grandfather was still puzzling over the weird events of the night, he fed his new pet and made him a bed for the night.

The following day they decided that the dog could stay and they named him Kim, as his collar had the initial 'K' engraved onto it. He was a black-and-white Alsatian, lovely and soft-natured, with a shiny coat and healthy physique. Kim soon became a member of the family. He was an excellent guard dog and he'd stay with Grandfather throughout the day at his garage. Kim was also great company and Grandfather was thrilled to have him by his side. A full year passed, and then on the anniversary of the mysterious day that my grandfather had found Kim, he lost him.

The day seemed like an ordinary one, and my grandfather went to work with Kim as usual. Finishing early, he decided to take the rest of the afternoon off, and so he quickly packed up and headed home. After parking his car, he stepped out with Kim, his shadow, right behind him. The chimes from a local ice-cream van rang out, and Grandfather turned to cross the road and buy his children an ice cream before going indoors. After he was served he walked with his neighbour to the back of the van and started to cross the road. Milliseconds later a car carrying a gang of youths went speeding past the ice-cream van and was about to plough into my grandfather. Kim saw the danger and jumped up at him, pushing him and the neighbour backwards. Poor Kim was hit by the car and killed instantly.

Distraught at his loss, Grandfather couldn't believe the bravery of his beloved pet. Kim was cremated, and Grandfather chose to bury him with his family in Allerton Cemetery, right opposite the place where he'd first found him.

Two months later, while he was driving down Hillfoot Avenue, Grandfather spotted the same hitchhiker he'd seen there before, and sure enough his dog was standing beside him. Stunned, Grandfather pulled over, and watched in disbelief as the man vanished before his eyes again, only this time Kim disappeared, too.

Had Kim been sent to save my grandfather's life and had the connection of my mother's father's ice-cream van united them? Or had Kim simply returned to his previous owner after having been looked after for a year? Many people still report seeing the hitchhiker and his pet and, we wonder, will Kim return again one day to save another life?

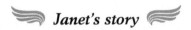 *Janet's story*

Russ is a short-haired miniature Jack Russell. He was given to my parents by my niece as a 'therapy dog' for my mum, who wasn't well. He arrived in December and we always celebrate his birthday on the 7 November with a cupcake with a candle in. Nowadays, when we sing Happy Birthday to him, he starts to sing with us. Mum and Dad think this is great. I've also taught Russ to say hello, and it almost does sound like he is saying that. He's seven now and he sleeps with Mum and Dad in their bed.

Russ seems almost human at times. He has to sit at the dinner table with us, and eats his dog biscuits there while we have our breakfast. He has a sweet tooth and he likes to start the day with something sugary. He loves to lick Mum's cereal bowl (after she's finished with it of course). He insists also on licking the dessert bowls, because as I said he has a very sweet tooth. Most of the time he's an all-round family dog, but he gets a bit weird when he's given his main meal at night. He won't eat it unless I'm sitting in the lounge with him. I have to play with him to get him to eat it. The reason that it's so weird is that, to be honest, I don't really like dogs much. He wasn't bought for me and I just can't understand why he acts that way.

This might sound really silly, but I've been thinking that Russ is someone I've known before, someone who's been reincarnated as a dog. This is because his eating habits remind me of my grandfather, as he liked to eat his dessert first and then his main meal. Also, the way he fusses around all of us, especially if someone is sick, is just like my grandfather. He does this more if it's me, and sometimes it just feels like my grandfather is back.

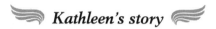 *Kathleen's story*

My stepson Andrew's father-in-law passed last spring. We took care of Andrew's daughters when they went back to Illinois for the funeral. Now, his widowed mother-in-law, Carolyn, has left her home in Illinois and moved here to Port Orchard. She and her late husband had been planning to move here before he passed suddenly from a massive heart attack following major surgery. She felt she was doing what he wanted her to do by coming here. She's here now with her daughter (Andrew's wife), dealing with the loss of the love of her life.

When she moved Carolyn brought the dog that had belonged to both of them with her. He's a white dog, named Polar Bear. She feels that the spirit of her late husband is there in the dog to comfort her. When she told me about this it reminded me of a movie I saw years ago called To Dance with the White Dog. The story was based on actual events in the life of the author, and is about a man whose wife passes away suddenly. A white dog then appears, which becomes his close companion and guardian, and he feels the spirit of his late wife is in the dog. Anyway... I have ordered the DVD of this movie for Carolyn. I will be giving it to her soon to watch, as I told her about it. She feels strongly that her husband's spirit is now in Polar Bear.

Chapter 4

THE
BABY ANGEL

Should someone suddenly die, all those things they worried about will count for nothing. Those worries will mean nothing to the world in general. Love is the only thing that is really for ever, and children know that. I think that's why there's a specific 'Baby Angel'. Mums are always telling me their experiences with this angel, and they are similar enough to prove the angel is real.

This baby angel has appeared to many people who've bravely recounted their story to me, and I've been given a name: Mayura, which is a Sanskrit word for 'peacock'. As peacocks are symbols of great integrity, mothers who lose a child can certainly trust this angel to bring their babies home.

With the loss of a child, there is also of course the possibility of the parent feeling guilty, and thinking that there was something they missed seeing or could have done to prevent the death. In many cases Mayura will visit the parent later in life to absolve them of this guilt once and for all.

I recently had a message from a very good friend and medium called Ann. She told me about a client who had recently come for a reading, and had been terribly distressed. It turned out that she had miscarried two babies, one after the other, and had been traumatized, as many mothers obviously are, by these events. Ann said that within seconds of the woman entering her cottage, Ann, who is a clairvoyant (one who sees spirits), could see a fairy standing in front of her, accompanied by a tall man wearing a hat. The fairy told Ann that babies who are miscarried and don't return to their mother in a new body later, become what we would call 'fairies'. She was delighted when I was able to tell her I could confirm what she'd seen because her description of the man fitted reports I'd had of the Baby Angel. I thought it was a wonderful thing to know that babies who elect not to become human, instead become wonderful fairies. The client was also astonished, mostly because since she was a child she had been fascinated by and collected fairy items, and even today her house is full of them. Now she knows why.

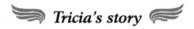 *Tricia's story*

My mum lost my little brother, Toby, when he was only about 17 months old, some 35 years ago. He was a late baby, born when my mum was in her forties and I was already 20. She found Toby still and lifeless one morning. It was a cot death, but that didn't make it any easier. He'd been sickly because he'd been born very early, but that didn't help either. In the night I'd hear her crying and Dad trying to soothe her. I thought her heart would break. I thought she'd die, too, from the grief. She felt very guilty and she'd cry out that he was alone now and she needed to know if he was OK.

One day when she was really down she told me that in the night he'd died she'd been woken up – maybe he'd made a noise, but she'd been too sleepy to know for sure. She said she'd thought she saw the lit-up figure of a man standing in the corner of the room. He held out a hand to her and smiled sadly. She thought he was carrying a bundle in his arms. She'd slipped back to sleep while she was seeing this, and later thought it was a dream. After the next day's events, though, she thought an angel had come to warn her that Toby was ill, and she'd ignored it. That was why she felt so guilty. What kind of a mother, she asked, would ignore an angel trying to warn her to check on her baby?

I tried to console her, but it didn't work. She never told Dad, I guess because she thought he might blame her, too.

Then something happened. It was right after the funeral, when we'd had to watch that little coffin being lowered into the ground. Mum suddenly cheered up. She was still sad and cried a lot, but it was more like the tears just spilled out of her eyes, rather than she was heaving hysterically with grief as she had done before. Eventually I broached the subject, gently asking if she felt a bit better. She turned to me with tears glistening in her eyes, and joy, actual joy, gleaming there. She told me that at the funeral she'd looked across the grave to see the same man she'd seen the night Toby passed, standing there in broad daylight. He'd smiled and pointed behind him and over to a tree. There on the grass in the shade was Toby, crawling around and gurgling happily. My mum said she took a step, wanting to run to Toby, but the man shook his head to say no, and mouthed at her 'He'll wait for you.' With that the spell was broken and the man and my brother disappeared. Mum said after that she knew that Toby was safe and being looked after. She never told Dad about that either, because he was a bit cynical about that kind of thing. She didn't want him to spoil it for her and make her doubt, I think.

My mum passed away unexpectedly five years ago. The night after she died my dad said he'd had the weirdest dream the previous night. He said he'd thought he was awake, but couldn't have been because he saw a young man standing in the bedroom doorway. He was all lit up and smiling. Dad said there was a man standing behind the youth – and he was lit up too. In the morning Dad forgot about it and Mum collapsed suddenly later in the day. She never even made it to hospital.

That evening was when Dad told me about his dream. I felt I had to try and explain, and I told my dad about what had happened years ago when Toby died. I explained that I thought the man was the angel who'd been caring for Toby and that the youth was Toby, who had come back for Mum.

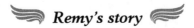 *Remy's story*

Remy didn't send me a story to begin with, she sent a photo – and it was extraordinary. This photo was a still from her son's baby-monitor, which took videos. It showed a small boy (her son was about two at the time) sitting in his bed. In each of his arms he cradled the form of a baby. On the bed was the ghostly outline of a woman. And standing next to the bed was the tall figure of a man wearing a hat. In all the descriptions I've had of the Baby Angel, he has been a tall man in a hat, so I had no doubt who he was.

I suggested to Remy that the babies in her son's arms were siblings who had passed to spirit, and that the woman was the grandmother of these babies. I told her that I believed the Baby Angel had brought her son's siblings to visit him, as well as the woman, who by her presence was assuring Remy that her babies were well-cared for.

I wasn't really surprised when Remy told me that she had indeed lost two babies. One had been miscarried and the other had died a few hours after birth. She also told me that the children's grandmother had lain on the bed in the same position as in the photo, shortly before she died.

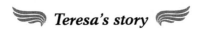 *Teresa's story*

I had a son who was born 15 weeks early after an unexpected pregnancy. I already had a daughter who was just a few months old when I discovered I was pregnant again, and I knew having another child so soon was going to be tough, but I got used to the idea. I was scared of labour, having had such a painful time before, and I had still only just turned 18. I went into early labour on 21 March 2000, and when my son was born at 4:30 p.m. he was fighting for his life right away, because he was 15 weeks premature. He only weighed 1lb 5oz, and I called him Paul. I prayed to God to let him live.

Watching my little boy fight for his first few months of life made me feel so helpless. I had instant, unconditional love for this child and couldn't wait until I could take him home, and that day finally came on the 16 July 2000. I thought that at last the battle was over and I could enjoy life and move forward.

Both my children made me very happy, so I looked forward to each morning and seeing them again. Because Paul was born early he had a few medical conditions, and had to visit the doctor often, mainly weekly. Eventually the doctor told me that he was doing very well, and she wouldn't have to see him so often. Paul's first birthday was coming up by then, so I felt confident enough to let my guard down and stop worrying every day. The doctor's words made me feel that everything was going to be all right. Of course, my little man might have been small for his age, but he sure did have a big heart and he was strong.

But on 21 April 2001 my life came to a standstill when my baby Paul passed away, leaving me in a world of sadness. I didn't know what to do, as I didn't feel I had anything left to live for, even though my daughter Lucy was soon to turn two years old and I knew I had to carry on for her. I wanted to keep busy, so not long afterwards I went to college to study childcare. It was the skill I was good at.

From time to time I get sad and think of Paul. It gets too much sometimes, and then I hide away in my home and don't answer to people. One night, a couple of years after he'd passed away, when I'd shut myself off from the world and was clinging to my grief for Paul, I heard a noise. Rachel, the other little girl I had by then, was lying across my leg and Lucy was in the bed with us as well. I had cramp in my leg from Rachel's weight and I looked up to see where the noise was coming from. I could see a little kid playing with the children's kitchen set. I nearly had a heart attack, and then I remembered something from before Paul had died. I had seen a man with long curly hair, sky-blue eyes and a long face, in my house. Of course, that man hadn't said a word to me and I don't know how he had got in because the door was locked, because I didn't like people walking in without knocking. I knew at that second that I was now seeing my son Paul again, and I was no longer scared, only sad because I knew I couldn't hold him in my arms again.

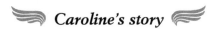 *Caroline's story*

I'd lost five babies during pregnancies and they were the worst kind of loss – where the baby had died inside me and had to be removed. There were no sadder moments in my life than when I had to sit in a ward of women with live babies inside them, waiting for mine to be washed away like unwanted garbage. This happened many years ago, and I understand things are done a little more sensitively nowadays, thank goodness.

Anyway, we'd tried everything. I'd had stitches to hold the baby in place. I'd spent weeks scooting around everywhere on my butt, not daring to stand erect or walk anywhere for fear of triggering a problem, but nothing worked and the babies died. So, having only surrogacy left to try (which was practically unheard of in those days), I felt I was never going to be a mother or give my husband his longed-for son. Then I met a remarkable woman. She told me that she could 'see' I'd had past-life problems, and that all I needed to do was to resolve them; then, if I was ever meant to have a child, I would. I have to confess I didn't really believe her at the time and thought I had enough 'real' problems in life without stirring up old issues that may or may not be real. But I guess my angels heard my cries for help somewhere along the line, because they took a hand in things.

I had a dream. I saw myself as a raggedly dressed woman, I think on the streets of Victorian London. There were horses and carriages and people dressed in clothes of that time. I felt like I was floating above myself (I was told later that I might have been doing what they call 'astral travelling', where you go somewhere else in time and place in a sort of real dream). In this dream I had two snotty-nosed kids with me, both boys. They were dressed in rags, too, and it was freezing cold. I could see all the breath clouding white from their mouths. The boys were crying, hungry, begging their mother (me) for food, but she didn't have any. I couldn't believe how people were just passing them by, not caring. No one even looked at them, and it was as if they were invisible. No one seemed to see me either where I drifted above the scene. I remember thinking how great it was not to live in those times. It was obvious that the three of them were dying, and in 'my' time, today, there was help for people like that. I felt that the world had learned to care a bit more than it used to about poor people. I remember thinking how glad I was to live in the Western world, where the state helps us, and with that thought I woke up.

I realized straight away that this had been more than a mere dream and I felt that my angels had taken me back to my past, not to suffer, but to help me realize that things were different now.

I went back to sleep and had another dream. This time I saw an angel and he spoke to me. He told me that I'd been subconsciously telling my body to let my babies go because I was afraid I wouldn't be able to take care of them, just as I hadn't been able to back in the past life I'd seen. The angel told me that if I let that past go and understood that I had plenty of safety nets in this life, things would change. By the next morning I felt very optimistic, as if a weight had lifted from me.

Today I have two grown-up sons and I believe they are the same boys I lost back in Victorian England. I also believe they are the same souls that I lost five times, (as they struggled to get through what I now see as their 'rehearsals' for being born), and would have gone on losing them if my angels hadn't helped me.

Chapter 5

ANGELS WHO USE ANIMALS TO HELP US

Animals have much purer souls than we humans. They often come to us in order to help us with a difficult time. They do this with no sense of grudge, no sense of not living their own lives, no sense of giving us their time, and it's these things that show the purity of their soul. Of course they will sometimes be 'just animals' and live as nature intended, but when asked by an angel to give up their lives to help their frailer human partners, they will do so immediately and without question.

Animals live in the moment, something that as humans we find almost impossible, which is also evidence that in many ways they are more evolved than us. Some people will find this impossible to accept and claim that humans are the ultimate lifeform, and in some ways they are right. I believe that the transition of a soul through bodies from life to life almost always starts with a 'lower' lifeform and then progresses up through the sentient animals until finally becoming human. This sometimes changes, though only in certain circumstances. However, the way I see the normal progression is that we need to spend time first as animals in order to be capable of facing the challenges we will face as human beings. Humans do not live in the moment naturally, do not give all their time to help others naturally and, most importantly, are this way because they're brought up by society to be greedy and vain and to judge their success or failure by their possessions and wealth against those of others. So we humans need all the help we can get, and 'grounding' lives as animals can give us the experience we need. Angels will also send us pets to help us heal, to save us from danger and to turn our lives completely around!

Included here are also stories that demonstrate pets that are very close to us can have a telepathic connection with us. The story of Patch's kidnap and rescue is particularly amazing.

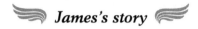

James's story

Pamela and I have been married for over 28 years and have always had beardies (bearded collies) as pets. In fact, our first one was a wedding present requested by Pamela. She had in fact asked for a wolfhound, but I thought it would be too big and too much work to look after, so I compromised when she came up with the idea of a beardie (I thought they'd be easy to look after. I know, I was young and innocent and knew nothing about the breed!).

Anyway I'll skip on through the happy, happy years, to very recently. We currently have beardies numbers four, five and six: Star, who'll be 11 in November, Amy, who'll be five this week, as I write, and Fliss, who was one back in February.

My darling Pamela had a stroke on the 12 July 2009. It was a massive bleed and my sister-in-law and I spent an entire week camped up in the hospital by her bedside, willing her to pull through. The girls (our dogs) would spend the daytime in our car in the hospital car park. I would regularly get them out for a walk, and as soon as I had gotten them out of the car Star and Fliss would try and drag me off for a walk anywhere; however, Amy would pull me towards the hospital. She obviously knew 'Mum' was somewhere in there and wanted to go and see her. This happened several times.

Five days after Pamela was admitted the doctor pulled me aside and regrettably asked me to face up to the fact that Pamela was not going to regain consciousness, and so we had to decide whether or not to go on to palliative care. I knew that Pamela had never wanted to be a 'vegetable' in a bed, so over the course of the next few days the nurses and doctors made her as comfortable as possible, so that she could slip away in peace and dignity. Vivienne (my sister-in-law) and I were convinced that she would slip away on Sunday 19 July, as the 19th is a significant date in both our families, being both Pamela's birthday and my own, also her older brother's, my parents' wedding anniversary and the date Pamela's dad died. But she didn't.

On the Monday the charge nurse for the ward came back after being off for the weekend, and asked how we were doing. We relayed the story and she asked if Pamela could be hanging on to see anybody. We couldn't think who. We had also mentioned the story about Amy trying to get into the hospital. Shyvonne, the nurse, immediately said maybe Pamela was waiting to see at least one of her girls, so we should go ahead and bring the dog in. A good friend who was looking after our girls during the night brought Amy in on the Monday afternoon for about an hour. Amy was as good as gold, just enjoying being next to her 'Mum'. Pamela sadly died that evening. So I'm convinced that Pamela was indeed not going to go without seeing Amy. Although we were very careful about not having favourites, Amy is very special. She's so sensitive.

When I'm having one of my meltdown moments at the loss of my beloved wife, Star and Fliss will come and sniff me, knowing something's wrong, but Amy keeps her distance for a while until they move off, and then after a few minutes she'll climb on board my lap and give me the most therapeutic cuddle imaginable.

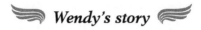 *Wendy's story*

When my mum died, because none of my family was at all religious or church-going, we arranged her funeral ourselves. My biggest contribution was to write her eulogy. I wasn't with her when she died and it was my way of saying everything to her that I needed and wanted to say. I shut myself off from the rest of the family to write it, but Paddy (Mum and Dad's much-loved Labrador) came into the room with me. I sat down and wrote for about two or three hours, pouring my heart onto paper. Of course, I cried and cried while writing and felt much better for it. It never struck me as strange that, while I was writing, Paddy stayed at my feet also crying. He never usually whined or whimpered, but on this day he did just that. I honestly believe he had somehow connected with my emotions. Whether he was crying because I was, because of his own loss or because he understood that it was about Mum it's impossible to know, but there is no doubt that this was heartfelt and I have no doubt that Paddy was aware of the emotional pain in that room.

Soon after that I was walking Paddy with my two youngest children, then aged two and three. They'd grown up with Paddy and were not at all frightened of dogs, but on this particular day a large, quite aggressive-looking dog came running over to us. I could feel the children's fear immediately, but before I could react Paddy placed himself between the dog and my children and stood his ground, growling until the other dog went away. There is no doubt in my mind that Paddy was protecting my babies and me from danger. I remember feeling very proud of him and utterly grateful, because I was strung out and emotionally weak and he did all the thinking and reacting for me.

A few months later my dad went to the Philippines for several weeks to see an old friend. He left Paddy with me and Paddy was just his normal, playful, happy self and showed no signs of missing my dad or being homesick. The day my dad was due to fly home, however,

Paddy changed. He sat by the door and started to whine, like he was expecting someone to appear. When we worked it out, it appeared that this change in Paddy's behaviour coincided almost exactly with the moment Dad was getting on the plane in Manila. Somehow, Paddy knew that his best friend was coming back to him.

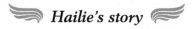

Hailie's story

I had a very close bond with my rabbit, Tyler. He came to me at a very low time in my life and helped me through it with his love and affection, and he made me realize that the world was not such a bad place, by showing me what true love was. Sadly, two and a half years after I got him, he passed away, which devastated me.

Looking back I wonder whether he was sent to heal me and once his job was done he had to leave, as by the time he passed I was settled in a relationship and had my son and was pregnant with my daughter. Tyler also had markings on his nose that resembled angel's wings, which could be purely coincidental, but he helped me in so many ways that, to me, he will always be my guardian angel.

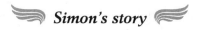

Simon's story

On this journey I've been fortunate to have had many wise and compassionate teachers, including some of the world's top personal growth experts, and yet in all this time my most insightful, wise, gentle and caring teacher was not a guru or an expert, or even a human being. He was my faithful and utterly adorable darling dog, Tyson.

Before I met Tyson, I already wanted to be a success coach, but I had a wound deep in my heart that stemmed from not fully loving myself, which prevented me from being truly successful, just as it does for millions of others. Now, thanks to Tyson, I am a success coach, my wound is healed and I'm living my dream life helping others heal theirs. And all because one kind-hearted dog was able to do what no one else ever could: he taught me how to love myself!

Tyson came into my life in the most remarkable way nine years ago, at a time when I had lost my way professionally and my relationship was on unsteady ground. But worst of all, I was suffering from a self-imposed sense of isolation brought about by the growing realization that, although I had many friends, I'd never met anyone in all my years – and all my travels – who was like me. I kept thinking one day I would. But after 42 years, 'one day' had never come. I felt like a misfit, an aberration, an alien in a foreign world. I mean… I had two eyes, two ears and a nose. But the thoughts in my head and the feelings in my heart seemed to be different from everyone else's. I seemed to feel emotions more acutely than others. For a grown man, I wept a lot – mainly at the images of suffering on the nightly news. Stories about war, hunger or – worst of all – animal cruelty pierced my heart as though it was me who was experiencing them.

I yearned to give love unconditionally and yet I didn't know how. So I shrank back into myself and slipped deeper and deeper into depression.

Then one day I received a phone call from a close friend of mine called Nicole. She knew I was struggling, and she knew that my beautiful and loving partner at the time, Dana, was also struggling. So she suggested we might like to look after a dog for some friends of hers who were returning to England and needed someone to mind him for six months before sending him on to join them. The way rabies quarantine laws work in the UK is that if you live abroad and you want to bring your dog into the country, you have a choice: you can either bring them with you and put them in a cage in some ghastly quarantine facility for six months or you can choose the much kinder option of giving them an anti-rabies shot and leaving them with a foster family, who after six months can then put them on a plane to the UK where they will be cleared to go straight home to you. So that was the deal. Look after the dog – whom Nicole described as being the size of a small lion – for six months and then put him on a plane to England.

I declined Nicole's offer, partly because I felt at the time that having a large dog to look after would be a burden, and also because we only had a small garden and I felt it would be unfair to him. I'd never had a dog before. When I was young my father had had a black Labrador called Bess and I loved her with all my heart, but I was still a child when she died and I felt I might not have what it took to look after a dog properly. Nicole pushed the issue. She knew that her friends were starting to panic because they were due to fly out in a few weeks and they hadn't yet found someone to take care of their dog – which, after further questioning, I discovered was a very large, four-year-old Rottweiler–German shepherd cross called Tyson. Now, if I asked you to picture a huge dog that was half Rottweiler and half German shepherd, weighing 110lbs (50kg), the image that would spring into your mind is probably much the same as the one that sprang into mine! I pictured the kind of intimidating attack dogs the Nazis used to patrol the perimeters of their evil concentration camps, all muscles, teeth and salivating jaws powerful enough to bite your leg clean off! I refused politely. Nicole sounded sad but said she understood and I thought that was that.

Then the following week she called again. 'Are you sure?' she said. 'I think a dog would be so good for you. Why don't you just go and meet him?' It was now just two weeks before Chloe and Paul, Tyson's owners, were due to fly and they still hadn't found anyone willing to take care of him. It was looking as though they would have to put him in a cage for six months and they were clearly distraught. 'He's a beautiful dog, not at all like you imagine,' Nicole went on. 'I know you'll fall in love with him and I just feel, I don't know… like you're meant to be together.'

But my mind was made up. A few days later she rang yet again. 'Something is telling me you should be the one to care for Tyson,' she said. 'I don't know why, I just have a feeling about it.'

Looking back now, I can't recall if I was swayed by what she said. All I know is that I rejected her a third time and that when I hung up the phone I felt how Jesus' disciple, Peter, must have felt after his third denial… as though I had just done something very wrong, although I didn't know what.

The following Wednesday – four days before Chloe and Peter were going to put Tyson in a cage and board their flight back to the UK without him – I found myself waiting outside a motorcycle repair shop more than 18 miles (30km) away on the other side of town while the mechanics gave my beloved Kawasaki its annual service. My mobile phone rang. It was Nicole.

'I know you don't want Tyson,' she said immediately. 'But I thought I'd just try one last time. They haven't found anyone to look after him and they fly out on Sunday.'

Hearing the desperate tone in her voice, I realized how selfish I had been and suddenly felt deeply sorry for the poor dog. No animal should ever be put in a cage, let alone for six months far away from his family.

'All right,' I said. 'I suppose the least I could do is meet him, but I can't promise you anything.'

Nicole sounded ecstatic. I asked her where Chloe and Paul lived, thinking I would ride over when my bike was ready. What she said next made the hairs on my neck stand up and I nearly dropped my phone. I was miles out of town, far from where I live. And I only went there once a year to have my motorbike serviced. But that day, at that precise moment when she rang, I was standing about two minutes' walk from Chloe and Paul's house!

I often wonder what it must feel like to be 90 and to look back on my life from the comfort of my favourite rocking chair. What would I regret the most? What would I be most proud of? What would my happiest memory be? The first two I can't answer yet. The third is easy.

Chloe and Paul answered the door together and almost fell into my arms with excitement. I tried to calm them down and explained I was only there to meet Tyson, and I hadn't agreed to look after him. But my words trailed off into stunned silence when I saw behind them, bounding towards me like a giant woolly bear, the happiest, most strikingly beautiful dog I have ever seen. Tyson, all big boofy paws and wagging tail, bowled straight past Chloe and Paul and leapt into my arms like a long-lost lover, kissing me and licking me and sending me tumbling backwards against the door.

To this day I don't know if he knew I was his saviour from the dreaded cage, or if he recognized me immediately as his soulmate. All I know is that it was love at first sight – for both of us! For me, as we hugged each other, it felt like coming home – or, to be more accurate, like finding my home for the first time after 42 years of searching for it. In that instant something shifted inside me. I didn't know what it was at the time but, looking back, I know now it was the moment my healing began.

When I think back about the way we met – and the fact that, today, Nicole says she still doesn't know why she pushed and pushed so hard for it to happen – it is clear to me that Tyson and I were destined to be together.

Chloe and Paul dropped him off at our house on Saturday, along with their cat, Ginola, a huge, Garfield-like ginger tom whom Nicole had forgotten to mention and who also needed to be cared for and put on a plane with Tyson in six months' time. It was immediately apparent that Tyson and Ginola weren't like other dogs and cats. They had grown up together and were more than just best friends – they were like brothers.

They cuddled together, kissed each other often and even slept on the same bed, with Ginola curled up against Tyson's stomach. Throughout the years they lived with Dana and me, and then, after we broke up, with me on my own, Tyson would always tend to Ginola's wounds after he got into a scrap with one of the neighbourhood cats, which he did quite often. As soon as Ginola came home, Tyson would hold him down gently with one paw while he licked his cuts clean. And if ever Ginola was out on the tiles and Tyson heard the sound of a catfight, he would leap up – even from a deep sleep by the fire – and run out into the garden, where he would bark loudly and watch the top of the fence at the end of the garden until Ginola eventually returned home.

Sometimes Tyson would wait for an hour or more, never relaxing until he saw Ginola scramble back over the fence and plop noisily to the ground. The unwavering loyalty and kindness Tyson showed Ginola taught me the true meaning of friendship in a way no book, no seminar and no human being had ever done, or ever could. I know that if I can show my friends – and my supposed enemies – even a quarter of the loyalty and love Tyson showed his 'little brother', I shall live a very rich and happy life indeed.

From the day Tyson gallumped his way into our lives with his eternally wagging tail, massive bear hugs and unquenchable enthusiasm, Dana and I knew it was going to break our hearts to have to say goodbye to him in just six short months. In fact, after only one week it was impossible to imagine life without him. Everywhere I went, Tyson would walk calmly by my side with no need for a lead or a collar. He would stop at roads, obey all commands and wait patiently outside shops until I came out again. Passers-by would invariably marvel at how handsome he was and how immaculately well-behaved and friendly he was as well. No matter who he met, Tyson would always go straight up to them and lean on them, giving his love without caution or condition.

'Where can I get a dog like that?' they would ask. But I had to explain that, unbelievably, he had been abandoned as a puppy by his first owner and had been rescued from a pound (by Chloe), which meant he had been neutered. Sadly, I would tell them, there could never be a 'Son of Tyson'!

From day one, Tyson and I were inseparable. At picnics and barbecues, friends and strangers alike commented on how perfectly matched he and I were and how he was so obviously 'my' dog. Then, after I told them he wasn't my dog and I was only minding him for a short while, they would say, 'Well, he should be. You're perfect together.' My thoughts exactly!

Dana got the same treatment. Tyson absolutely adored her and wherever they went people would comment on the strength of their bond. But as the months flew by and the dreaded day grew closer and closer, Dana and I grew more despondent. We thought seriously about moving house and just disappearing with Tyson and Ginola where no one could find us. But we also knew how much Chloe loved both of them and that it would be grossly unfair. No, there really was no way we could prevent the inevitable from happening. Then one day, a light bulb went off in my head. I knew the purpose of life is to learn and grow, so I looked at our predicament from that perspective – and in a flash I realized the lesson we were supposed to be learning from Tyson and Ginola was to live in the moment. Like life, nothing lasts for ever. We only have so many days, so rather than spend our lives worrying about dying, we are supposed to enjoy every moment we can while we are here. Our six months with Tyson was a microcosm of that. Rather than mope around knowing that one day it would be over, we decided to relish every moment we had with him while we could.

And as soon as we got that lesson, we were rewarded with a miracle.

Just two weeks before D-Day, Dana and I were sitting at home one evening watching television. Ginola was asleep in her lap and Tyson was asleep at my feet when the phone rang. I answered it, and Dana knew immediately who it was by my expression.

We hadn't spoken to Chloe for several months, and all I could think was that she was calling to make sure the boys were all set for their big journey. But this is what she said, 'Simon. I'm so sorry to put this on you – but Paul and I have split up and we are both moving out of our house. I know this is a lot to ask, but would you by any chance be able to keep Tyson and Ginola, as we can't look after them here?'

It took every ounce of restraint I possessed to commiserate with Chloe and get off the phone as quickly as I could before the volcano of joy erupted inside me and I danced around the room shouting and laughing and crying all at once. Dana and I whooped and hugged each other, tears rolling down our faces. We hugged Tyson and Ginola so tightly we must have squeezed them half to death! In all my 51 years, I never received a better phone call. And I know I never will. Most important of all, I have never forgotten the lesson we both learned about living in the moment – and the fact that when we learn such an important lesson, our angels always reward us immediately with a gift of pure joy.

One morning, about a year later, just after Christmas, I was up early and sitting on the patio making notes for a book I was writing at the time about the dynamics of human relationships and why they so often break down. The chapter I was working on dealt with the agony and confusion that many people feel when they start to doubt whether their partner truly loves them because they just don't feel loved by them. Tyson, as ever, was at my feet, looking up at me with his big, wise brown eyes, waiting patiently for me to take him for a walk. As I smiled at him, a question popped into my head. It almost felt as though he put it there via telepathy, or something. 'Why do I love you so much?' I said out loud, bending down to kiss him on his nose. 'I mean, you are the gentlest, kindest and most loving dog in the world. But you never tell me you love me, and you never buy me things or take me places to show me you love me!'

And then it hit me. I loved Tyson so much because he LET me love him!

It was that simple. I kissed his nose again in delight and started to write as fast as I could as the words literally poured out of me onto the page. So many people feel unloved by their partners because their partners disappear into themselves whenever a challenge arises. That's how some people deal with things, but it leaves the other person feeling abandoned and unloved. We all crave openness. We want our partners to be fully present, to share their feelings with us and to open up the deepest, darkest recesses of their hearts. But so many people are uncomfortable with that. It makes them feel vulnerable. And besides, they mistakenly think that what we really want is for them to be strong, and that involves shutting down their emotions – closing up their hearts, if you will – so that they can 'get the job done'. Sure, we love a strong partner who makes us feel safe and protected, but not if it means they shut themselves off from their emotions, thus denying us the opportunity to love them at the deepest level. You see, the bottom line is it feels better to love someone than to be loved by someone. We long to be able to love fully, and if our partner doesn't let us – by not opening up – we will take this as evidence they don't truly love us.

The terrible irony is that throughout all this, the other person believes they are being a good partner. They love us. Take care of us. Work hard to provide us with all we want. Even tell us they love us over and over again. And they simply cannot understand why we say we don't feel loved! This fundamental misunderstanding can quickly turn to resentment, which turns to anger and fighting, and worse. And, often as not, we split up, thinking the other person never truly loved us, while they're left thinking we must be mad because all they did was love us. If only they had simply opened up their heart and let us love them! By doing this, of course, they are not really 'doing' anything at all, which is why it almost never occurs to them. It is entirely passive, and yet can make us feel as though we are actively being loved.

A few days later, at a New Year's Eve party, I shared my insight with a man I met who had confided in me that he was having some difficulties with his relationship. As soon as I had finished, his eyes lit up. He handed me his drink, thanked me profusely and rushed off to find his wife. I watched him run up to a beautiful woman sitting all by herself and give her a long, tender hug, and I knew instantly that Tyson had saved their marriage.

Sadly, my relationship with Dana couldn't be saved. We went our different ways, but our love for Tyson has kept us together and today, seven years later, we are closer now than ever. I am also proud to count Dana's boyfriend, David, as one of my dearest friends. Everyone I have met in the past seven years – and I mean everyone – who learns that Dana and I lived together for four years is flabbergasted at how we have managed not only to stay close friends, but to grow our love and friendship to an even deeper level. They all ask me how on Earth we did it. And I always give them the same one-word answer: Tyson. You see, after we broke up, whatever feelings we may have had about each other were always of secondary importance to the need to care for Tyson. Ginola, being a cat, was much more adaptable. But Tyson was a very sensitive soul and he absolutely loved Dana as much as he loved me, so it was important that he spend a lot of time with both of us. The conversation of who should have Tyson never once came up. Dana and I never spoke about it even for a second because we both knew that he was neither 'her dog' nor 'my dog' – he was an angel who had come into both our lives, and wherever he was needed was where he would be.

I know how much Tyson helped Dana immediately after we broke up, and then when she moved north to live with David, Tyson came to live with me. And that's how he was able to heal both our hearts.

Whenever I went away, Tyson stayed with Dana and David. And as often as I could, I would drive him to their house three hours north of Sydney on a weekend so he could spend a whole week with them, and they would drive him back the following weekend.

To give you an idea of how much he loved Dana, four years after we broke up Tyson and I were walking down the main street of the suburb where I lived and we both heard the distinctive 'beep beep' sound of someone disarming their car alarm by remote control. It was exactly the same alarm that Dana had had on her old car, which she had sold several years earlier. Despite it being years since he had heard that sound, Tyson's ears pricked up immediately and his eyes opened wide with an ecstatic expression of 'Mum!' In a flash he was off, running up and down the street as fast as his legs could carry him, searching for her.

I called after him that it wasn't his mum, but he ignored me. He raced up and down the rows of cars for a good 20 minutes before I could get him to agree, reluctantly, that it wasn't Mum's car, and he eventually followed me home with a pitifully forlorn look on his face, the kind of 'woe is me' expression only genuinely sad dogs are capable of, and no human can ever hope to emulate!

Tyson lived with me for seven years before he died, and in all that time he always welcomed everyone who came to the house with the same joyful greeting. But there was a very special welcome he reserved just for Dana. He literally turned cartwheels and jumped for joy every single time he heard the distinctive sound of her voice calling his name from the car as she pulled into the driveway. I'm told he did the same thing when I went to pick him up from her house. So you see, Dana and I could do nothing but love each other, when the object of our adoration loved both of us so much. Our deep and enduring friendship is yet another of Tyson's legacies and a lesson to us – and all of you – that love never has to die. The years I lived with Tyson have been the happiest of my life by far. And in all that time he taught me so many valuable lessons about patience, loyalty and unconditional love, just by being himself.

But the most powerful and life-changing lesson of all he decided to save for last.

I knew Tyson was getting old, and that my nightmare was not far from becoming a reality. He was 13, which for his two breeds and his size was well above the average life expectancy. His arthritis meant he had trouble getting up from his bed, and he walked very slowly. And he had a brain tumour that caused him to have terrifying seizures like epileptic fits every few weeks. But he never complained once, and he never showed even a hint of grumpiness right up to the end, another lesson that we humans would do well to learn! The most difficult challenge of having a pet is the knowledge that one day you will have to say goodbye to them. We love them like our children, and yet when we have a child we assume that the natural order of things is for us to die before they do. We love them like our husband or wife, and yet when we fall in love we never think about who is going to go first. Not so with a pet. Right from the start we know that, barring some tragedy, we will have to bury them one day. And the pain of that is almost too much to bear. I was never able to even contemplate life without Tyson. He was my partner, my son and my whole world. And I knew that when the day came, I would fall apart. But Tyson had other ideas.

One Monday morning, about two months after his 13th birthday, I took him in to be washed by the groomer who worked at the vet surgery just up the road where Tyson always went when he was sick. The vets and nurses who work there had become Tyson's second family. They adored him like he was their own, and they always gave him special treatment. In Tyson's later years I decided to have him washed at the vet surgery rather than at a grooming salon, just in case anything happened – in which case he would be in the right place to get immediate expert care. That turned out to be one of the best decisions I have ever made.

A few hours after I dropped him off, I got a call from the vet saying that Tyson was having trouble breathing. I rushed over at once and found him in the surgery being examined by two of the emergency doctors. Tyson was by now completely unable to breathe and was starting to turn blue, so they knocked him out with a powerful anaesthetic and placed an oxygen tube down his mouth and into his windpipe. We then rushed him across town to the emergency 24-hour veterinary hospital where he could receive round-the-clock care. The first thing the doctors did was shave him from head to claw – including his tail, his ears, face and paws – in case he had been bitten by a paralysis tick, an all-too common occurrence in Australia. There was no tick. Instead, a CT scan later revealed that the tumour in his brain had ruptured and this was what had caused him to be partially paralysed.

For three days the doctors fought to save him. A nurse told me later that in her ten years at the hospital she had never seen them try so hard or care so much for a patient. It didn't surprise me – Tyson had that effect on everyone he met! But by Thursday, although he had recovered the ability to breathe and eat, most of his body was still paralysed and I was told he would never sit or walk again. They also said that if the tumour ruptured again, it would likely be fatal. I asked the doctors to give me some time alone with him, and I lay down on the floor next to Tyson for what seemed like hours, crying and holding him until I plucked up the courage to ask him if he wanted to stay or go.

He was drugged, shaved, paralysed, terrified and exhausted, and yet that eternally loving and devoted look was still there on his handsome face as he gazed deep into my tear-filled eyes. It was not a look of pain, or self-pity – but of pure love for me. I will never forget it. And it told me all I needed to know. Dana and David were on holiday in Indonesia and they jumped on the first plane back to Sydney, which was due to land early on Saturday.

That morning I drove Tyson home very slowly from the hospital on his final journey. I carried him into the house and laid him down on his bed, which I had moved into the living room and surrounded with all his favourite toys and teddies. He looked so frail without any fur, and although he could move his head a little, his body was broken and motionless. I did my best to be cheerful for him, singing to him and cuddling him until Dana and David's taxi arrived from the airport.

For the next four hours, the three of us stroked and kissed Tyson and thanked him over and over again for all the joy and love and wisdom he had given us. He was completely calm, despite not being able to move, and was clearly happy to be home again and to be surrounded by his family. Ginola came in and gave him a kiss, and with a determined effort Tyson lifted up his head and gave his little brother one last lingering lick.

There is no doubt in my mind that Tyson knew exactly what was happening. In the hospital the night before, I had spent hours lying with him, explaining that in the morning he was going to come home, and then he was going to go home. I knew he understood.

Nicole arrived and joined in the hugs. She was the reason we had been blessed to have Tyson in our lives in the first place. She had brought us all together, she was part of his family, and we wanted her to be there. She brought out some delicious chicken she had cooked specially for him, and together we gave Tyson his last meal, which he wolfed down with a wonderful final burst of puppy energy. Then it was time.

The vet arrived with a nurse. As she injected the fatal overdose, all four of us held Tyson and smiled and kissed him and told him how much we loved him. I looked into his eyes and said over and over again, 'Thank you, thank you, thank you! Thank you for choosing to share your life with me. Thank you for all your love. Thank you, darling. Thank you!'

Tyson didn't even notice the deadly liquid being pushed into him through the catheter in his leg. And his eyes never flinched or broke contact with mine even for a second as it raced through his veins towards his heart. Then, at the exact moment that it hit and he slipped away, two things happened that changed the lives of everyone in the room for ever. The front door suddenly swung open with a loud bang and a split second later, despite his tail being paralysed from the stroke he had suffered five days earlier, Tyson wagged it strongly four or five times, and then was gone. It was not physically possible, but somehow it happened.

In an instant, our tears of sadness turned to tears of joy because we knew he was safe. He must have seen an angel coming for him and had somehow managed to wag his tail just as he passed over into spirit form. Earlier in the day I had asked my father, who had died many years before, to come and get Tyson and make sure he was all right. So whether it was him, or an angel, who came in through the front door, I don't know, and it doesn't matter. All that matters is we quite literally saw Tyson going up into Heaven, and what was left behind was nothing more than an empty vessel – a frail, broken old body that had served its purpose well and wasn't needed any more. By showing us this miracle and wagging his tail, Tyson in his own inimitable way had given us one last, life-changing lesson … that there is a Heaven, and we have nothing to fear from death.

I know that in the years to come, Tyson will continue to teach me and guide me from the spirit world. And I know that when it is my turn, he will be there to welcome me and we will be together again for ever. Until that day comes, I will spend my life teaching Tyson's lessons to as many people as I can through my books and my seminars, so that his remarkable love and wisdom can heal others, just as they healed me.

 *Alice Jean's story*

Last time we were in Ireland, my brother took my hubby and me to a pub for lunch. All three of us sat right inside the door, facing the next room where there was a pool table. I could see two large Labs asleep under the pool table. After about two minutes each dog popped up its head and trotted towards us. I was sitting in the middle between my hubby and my brother. Both dogs were trying to get to me, almost pushing my hubby's chair out from under him! My brother, Gene, was laughing his head off as he got up and moved out of the way, all the while explaining to my hubby that this kind of thing had been going on all our lives and that his sister seems to attract the animals. Turning to me, he quickly added that that was a compliment!

As a child I never heard anyone warn me not to look animals right in the eyes, like I hear these days, so I never knew better! I always looked into their faces and wondered what they were thinking and feeling. I've always loved them, pets and wild ones, too.

Probably anyone who has lived with any kind of animal has wondered what animals think and feel. What do they know that we haven't a clue about?

I feel like I was given an answer the day my dear Laban died. He was a huge Great Pyrenees Mountain dog that lived with my dairy goats, and was my dear pal. We hadn't a clue that he was sick, or even feeling bad in any way.

One day I was trying to make my way through the many goats crowded around me without tripping and I had a long pipe-feeder over my head, I felt Laban lean against my legs for a moment, like he did sometimes. 'Oops, move pup,' I said, as I made my way to the fence to rest the feeder on the ground. I looked back at him, went and gave him a pat on the head and headed out. I then walked to the little store just down the road for ice cream, and was back in minutes. When I got back I noticed that the goats were gathered around something in a circle in the pasture. All I could see were goat backsides, so I walked over to them. Before I got anywhere close to them they decided to slowly walk away. There on the ground lay Laban – he was dead. The vet thinks his heart just gave out. Do I think the goats were honouring him? Yes, I do. Do I think they loved him as much as he loved all of them? Yes, I do. For three days everyone in the barn was very quiet and Nubian goats are not normally known to be the quiet kind. Of course, I cried my eyes out for three days. Then we all carried on. I still miss him.

Nelson was a Great Pyrenees male given to me when he was three years old. I hesitated about taking him because the woman who made this gift told me that she had never really bonded with him. She preferred another one of her dogs and paid no attention to Nelson. Besides, if I wanted another livestock guard, I wanted to get one from a small puppy, not three years old! I needed that dog to bond with my goats and me like Laban had done. The reason we chose the Great Pyrenees over other breeds of livestock guard dogs is for their wonderful gentle temperament. I'd never be afraid to send my little grandchildren out there with them. They look like big lazy goofs during the day, but that's deceiving because they'll give their life to defend the ones they love.

Nelson had never had a collar on and had never been told what to do. He and I had a 'stand-off' one day, right after we brought him home, when he wanted to go into a yard I didn't want him in. He actually growled at me! I never, in all my life, had had a dog growl at me! It scared me a little, but mostly I knew I had to fix this. I couldn't live with a dog that was bigger than me and thought he was my boss! So I walked into the barn and got a collar and leash, and quickly put them on him, all the while shaking my finger in his face and telling him that I was the boss, and wondering if my finger would be bitten off! He didn't argue with me at all. I didn't even speak to him the rest of the day, which my husband thought was a little cruel on my part. It worked, though. The next day Nelson did everything he could, which included acting goofy and flopping over on the ground at my feet, to make up for his bad behaviour. We loved each other for many years after that, Nelson and I.

Then one day I asked him if he would be willing to live with a family he'd seen many times, and make puppies. He loved the children in that family, so I knew he'd be happy with them. They'd lost their male dog and loved Nelson. He sat up straight and put his head up for a collar and lead, then walked like a little prince out to their truck. I was so proud of him and he knew it. They brought me one of his pups and that dog lives with me now.

Some time later, I was standing at the kitchen sink one day, off in a trance as usual, when I saw Nelson lying there out on the hill in the pasture, with his head up looking around. Suddenly, I realized that

Nelson didn't live with us any more. The next day I called the people who now had him. They told me that they had been planning on coming to tell us that Nelson had died during the recent bad storm we'd had, he'd maybe been struck by lightning. I know he came back because he wanted me to see him here at home again. I think he's always around.

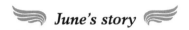

June's story

I can remember the day Rover came into my life as if it was yesterday, although I was only six years old at the time. My dad rescued him from a boy who'd been about to drown him. He was a Border collie with a black-and-white coat. I was at exactly the right age to have a dog, and I always felt so safe with Rover at my side. I loved him to bits, and he would never let anyone harm me. He would even watch over me protectively if my mum was telling me off for something. He wasn't a particularly healthy dog, though, I suppose because of his bad start in life, and by the time he was nine he was going downhill fast.

He started getting lumps on his body, and his back legs went so he couldn't walk on his own. I still loved him very much and, despite his heaviness, I'd carry him around the house and outside to do his business, and then at night upstairs to bed. I thought we were doing all right, but of course my parents knew the end was in sight for Rover. He couldn't be allowed to carry on suffering that way. When dogs can't do normal 'doggie' things, they aren't happy. My dad was off work as he'd a slipped disc and so money was very tight at that time.

As soon as they had enough money for the vet, my parents waited one morning until I had gone off to school to take him, and when I came home that day my precious friend was gone. My mum and dad had loved Rover, too, and the three of us cried and cried together. When I went to bed that night the bed felt so empty without him at first, but then I pulled my pillow down the bed as I always did to make room for Rover at the top and I felt that he was still there with me.

The next morning I set off for school, thinking about Rover with every step. Suddenly I became aware of a clicking noise as I was walking and I finally realized that with every step I took there was the sound of claws on the pavement keeping up with me. Rover was trotting alongside me, keeping watch on me, just as he always had when he was alive and well. This continued, every day, for nearly two years, until we were ready to get another dog.

This was another Border collie, and her markings were like a negative of Rover. They were the same but in reverse: she was white where he'd been black, and black where he'd been white. I named her Sheba because this was the name that was shouted in my head and I knew it was her name. My dad was very strict with our dogs, in as much as he would never let them out in the street, except with him and then only on a leash. They were only allowed to run free in an open field where there was no danger from traffic.

Sheba and I had a close connection. I was 18 by then, and sometimes felt down, as teenagers do. Sheba would understand how I was feeling when it seemed no one else did, and she would nuzzle up close to me, licking my tears away.

But tragedy struck when Sheba was just four years old. It wasn't like her, but for some reason that day she jumped the fence into a neighbour's garden and ran off. I didn't know about it, as I'd already gone to work. Maybe she was trying to find me. I'll never know for sure.

Out of the blue, I suddenly got this awful feeling deep in my stomach. I didn't know what it was, but I knew I had to go home immediately, so I told my staff supervisor that I was feeling ill and had to go home. As soon as I got into the house and my lovely Sheba wasn't there to greet me like she always did, I knew.

My mum told me that Sheba had been knocked over by a car and killed, while running away from another dog. The man who had run her over had lifted her to the side of the road and gone into our local police station to report it. They had called Mum to tell her. What was odd was that the accident had happened at exactly the same time I had felt sick and said I had to go home. It was like Sheba was calling out to me to say goodbye.

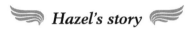 *Hazel's story*

Millie, our Maltese Terrier, was the most beautiful little dog, and so smart. She knew every word we were saying and could communicate 'yes' and 'no'. She would nod and sneeze for 'yes', and give a shake of her head for 'no'. She'd do her 'Bob-a-job' work, as we'd call it – we'd get her to pick up washcloths and other small items for the laundry basket and carry them in her mouth to the basket or the washing machine.

Once the job was done, she'd get her treat. My dad also taught her to bring her plastic dish for a cup of coffee. He got down on the floor with the dish in his mouth and crawled round the floor to show her how to carry it. Mind you, if Mum gave her a drop of tea instead of coffee, she'd upend the dish on the floor because it wasn't coffee. I guess she was more than a little bit spoiled. We wouldn't allow Dad to put a kennel outside for her and she was very much an inside family dog all her life. Dad and my sister would often tease her and ask her to show us her teeth, which she did. She'd bare her teeth and growl. Some of her 'human antics' were great.

She was named Millicent by my dad, but that quickly got changed to Millie for short. She was only called Millicent when she was in trouble. Her nickname was Mim, which also came from my dad. I think she really understood everything we said to her, and she was such a loyal pet that one time when my mum took her for a walk and fell over on the way, Millie took off and started running for home to get help. Fortunately Mum was able to pick herself up and stop Millie from running all the way home.

Our Millie died in September last year and every so often she visits us. She leaves behind little tufts of white fur that I find on the floor, usually near the sliding door she went through into the back garden, and I'm convinced that it's her way of letting me know she's still around.

We bought a new puppy in January this year, a cavalier King Charles spaniel we call 'Lady', and she sometimes looks straight at Millie's picture on the wall and barks, and I'm certain she sees Millie sometimes. I've also seen a small white light darting across the kitchen early in the morning around breakfast time.

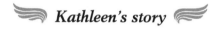 **Kathleen's story**

It was a cold winter day but the roads had thawed for the first time in a week – enough so that we were able to drive to the nearest grocery store for provisions. We had no intention of coming home with a pup, but then we saw two young children with a box of blue-eyed puppies. We didn't care about gender when we got Ubu, as we were rescuing her and she was the least attractive puppy. We figured the others would find homes as they had pretty markings. The children told us the pups' mother was a blue heeler (Australian cattle dog) and the father an Irish terrier. I carried her home, cuddled against my body inside my shirt. She was such an odd-looking animal that when my daughter saw her peeking out of my jacket she exclaimed, 'What is that?'

Ubu would have never won any beauty contests but her loyal devotion made her a winner in our eyes. We had her for 17 wonderful years, and even towards the end she would do her best to stand guard, despite being old and frail.

Just when I was thinking that I'd have to make the awful decision to let her go, one hot day Ubu passed away quietly at home. It was as if she wanted to make it easier for me. We buried her in the backyard under the Ponderosa Pine we brought from the old house when Ubu was just two years old. Then we went out and got a rose bush to mark her resting place. I went through the day feeling that the world seemed so different without her. She had been with us for so long.

I'd been thinking, too, about what a psychic had told me about how Ubu's final moments would be. And now, looking back at all that happened, I see how everything fell into place for us to be together at that time. I had hoped that she would pass peacefully in her sleep but I'd wanted to be with her. I didn't think it would be likely that that would happen, but it did. On that day I was meant to go on a shopping trip with my daughter, but there was a strange mix-up with our communications and she left without me. If all had gone as planned I would have gone out and would have missed Ubu's passing.

She was so faithful to her job watching over us that I had hoped she'd be able to work up to the end, and I was happy that she did. I'm looking forward to meeting that sweet soul again some day.

Oh yes... the rose we planted on Ubu's grave is a variety called Oranges and Lemons. The flower is striped and two-toned – it's unique, just like Ubu. The rose didn't have any flowers until my birthday in July and then there it was – one perfect bloom – a gift from my wonderful and amazing dog, Ubu.

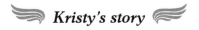

Kristy's story

We were aged 12 and 15, my brother Danny and I, when we went for a week's holiday with our auntie in Dorset. It wasn't much of a holiday, to be honest, as it was on a farm and we already lived on a farm at home in Wiltshire. I think Mum sent us there just to get us out of her hair, rather than for our own sakes. The six-week school holidays must have seemed like years to her. Anyway, it was a pleasant week and we enjoyed the different countryside, but we were both a bit bored and itching to get back to our computers at home.

If it had just been down to me I don't think anything weird would've happened, because I would've gone home the conventional route that day, no matter how long it took, as I was not keen on trudging round the wet countryside in the dark. What happened though, was that by the time we got all the connecting trains and ended up at our home station, it was about 9:30 p.m. and almost dark. There'd been a delay and we'd just missed our bus, the one that passed right by the end of our driveway. There would be another one, but we'd have to wait a whole hour.

Danny reckoned we could walk the rest of the way in about half that time. I didn't want to because I thought it would take twice that. No, he said, not if we go 'as the crow flies'. We could, he insisted, walk cross-country, along footpaths, tracks and across fields, and cut the time in half. It sounded logical so I reluctantly agreed. I don't think either one of us took any notice of the fact that it was clouding over, so the stars and moon wouldn't be out to guide our way once it was fully dark. We set off, both tucking our jeans into our socks to avoid getting them wet in the long grass.

It was perfectly fine at first and we made good time, but that was because we were on stone footpaths and mown fields. Once it was really dark I realized how silly we'd been, because we couldn't see more than a few feet ahead. People who live in towns have no idea how dark the countryside can be once you move away from all street lighting. We didn't get lost, exactly, because now and again we saw the twinkling lights of a cottage or a farmhouse that we could identify. I was just about ready to go and knock on a door by then, though, because my legs were soaked despite my precautions, and I was sick of having brambles and other branches whip suddenly across my face in the dark, but just in time Danny said, 'Here we are, in the back meadow, we're almost home.' Immediately, thoughts of a hot shower and a pleasant hour of checking and answering my e-mails cheered me up and I pressed on happily. We both knew that we just had to cross the railway sleeper bridge from this meadow to the next, then we could walk across the last field and we'd be in our yard.

We stumbled along, feeling for the gap that would signal the end of the bridge. Just at that moment we both nearly had a heart attack as Dad's collie, Merle, appeared out of the darkness. Merle could be a bit of a pain as she thought she was meant to herd everything, including us, but we were pleased to see her as it confirmed that we were home.

Danny let out a whoop when his searching fingers found the gate on our side of the bridge and he started fiddling with the latch, moaning because the gate was usually open while the field was empty, and he knew that the cattle weren't in that field yet. They never went in there until late August and this was only mid-July. Finally he managed to flip the bolt, but before he could actually swing the gate open, it all went wrong because Merle wouldn't let us cross the bridge. She kept barking and bouncing in our way, and when that didn't work she actually growled at us, showing her teeth. I'd always been a bit wary of her, so I told Danny that we should give up and go the long way round. Reluctantly, he agreed. Even his bravado had gone by then, so we backtracked to the hedge and climbed the gate that led into the lane. By following the lane for a few hundred yards we came to the end of the drive and we could walk from there easily, even if it added about ten minutes to the journey. Merle had vanished, thank goodness, and we made our way home with no further adventures.

When we got in, Mum first of all exclaimed and complained at our scratches and the mud plastered all over our trainers and jeans, and then told us she had some sad news. She said that Merle had run off down the lane and been killed by a lorry. We were shocked and upset, but also totally amazed. How could Merle have been dead when we'd just seen her? Mum's face turned white as we told her what had happened, because Dad had already put the cows and calves in the field Merle had stopped us going through. Cows can be very dangerous if they think their babies are being threatened, and two kids feeling their way through a dark field would certainly have aroused their aggressive, protective instincts. In the dark, if they'd tried to trample us, we'd have been helpless. Merle had come back to protect us.

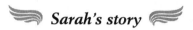

Sarah's story

When I looked at the puppy in the basket, she looked more like a drowned rat than a dog. She'd just been bathed by the rescue centre staff, and although she'd been more or less dried, her very short coat was lying so tight and damp to her skin that it virtually wasn't there at all. Her grey colour didn't help dispel the likeness to a rodent. She was a Chihuahua crossed with something unknown, and my hubby, Ray, always said perhaps she was crossed with a rat, which I thought was a little unkind! She wasn't the prettiest dog in the world, having a slightly overshot top jaw that made her teeth look a little goofy. It didn't matter to me. I picked her up, looked into her big brown eyes and it was love at first sight. From that moment on, she owned me. Ray loved her too, even though he tried not to show it. The day I brought her home, all skinny and nearly hairless, she found a place in his heart.

I called her Teacup. A silly name, but it suited her because she was as dainty as bone china. She didn't have a china nature, though. She was mischievous and bright and when she wanted me to pick her up she was a tyrant, screeching and wailing as if she was being attacked by a giant Rottweiler! It was naughty, really, but I loved the attention she gave me. She'd embarrass Ray if he was waiting with her outside shops while I was inside doing the shopping. Pirouetting around on her hind legs and crying, she'd make a complete exhibition of herself.

She had a passion for custard cream biscuits and would behave really badly over them. It was her worst and naughtiest fault. You couldn't trust her at all if you had one; she'd use every trick in the book to get it from you, even sneaking up the back of the chair and whipping it out of your unsuspecting hand with all the skill of a marauding seagull! Such a tiny dog, she barely grew much bigger than she had been as a pup, but she had the heart the size of a lion's.

She lived a long time and I was very glad of that. There was a while when I thought she'd live for ever, but of course she didn't. The dreaded day that all dog owners have to face eventually came. I was very lucky, though, as apart from having had to have her sticking-out teeth cleaned a couple of times a year, she hadn't had to see the vet at all during her lifetime. The night she died was just like any other. She went out to do her business, got on her bed, snuggled up with the fur-covered hot-water bottle we'd never been able to wean her off, and I told her, 'Goodnight, sweetheart,' as always, and went to bed.

The next morning when I came down, I knew immediately because she never would have stayed in her bed when I was up. She looked so peaceful, still curled round her bottle even though it was cold now. I picked her up, and I could tell by her slight stiffness that she'd been gone for hours, probably soon after I'd left her. I cried and cried, and Ray came down to see what was wrong, and he cried, too.

The next few months were full of hurt, coming home and forgetting as I turned the key, only to be reminded by the silence and stillness. Ray kept asking if we should find another one to rescue, but my heart still belonged to Teacup. I honestly thought it always would. Then a couple of years later something completely miraculous happened while Ray and I were on holiday, in a cottage in the Lake District. It was somewhere we'd been many times before. We loved the area and knew it very well. Our cottage was remote, so remote that Ray said that, as we were getting on a bit, we should think about looking for somewhere less cut off, but I loved it there.

One morning I was making a brew. Ray wandered into the kitchen, answering the call of the smell of frying bacon. I heard a scratch at the door.

'What's that?' I asked.

'I don't know,' answered Ray, settling in front of his plate. I took the hint and went and opened the top of the stable door myself. There was no one there. Then I heard a whine and looked down. There stood the prettiest dog I've ever seen. It was a little fluff-ball with the most gorgeous black coat. It was gazing up at me with the biggest brown eyes through a Beatle-style fringe. I looked down and the dog looked up.

'Who are you?' I asked.

'Who're you talking to?' asked Ray.

'It's a little dog,' I said, opening the bottom of the door.

The dog came in. Ray looked at it, smiled, and offered it a scrap of bacon. The dog, with no questions asked, jumped up onto the chair opposite him as if it had done it every day for years. We took the dog home at the end of the holiday, because no one claimed her and we were so far from anywhere that she was surely a stray.

Penny, as we called her, was a member of the family within a day, but I felt a bit uneasy. I felt I'd betrayed Teacup. Ray said I was being silly. Then that evening I was sitting looking at her while Ray was making a cup of tea, and her face just changed. The black shaggy hair vanished and was suddenly grey and smooth. Her pretty face suddenly had buck teeth. I blinked. It was Teacup's face looking back at me. Then she sneezed. Her face juddered and she was back as Penny. I thought I was going bonkers and decided I wouldn't mention it to Ray. He came in from the kitchen at that point and handed me a cup of tea and two custard creams. Like a flash, like greased lightning, Penny launched herself from the chair next to me, latched her little teeth onto the custard cream and was gone behind the sofa with it before I could move.

'My God!' shouted Ray. 'That's weird!'

Not half as weird as what I saw, I thought. There was no doubt in my mind that Penny was Teacup. I had my baby back.

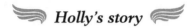 *Holly's story*

My interest in horses first began when my daughter, Charlotte, started riding lessons. Soon after that we were offered a beautiful Arab crossbred mare called Kayleigh, to buy. Knowing little about horses and so not being very cautious (and probably not very wise), I jumped right in and bought her, and she soon arrived home with us. We were quick to find out that she wasn't a novice ride, and yet within three months I was riding her out on the road in her head collar. It was just as if, for no real reason, we'd just trusted each other right from the start. I found I could calm her just by thinking soft thoughts to her.

After we'd had her around three months, Kayleigh fell desperately ill one night, and she was diagnosed with surgical colic. It appeared that a tumour had wrapped around her intestines and had strangled them, and she was quite literally dying.

The next few weeks were a roller-coaster ride as Kayleigh went through not just one but two operations to save her life. The second operation was very drastic but it was her only hope for survival. All the time the operation was taking place I found myself listening to the John Denver song Annie's Song, or as I later renamed it, Kayleigh's Song, because whenever I hear it I always think of her. Kayleigh came home from hospital and slowly recovered, though it took many months. She was only around 13 years old and yet by this time it was becoming obvious that she also had a dreaded disease called Cushing's syndrome, which is a metabolic disorder.

Still, life was good for a while, but over time it became obvious that Kayleigh had a lot of bad things going on in her body for a horse of such a young age. During this time Kayleigh passed a message to me through a friend, telling her, 'I'm going to push you to your emotional limits. Stick with it, because this is for you and your beliefs. My body is not my own. It's a test.' I was panic-stricken by this message, but over time I pushed it to the back of my mind to a place where it was almost forgotten.

After this time Kayleigh continued to go downhill, including suffering chronic laminitis in her hooves, which made them painful. But Kayleigh, who'd always been able to send me telepathic messages, kept on telling me, 'You know how to make me better, you know how to make me well, and I will die of old age.' So I continued to do everything I could for her to make her comfortable. On reflection, if I'm honest, I can see now that to a degree I refused to see just how ill she was, as I couldn't bear the thought of losing her, not my mare.

I clearly recall the day I walked into the field and Kayleigh broadcast straight into my mind the words that I'd dreaded hearing. She was ready to go. I burst into tears, ran indoors and cried on my bed like a baby. Still she spoke in my mind, in a loving but firm way, basically telling me to pull myself together and to go back outside, which I did. She then showed me in my mind's eye an energy cord that ran from my stomach to her. She explained that I'd been feeding her energy in order to help keep her alive, and it had to stop. In the vision, the end that was attached to me was red and swollen, and sure enough I'd been suffering from stomach problems for many months. She told me that now was time to cut the cord and let her go. But, she told me, in order to do this I first had to love her 100 per cent – that the 97 per cent I now felt wasn't good enough! I can honestly say that it took me only minutes to feel the 100 per cent love as I cut the cord to let her go.

I stood in the field and looked at her, and for the first time I actually saw the reality of her. I almost gasped at the realization I'd been refusing to accept for months. At only 15 this mare was dying of old age. The poor girl looked about 30. Kayleigh explained to me that we both needed a few days to get used to the idea of her passing. She said that during this time we needed to spend time talking to each other and coming to terms with her passing. That was a Saturday, and she told me that Thursday would be a good day for her to go, so I booked the vet for her. The following day I had booked a stand at a local horse event and I didn't want to go and leave her, but she told me I was still to go as I needed to look out for a little yellow dog that had a message for me.

So the next day I dutifully set off on my travels, not really wanting to leave her at home, as the time we had left together was to be so short. On the way I decided to pull off at the motorway services for breakfast. As I sat eating my food I did something I'd never done before. I picked up the receipt that I had been given at the till and read it right through. At the bottom of the piece of paper I read the words, 'You have been served by Kayleigh.' As I read the words a cold shiver of realization ran down my spine. Yes, I had indeed been served by this horse. I tucked the piece of paper safely in my pocket, got back in my car and made my way to the event. As soon as I got out of the car I was greeted by the little yellow dog, who belonged to a vet who was there. I asked the dog if it had a message for me, and quickly heard her clear reply, 'It's been a pleasure to serve you!' At hearing this I couldn't help but laugh, because it seemed there were no limits to what this mare was going to do to make me feel at ease and know that she was around me, helping me. I spent the day happily working with people and their horse-related problems, and then made the long journey home.

The next few days, I'm glad to say, went slowly and I felt as if something had changed in me. Something had become peaceful. When the vet turned up on the Thursday morning I felt calm and happy in a strange sort of way. Kayleigh was first injected with a sedative followed by a lethal injection. I just stood and watched as she gently slipped to the ground. Somehow I could no long identify with the old worn-out body that lay on the ground at my feet, because this old used-up shell was no longer my mare. Little did my vet know at the time but I had been silently talking with Kayleigh throughout the whole event, and can honestly say that never once was there any break or distress in the conversation. It had been as if she had been stood there talking to me all the time.

I thought this was the end of it until later that evening when I received a telephone call from a friend. She told me she had just been on an internet forum that we are both members of. There had been a new thread put on there only that day entitled, 'I don't know where this is from or who it's for,' and my friend felt I needed to go and read it, so I did. The message read…

> *'We are but one, I have not left*
> *I stand by your side and guide you*
> *Your dream is my dream and I will defend it to the last*
> *We will walk together side by side*
> *As you are my trusted friend and I your guide*
> *Stepping silently in the sand.'*

'Is this you, Kay?' I asked.

'Yes,' she answered in my mind. 'Did you get the bit about stepping silently in the sand? It's from your favourite poem, Footprints.' I had to laugh, as I e-mailed the lady named Jay who'd put up the post. She e-mailed back and asked me if 'sweets' meant anything to me, as in candy. Before the vet had arrived I'd given Kay two packets of Polo mints, something I hadn't given her in years.

That night as I walked down my driveway to lock the gate I heard Kayleigh's voice loud and clear. 'Look up,' she called, and as I did I saw the most beautiful shooting star. 'That's me,' she said softly. 'Each soul has a star.'

Rather than being the end of our story I feel that this is only just beginning. You see, Kay has never really left me. Just days after her death while I was standing in the field, I heard her ask me for a cuddle.

I turned around and I saw Anam Cara, my other beautiful Arab, looking me straight in the eye. It was her voice coming from him, and I instinctively threw my arms around him. It seems that Kay never really left completely. She chose to leave her body physically, but her wisdom, knowledge and, undoubtedly, her love, live on in the form of this beautiful boy, so that we can fulfil our journey and live out our shared dream together. Anam Cara totally changed that day, picking up all of Kay's mannerisms, and it left me in no doubt that Kay had chosen to pass her spirit into his body.

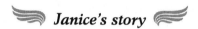

Janice's story

My dog Regis and my cat Portia were inseparable. We got them both together as tiny bundles of fluff, and they went everywhere together, slept together, investigated things together. Quite often it was hard to tell which one was the dog and which the cat. Regis played like a cat, and Portia sniffed around like a dog. So it wasn't all that strange, I guess, that they also started seeing spirits together.

It started one evening in 2004. We'd just moved into an old house with a bit of history, and as Jake, my husband, and I were both interested in ghosts and stuff, we were kind of hoping the old place might have a ghost or two. Regis and Portia weren't so keen! It was a really hot evening and we had no air-conditioning, so we had all the doors and windows open. We were still hot, though. It was breathless, no wind at all, and the air hung heavy around us.

Suddenly I felt a shiver as a draught of cold, almost icy air swept around my ankles. It was really odd as none of the curtains was moving at all. At the very same second Regis, who'd been fast asleep on the rug, and Portia, who'd been right next to him, both jumped up in the air and spun round to face the stairs. Jake and I looked, too, naturally, but nothing was there. Regis growled and Portia hissed, both of them with their hackles up. This kind of thing happened many times, until eventually the animals started to almost ignore whatever it was. They resorted to just staring and following it with their eyes, but Jake and I never saw anything.

Years later Regis got a bit rickety, and didn't move so well. He'd still romp with Portia and the two of them would cuddle up together in the evening, but he was getting old. At 15 he was a good age for a dog, but of course Portia was still quite sprightly, cats generally living longer than dogs. She was very sweet with him, waiting if he got left behind and, when he didn't see too well, guiding him around. She didn't even moan when he ate her food by mistake.

Jake and I discussed what on earth we'd do if Regis died. How would Portia cope? Finally the day came, and Regis died in his sleep. We left him where he lay so that Portia might understand he'd gone, rather than snatching him away from her. She was completely disinterested in his body, which surprised me. I thought she might push him with her paw or something, to try and make him get up. But no, instead she went off into the garden, as if for all the world Regis was with her.

But by night she wasn't so happy. We'd had to take Regis' body away and she didn't seem to know how or where to go to sleep. Jake and I did our best and tried to comfort her, but she didn't want to know. Finally, at about 9 p.m., she suddenly jumped up and started meowing, looking towards the stairs, and we were put in mind of that first time they saw our 'ghost'.

Her meows got more and more excited and she went bounding up the stairs, as if she were chasing something. Jake and I got up and followed her, but she was too quick for us and all we saw was the flash of her tail as she rounded the top of the stairs. By the time we got up there she'd vanished into the bedroom. We went in. We were staggered and pretty upset to see Portia lying stiff on the bed. She must have died in a second as we were still coming upstairs. Then we realized what had happened! Regis had come back for her!

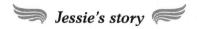

Jessie's story

I got my dog, Barney, as a pup. He was a cross between a springer spaniel and a Labrador, black with piercing brown eyes. His eyes are amazing, golden brown with flashes of amber in them, and everyone remarks how they shine against his jet-black coat. He's always been very 'knowing', either taking a liking or a dislike to people from the word go. I often wondered if he could see their auras, and in the end I think I wasn't far off track. As a family we got very used to seeing him watching an invisible 'something' as it moved around the room. He'd wag his tail at it and usually the 'something' would end up leaving through the ceiling while Barney stared up at it, transfixed. Then after a few seconds he'd just turn and walk away, game over.

Sometimes Barney would get up on his hind legs and 'play snap' at something mid-air as if he was trying to grab it. One or the other member of the family would comment, 'Hello, Barney's ghost-busting again.' In fact he started to develop the nickname, 'Ghost-busting Barney'. Or we'd all say at once, 'Who you gonna call? Our Barney!'

One day I read an article about orbs captured in photographs. It said that if there were spirits about, even if you couldn't see them, a digital camera would capture them as orbs. So I got a camera and prepared to capture some spooks. I didn't really think it would work, and sure enough for the next few weeks Barney didn't do any ghost-busting, or if he did I wasn't quick enough with the camera. But then, because I was observing him closely, I was able to spot the signs of an imminent ghost-hunt. Barney would stand there wagging his tail for no reason, as if he could sense something coming.

So, more prepared, I was able to get snapping. Much to my amazement, and that of the family, I started getting orbs in the photos right away. Sometimes he'd be surrounded by them.

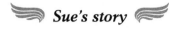 **Sue's story**

I was one of the lucky ones – I had a pony of my own from a young age. I was a huge fan of books like *Black Beauty*, and so I called my little dapple-grey mare Merrylegs, or Merry for short. She lived up to her name, and we spent many happy hours, just the two of us, roaming the lanes, fields and bridleways of Hampshire. I always felt safe with Merry, and after some trepidation my mum was relaxed about me disappearing with her for hours, too. She might not have been quite so keen if she'd known some of the adventures we had! Like one time I came across an old man in the woods who tried to persuade me to get off my pony and go with him. Merry seemed to sense the danger immediately, and although I would never have done what he said anyway, she left me no choice, rushing me away at a canter in the opposite direction, as if she'd seen a rattlesnake! Another time I tried to make her cross a ford, and although she usually went through water quite happily, she refused point blank this time. Then, while I was still trying to persuade her, a car came through and got stuck, because the water was much higher and running much faster in the middle than I'd realized.

The day that really scared me, though, was one I did tell Mum about, because I needed her reassurance. We'd had a nice ride and I decided that we'd take a shortcut through Berry's Wood because the day was hot and the shortcut would take half an hour off the journey. It all started out all right as we set off across a meadow. The entrance into the woods lay diagonally across the grass, and was swathed in deep shadows cast by the big, low-hanging oak trees that marked the boundary between woods and open field. As we were about halfway across the field, Merry suddenly stopped dead. She refused to move at all and tried to turn round. My pony wasn't normally spooky, so I should have listened to her, but I was only 12 years old, so I suppose I can be excused.

I kept turning her in circles, forcing her ever closer to the edge of the woods, but by the time we were about 50 yards away, Merry started shaking. She was staring at the trees and quivering with fear. That did make me think, because she'd never done that before, so I let her stand still. After a few seconds I saw it. A smoky shadow detached itself from the genuine tree shadows, and started swirling across the field towards me and my stricken pony. We were both frozen with fear. The shadow was as black as night and it writhed and twisted its way across the grass. As it got closer the air around us began to grow cold, and the bright sun shining overhead only made the chill feel deeper as the shadow came closer. The darkness inched nearer until it was only a few feet from Merry's front hooves. I could see the sharp line it cut across the bright green grass, and beyond was stark, Stygian darkness that the sun couldn't penetrate.

I dread to think what might have happened if Merry hadn't shown more courage than me, whirling around quickly – though carefully enough that I didn't get tipped off – and setting off across the field at a gallop. I never looked back.

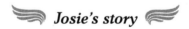 *Josie's story*

I developed agoraphobia when I was in my thirties. I'd had a daughter and the doctors said I was suffering from postnatal depression. But it got worse. First I didn't want to take Charity, my baby girl, out in her buggy. My hubby, Dave, bought me a big old-fashioned carriage pram because he thought maybe I felt Charity was too vulnerable in the little buggy. At first that did help, but gradually I started making excuses not to go out: it was too cold, too hot, too windy, there wasn't time, I had to wait in for a delivery, etc., etc. Soon we were only going out in the car. It took months, but eventually I had to ask Dave to leave the car in the garage until I'd got inside it. Then we couldn't go out at all after dark.

Then he'd have to drop me off right outside whatever shop I wanted to go in, and pick me up the same way when I'd finished. Soon I was having all the groceries delivered, and doing any other shopping online. I had always intended to go back to work, and I really wanted to, but there was no chance of that.

It finally reached its peak when I started rearranging the furniture so that I didn't have to walk through the middle of the room. Dave was patient, but he started cursing the fact that all the rooms were getting harder to get into. There was always something half blocking the way. I thought he was going to have me sectioned or something, but he didn't. He did something else – he brought me home a dog. It turned out that a mate at work had been desperate to rehome his dog. It was a Shetland sheepdog called Jay, and the mate's wife had got sick of dog hairs everywhere and having to keep grooming him. I'd always loved dogs, but I couldn't believe Dave's timing! I couldn't even take our daughter for a walk, so how could I walk a dog? I couldn't even stand at the open door, so how could I let Jay out into the garden?

Still, I loved that dog. I loved grooming him while Charity was asleep; somehow it soothed me. I didn't think of anything while I was brushing his silky coat. But of course he had to wait until evening when Dave got in to go for a walk. I got around to letting him out to do his business by only using the front garden. We had a small porch that had its door on the side, so I was able to open that because I wasn't facing the road. I don't know why that worked, but it did. I'd just open the door enough for Jay to get through, shut it quickly and then watch through the glass until he wanted to come back in, then do the same in reverse. This worked for a while, but Jay seemed to want me to go out there with him, and I just couldn't. Life was bad because I was so limited, and Jay would sit, his head on my knee, regarding me solemnly as if trying to figure out how to help me.

Dave had always made the postman swear to shut the garden gate behind him, and he always did. Tradesmen I would tell as they were leaving to shut the gate, and they did. But one day, in late spring, we had a relief postman, and I didn't see until it was too late that he'd left the gate swinging. Jay went down the path straight to the open gate. I called him, and although he looked back, he took slow steps forwards as if daring me to come get him. By the time he was on the pavement I was hoarse with yelling, and Charity had woken up and joined in with her bawling. Still Jay kept going. He walked two or three steps onto the road, glancing back to see what I was doing. Along the road, to my horror, I could see an oil tanker approaching. Jay had moved to stand between two parked cars. He took one look back at me and I understood. If I didn't go out there and get him, he was going to walk into the path of the tanker, which by then would have no chance of stopping. That did it. I unfroze my feet and ran down the garden path. As I got near to Jay I saw his mouth open in a triumphant grin. I grabbed his collar and the tanker swept past, bathing us in a shower of dust and displaced air.

That afternoon I put Charity in her pram and on shaking legs pushed it, with Jay attached by his lead to the handle, down to the park, around the park and back home. I even picked a few daffodils (which was banned!) to show Dave, or I feared he would never believe me.

After that I never looked back. The following year I was headhunted for a really good job, and everything fell into place for me. I found a great childcare facility and, just when I was wondering what I could do about Jay being cared for, I met a woman suffering from bulimia who was at her wit's end. When I asked if she'd care to have the company of an amazing dog during the day, the woman was very happy to say yes. I had a feeling Jay would work his magic on her, too.

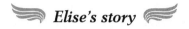 *Elise's story*

Shortly after my first marriage, on the day of my 22nd birthday, 19 January 1979, naïve, unworldly and wanting a baby, I went out shopping one Saturday morning with precisely £60 for the week's groceries. Passing the local pet shop on the way to the shops, I caught sight of one lonely black-and-white puppy in the window. I never did buy any groceries that week, but arrived home, to my husband's dismay, with a six-week-old border collie puppy. Dismayed due to the fact that we both worked full time, I had no idea how to look after a puppy, let alone a grown dog, and the choice of breed didn't fit in at all with our lifestyle. We called him Patch because he had a black patch on the back of his neck and, after a disagreement as to whether or not we should keep him, it was easier to choose a name that my husband had used for his own dog years before, which also fitted our new arrival. Somehow we got by.

I suppose you could say that Patch and I grew up together. I learned responsibility for the first time in my life and how to look after a dependent creature. He had his faults; in fact they were my own, because I was unable to give him what he needed as a young, growing and extremely intelligent, active dog. Hence he could be 'naughty' at times. He was, however, my best friend, substitute child and companion for over 16 years. He was the friend who kept me from totally falling apart during an unhappy marriage, the loss of a baby, my divorce and then the loss of employment. To say that he offered the only real stability in my life at that time would be an understatement.

Patch never strayed far from my side. He slept on the bed, lay on the sofa, ate his meals with me and was, I suppose you could say, spoiled. That is, unless you've read any books by Cesar Milan, the renowned dog behaviour specialist, in which case you'd probably say I was a pretty lousy dog owner! I admit that I do it very differently these days. My dogs are brought up and looked after as dogs, not humans; they're trained, well behaved and they accept the relevant hierarchical order in the 'pack'. They don't sleep on the bed and aren't allowed on the sofa. Oh, those were the days, though. We were soulmates of a kind. They say dogs take after their owners, and I firmly believe that to be the case. In those days, I was rather neurotic; hence, I owned a rather neurotic dog. And we adored each other for nine long years, until one day I will never forget in 1987.

I had gone to my mother's house in Esher, Surrey, and taken Patch with me. He pretty well came everywhere with me except for the times I was working or unable to take him, hence he would often stay at my mother's so he had company until I could collect him. On this particular day I was going to visit a friend in a nearby village and left Patch in my mother's garden, which backed onto a field where we often walked together. It was some time around mid-afternoon when I left, and I didn't return until about 6 p.m., thinking my mother would have brought Patch back into the house before I arrived to take him home with me to my own house in Byfleet. I let myself in (my mother always insisted her daughters had keys to the family house) and expected Patch to run and greet me as he always did. But he wasn't in the house. 'Mum,' I called, 'I'm back, is Patch still in the garden?'

'I don't know,' she answered. 'I thought he was with you.' And he wasn't in the garden either. In fact, he was nowhere to be found. Patch had simply disappeared. The date was 20 December 1987, five days before Christmas.

It was the worst Christmas I can ever remember. I'd recently lost my job, my lover and now the only real friend, ally, baby, soulmate – my reason for carrying on – had gone. With my family's help, I spent the entire Christmas scouring local fields, villages, woods, river walks – in fact, anywhere we had ever walked together. As I'd been something of a wandering soul (I'd moved several times with Patch), we covered a 25-mile radius of dog walks around most of Surrey.

The biggest marketing campaign for one lost dog was immediately under way, with coloured posters and descriptions of him hung in every conceivable location covering Guildford, East Horsley, Molesey, Byfleet and many other villages throughout Surrey; anywhere, in fact, where we'd spent our happiest hours roaming through woods and fields. The internet was still unknown to the vast majority of us in those days, so the only way to try to find him was to put up posters and get as much publicity as possible in the local newspapers, on local radio, at the vets etc. – wherever it was permissible to advertise a missing pet.

I recall becoming ill just after Christmas and having to take to my bed with a high fever, feeling even worse because I was unable to go out and look for my baby. I wrote long, sad poems mourning the loss of Patch with cries to the universe for angelic or divine assistance. I sent out thought messages to my dog, letting him know if he could hear me that I missed him badly, and begging him to be OK until I found him. What astounded me was how much people really cared. The phone calls over that period were profound, from people I didn't know, had never met, and may never encounter again. I received offers of assistance from complete strangers who would call and let me know that they were thinking of both Patch and me and would keep a lookout when they were out with their own dogs.

Many callers believed that they had seen him and, when I was able to get out again, I visited any area where reports of sightings had been made. One young couple with enough troubles of their own – a psychologically disturbed young man and his pregnant girlfriend only days away from her due date – insisted on coming out with me and helping me search some local fields. I really did feel that there was a little divine intervention in the form of some of the wonderful people who appeared in my life during the worst few weeks I can ever remember. And I was never convinced that I really deserved anything – after all, what had I ever contributed to the world to help others?

On the 28 January 1988 I received a telephone call. By this time Patch had been missing for 39 days. I had received so many calls that at this point I didn't get too excited, but the woman's voice sounded different to all the others. 'I'm calling about the dog,' she said. 'But I can't give you my name because I know who has him and it's too dangerous to tell you who I am.' A little dubious at this point, I asked her how she knew it was my dog. 'Well', she said, 'he's a black-and-white border collie and he's getting a little grey. He was stolen from a field in Esher before Christmas and I know who stole him.' Now I really was listening. 'The man who took him is a drug dealer and lives in Kingston. Your dog's still there. I've heard him bragging about the dog he stole in Esher and he brought him to the pub.'

She was frightened to tell me who she was even though a reward was offered for any information, and I got the feeling she really could do with that reward although it was more important to her that I found my dog. It was as though she knew what I was going through. Perhaps she'd been through something similar and could empathize. People who have experienced profound pain frequently are those who are able to feel acutely for others, and I felt she had probably been through her own traumatic experience of loss. Whoever she was, as far as I was concerned this woman was a true angel or had certainly been sent by an angel.

Patch had been reported missing at all the local police stations, but as this was the Kingston-upon-Thames area, after a brief conversation with Esher police they informed me that I would have to speak to Kingston police. *Stuff that*, I thought, and with my lodger, a charming young man (I shall call him Tim) who had been totally supportive throughout the few weeks of trauma, I drove to Kingston Police Station. I was in quite a state by this point, desperately needing to find out if Patch was where this woman had said he was and quite prepared to go with my lodger alone to the address she had given me. The police, however, had other ideas. 'Now, now, you can't go off to this estate on your own, and how do you know that this is your dog anyway?' they said, and took us into an interview room where I had to give more details.

'Well,' I said, 'let me give you an accurate description, then you can check for yourselves.' I was getting more and more agitated. 'Number 1: he has a white muzzle with a white stripe down the middle of his black head and a white chest and stomach. Number 2: he has three black legs with white socks, the front left leg is white with black spots. Number 3: he has a white tip on the end of a black bushy tail, he has a black diamond-shaped patch on his neck. And Number 4... he has been neutered!'

'Whoa... calm down, love,' was the response. 'We just have to make sure before we go barging into someone's flat that we have something concrete to go on... OK, OK... let's get a squad car.'

Three policemen, one squad car, a very agitated, verging-on-hysterical woman and her lodger drove through Kingston at about 8 p.m. that evening. That nearly hysterical woman sat in the squad car with Tim and one policeman while the other two police went into a flat in a block nearby. It seemed like an eternity and I am unsure exactly how long they were gone but at some point I saw them coming back to the car... smiling. 'Now love, we need you to stay calm... I think we've found your dog.' And as calmly as I could, leaving Tim in the car with the driver, I went with the two policemen into the block of flats and up to a front door on the second floor. 'We need to warn you,' one said, 'this man is on drugs, and he's not quite all there. His girlfriend is also in the flat and fairly drugged as well, so we'll just go in so that you can identify the dog.'

Patch barely recognized me and looked as if he, too, had been given drugs or was so traumatized by whatever he had experienced that he could only just stand up and wobble over to me with a slightly glazed look and a half-hearted lift of his tail. I burst into tears at that point and put my arms around my beloved pet. The police asked if I wished to press charges but, looking at the state of the two people in the flat, I said that they had probably suffered enough. The man was in tears, begging my forgiveness and claiming that he hadn't had any idea what he had really done, and the woman was so out of it that I don't believe she even knew what was going on. I just wanted to get home with Patch, get him checked by the vet as soon as possible and have him back by my side. We had to return to the police station to make a further statement, and then took Patch home where he remained, eyes glazed and detached, for a couple of days. The vet found nothing seriously wrong with him, although Tim was convinced that he had been abused, due to a strange reaction when the dog saw him taking his belt off to change.

However, Patch bounced back to his old self fairly quickly and we resumed some semblance of normal life once more. It transpired that the man had been fishing by the river in the field behind my mother's house and had driven his car into the field. Patch had jumped the wall at the back of my mother's garden and, seeing an open car door (he was crazy about cars and would frequently jump into any car with an open door), he had simply jumped in and the man had driven off with him, removing his name disc and collar first. So he had, in fact, known exactly what he was doing!

Patch remained a major part of my life as my best friend and soulmate for almost another seven years until he finally passed on at the grand old age of 16 in July 1995. If it had not been for the help of all those wonderful people, the local newspapers and especially the woman who had read an article in the *Esher News and Mail*, written by Animal Lifeline (Surrey), a registered charity for animal rescue, who I have no doubt were sent by the angels, the universe or whatever, I would never have found Patch again. In writing this story I wish to express my profound and sincere thanks to all for their help and love, albeit somewhat belatedly! The faith I kept in the possibility of divine intervention throughout that time was rewarded in full in the form of humanity at its most loving and the return to me of my beloved dog, Patch.

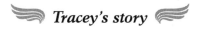

Tracey's story

I look after dogs in my own home when they need a temporary refuge. It was definitely love at first sight. Not the holiday romance kind, which is great while it lasts but is soon forgotten. This was the heart-stopping, life-changing, forever kind. When Misty first walked into our kitchen on Thursday 26 March 2009, I instantly knew she was a very special little dog indeed: a beautiful six-year-old cocker spaniel with a gleaming black velvety coat, huge shiny brown eyes and the most amazing character.

The other dogs didn't make the usual move forward to investigate and sniff her bottom; instead they quietly watched her enter the room and kept a respectful distance while she calmly looked around and then settled regally into her bed. They too knew we had a very special guest. It was like the Queen had popped in for a visit. Queen Misty had entered the building.

That first time she stayed for just three nights, which was over far too quickly. I admit it: I fall in love with every dog that stays for home-boarding. I love them and then I have to hand them back. I had been getting better at the handing-back bit, and I usually recovered quite quickly, but thoughts of little Misty were never far from my mind. I was over the moon when her owner booked her in again for a two-week stay in April.

Those two weeks were warm and sunny and we had some fabulous walks with Misty, our own dog Layla and all the other visiting dogs. In the evenings I'd sit on the living-room floor for the customary group cuddle with them all, and my husband would raise an eyebrow as Misty always had prime position on my lap, one paw either side of my neck while I showered her shiny black nose with kisses. When the dreaded day came, I sat on a bench in the garden on a lovely sunny afternoon, waiting for her owner to arrive. Misty-Moo was on my lap, snuggled into my neck and snoring gently. Her black coat was warm from the sun. All too soon the time came, and she jumped from my lap eager to be reunited with her owner. I watched the reunion with mixed emotions, happy that she was happy, but sad to see her go.

We see some dogs just once a year, but we only had to wait until July to see Misty again. I counted the days until she arrived, and my heart leapt when I saw her trotting down the driveway. Even Layla, the Black Beast of Dartmoor, couldn't contain her pleasure at the sight of her pal, and proceeded to wash Misty's face while Misty sat quietly, taking all the adoration in her stride.

As usual she settled in beautifully, got on with all the other dogs that came and went, and it was clear there was a strong bond growing between her and Layla. On walks Layla would charge into the woods after squirrels with Misty hot on her heels. Misty's little legs would be going ten to the dozen to keep up with her longer-legged friend, and they would re-emerge minutes later panting and excited from the chase.

I made sure I was out when Misty-Moo was collected. I cried as we said our goodbyes that morning, certain it would be a long time before we met again. I cuddled her close to me and told her how much I loved her as she licked the tears from my cheeks. My husband rang me to tell me she'd been collected. My heart broke a little as I wondered if I would ever see her again. Then I couldn't believe what I was hearing as he told me, 'Misty may have to be rehomed. Her owner asked if we knew of anyone who might want to give her a good home.'

Misty arrived three weeks later, at 2 p.m. on Sunday 3 August. Her lovely owner was heartbroken to hand her over, and it was incredibly emotional. Now it's like she's always been ours and I can't imagine life without her. Dreams do come true!

Gemma's story

I think that my dog Tobie sees spirits, because on nights his ears and nose suddenly start to twitch and he goes onto the landing and sits barking and growling at thin air. I check outside and downstairs, but there's nothing there. He then seems to be stalking something, but I can't see anything.

He saved us once. One day we left the gas on in the shop we live above, and Tobie wouldn't stop barking that night. When we woke up we found him scratching at the door to get down into the shop. We opened the door and let him into the shop downstairs and he ran straight to the cooker where the gas was on. He jumped and scratched at the cooker, and I tried to go and switch it off, but Tobie wouldn't let me go near it. He was rounding me up like a sheep and herding me away from the danger. Eventually I persuaded him to let me reach the cooker and turn off the gas, and then he calmed down. If Tobie hadn't warned me I could have died in my sleep from carbon monoxide poisoning, or I might have lit a cigarette and blown the place up. Tobie will also come and tell me if the bathwater is about to overflow. He really is my little star.

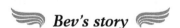

Bev's story

When I moved into my new home I was very happy. It was just an old terraced mill cottage, but to me it was home sweet home, a veritable castle. After being in rented places for so long, I finally had my own front door. That first night I slept like the dead, I was so tired, having moved in single-handed. But the next night it was different. I woke up. It was dark and I had no idea what had woken me. Then I heard it, a distinct thump, thump, thump. I had no stair carpet at the time and it sounded just like footsteps jogging really heavily down the stairs. My first thought was: *It's a burglar!* I was a woman alone in the house, but then I thought that the walls weren't that thick and I knew I had neighbours on either side, so that if I screamed someone would be bound to hear me and call the police. I must have been more tired than I thought, because the next thing I knew it was morning. I forgot all about what I presumed had been a dream.

The next night it happened again, only worse. It started with the sound of light footsteps coming close to my bedroom door. For a moment I was sure that something was going to come into the bedroom. The footsteps were quick and not very loud, and sounded stealthy, but the next noise wasn't subtle at all. It was the thumping noise again, and my heart echoed the thump, thump, thump. I knew I was wide awake and not dreaming. There followed an even scarier noise – chains rattling. Now, I was well into New Age stuff and I couldn't believe that if this was going to turn out to be a ghost, it was going to manifest in such a clichéd way as with chains rattling. Besides, this wasn't the Tower of London – it was an ordinary terraced cottage! I hid under the covers, telling myself it would go away if I didn't respond to it. It didn't. It happened every night. Finally, more exhausted than I'd ever been, I decided to call in a medium.

Of all the things I might have expected her to come up with, I had never expected what she told me. She said the noises were being caused by the ghost of a dog. She told me that a big golden retriever that used to live in the house was making all the noise. The muffled footsteps were actually 'paw-steps', the thumping was him dropping his ball down the stairs. And the chains? That was him taking his lead in his mouth and shaking it from side to side.

The dog told the medium that during his lifetime in the house I was living in, he had often been locked in a big cupboard under the stairs while the owners were out. He'd died in that cupboard. The poor dog had been waiting for years and years for somebody who was 'open' to live in the house, so that he could use their energy to manifest himself.

The dog told her that if he could be allowed to stay for a few more days, he would be ready to leave. Sure enough, true to his word, three days later the dog visited for the last time, and I never heard from him again. I was able to confirm with neighbours, though, that the previous owners had once had a big golden retriever.

Chapter 6

ANGEL RESCUERS

A lot of people, including myself, have talked about needing the right energy in order to get through to an angel and receive help. Generally this means positive energy, which tends to rule out feeling fear, anger, desperation, grief etc. However, this is not always the case as you will see. It seems that sometimes when we are totally terrified or completely depressed, or in some other extreme state, we will and do get help from angels. I think the explanation for this could be that either this high state of negative energy sends out such a strong signal that it still gets through, or that the angels can see something is going to happen to us that shouldn't, due to a third party utilizing their free will to make a bad decision and harm us.

A third possibility, and one I have experienced personally, is that sometimes depression pushes us down so far that we almost have no energy reading at all, and in this state we provide no help to angels, but neither do we provide any resistance. In this 'giving-up' state we can be reached and the angel that reaches out to us may have been trying very hard to help for a long time, but our destructive thought patterns and therefore energy have been too turbulent for them to get through.

If angels do come through to intervene to save a person from a physical accident or an attack, or even a suicide attempt, they can in fact become very tactile, and many a person has felt a shove from their guardian, which has pushed them out of danger. Even cars and trucks can be 'pushed' in this way. In other instances a warning voice is heard. Sometimes they bring someone into our lives just for a moment or sometimes for a lifetime to put us back on our rightful track. At other times the angels will send an animal to warn us or protect us, either from someone else or from ourselves. Angels send all kinds of signs and often use nature to provide the material for the sign, from rainbows to heavenly choirs, from feathers to numbers to car plates and posters. So keep an open mind.

You'll read some stories here in which angels have helped people who didn't even believe in them, let alone asked for their help. This just goes to prove that we do all have rightful paths, and although free will might take us off them from time to time, we're not allowed to leave this world until the time is right.

Some of these rescuer angels have sent signs meant to redirect people or make them come to the right conclusions and take actions to save themselves. If you ever get a day when you get the number of signs given in the 'sky' story, do take notice!

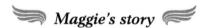 *Maggie's story*

Way back in the early 1980s I was working late nights in a milk bar in Perth, Australia. No ordinary milk bar, mind you. We offered wonderful ice-cream concoctions by the names of Merry Widow, Paluca, Sunset Dreams and heaps more. The American Navy had just begun its stops in Perth for 'R and R', so this Saturday evening we were really busy and I did not get away until after 1 a.m.

Now, usually I would have got a cab home, but with all those sailors lined up and waiting for cabs I decided it would be quicker to walk. Hey, it was only around 40 minutes and the night was warm and gorgeous.

But it soon became apparent that I was being followed. I crossed the street and so did he. I ran. He ran. He was so close at all times, roughly 10 to 15 feet away. I could see him clearly at all times. This must have given him a real buzz.

About halfway home I got to the causeway, a bridge that spans the Swan River. Ahead of me was a huge dark park area, and by this time I was in real panic mode. I remember shouting, 'Hey God! Anytime now, help!'

A cab drew up next to me, the other side of the metal railings. It was driving into oncoming traffic and the driver didn't seem aware that anything was unusual, and that the passenger door was on the wrong side.

The driver reached across, opened the door, and said, 'Margaret, get in.' Now whenever I was in deep trouble I was called Margaret, so naturally I did as I was asked. Somehow, I walked through the metal railings. They simply ceased to be there. I've tried this many times since, and only received the gift of bruises. I was driven directly home without the driver ever asking for the address. On reaching the house the driver asked for my house keys, opened the door and let me in.

Then he handed the keys back and said, 'We will meet again.' He never charged me for the cab or anything. I remember that the cab was shiny black and smelled of new leather and honey. The driver was shiny clean – that's the only way I can describe it – and wearing a really, really white shirt.

Now me being me and caught up in the day-to-day stuff of work and rearing three children, I let this miracle pass until around three weeks later when a newspaper article described how a girl had been found in the park by the causeway, raped, beaten and left for dead. I was really feeling sick and the indentikit photo only confirmed the feeling. It was the same man who had followed me. I will never know how close I came to a dreadful experience, or why I was saved, but I'll always thank the angel who came to my rescue. I now know that angel to be Gabriel, for we have indeed met many times since, and he continues to guide and protect me.

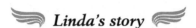 *Linda's story*

Quite a few years ago I was a single parent, struggling to bring up three children. It was a tough time. I was always tired and this particular night was no exception. I finally got all the kids to bed and was able to relax for a while. But I was too tired to enjoy TV or read, so I decided I'd go to bed, too.

I expected to be out like a light as soon as my head hit the pillow, but it wasn't to be. You know how it is when something's preying on your mind and it's almost like dreaming? You know there's something you just have to do before you can really relax, but you're so physically tired it's hard to make yourself get up and do it? All that kept running through my mind was that I needed to get up and pull the TV plug out of the socket. Something wasn't going to let me sleep until I did this. I resisted for a while, telling myself I'd never bothered before so why did my mind keep me awake about it now? But anyway, in the end I got up and went back to the sitting room and unplugged the TV. *There*, I thought, *now can I sleep!* I went straight to sleep as soon as I got in bed and didn't stir until morning.

Usually the kids put on the TV in the morning, so when I got up first thing I put the plug back in the wall socket to switch it on for them. As I did so there was an almighty bang and the fuse blew. I really do feel that my guardian angel made me get up and unplug the TV the night before, and if I hadn't listened and done it, we could all have been caught in a fire.

Georgina's story

Two things happened to me in January last year that turned my life around. The first was that I got attacked – well, as near as makes no difference! I was coming out of the mall late after having had a look at the January sales, and I was a little alarmed when I saw the parking lot was almost empty apart from a truckload of guys all laughing and the worse for drink by the looks of them. They spotted me and started making rude suggestions all the while. I thought I had three options: I could tough it out and keep walking to my car, which was the other side of their truck. I could run to my car, which would show my fear. Or I could run back inside the mall, which again would demonstrate my fear but would also take me away from them. In the end I decided on the third option, but as I discovered, there's nothing as scary as an empty mall!

The whole place echoed as I ran down between the stores, which all seemed already to have their lights off, or going off. All the staff must have been leaving by back doors, because I didn't see anyone, least of all a security guard. When someone grabbed me from behind I started screaming. Next thing I knew I was surrounded by the truck guys and they were all grabbing a piece. I don't know how far they intended to go, but when I found myself being lifted bodily, I started yelling for God to help me. They started carrying me over their heads, like some sort of weird trophy, back out to their truck. I knew if they got me in there I'd be finished.

As they charged across the lot, whooping, I suddenly went cold. I wanted my mom. Mom and I hadn't spoken since she'd left my dad. I couldn't forgive her for ages, and then when I could it seemed like it was too late, as she wouldn't answer my calls. I didn't know if she was mad at me, or if she just figured I wanted to bad-mouth her and couldn't handle it. Either way we hadn't spoken in months and months. But right at that moment a little voice in my head told me she was the one I should call for, not God. 'Mom! Mom!' I started yelling, 'Help me!' No one took any notice because the parking lot was still empty save my car and their truck. We reached the truck and they started bundling me inside.

At that moment I saw a car pull into the lot and I couldn't believe it was the same model and colour as my mom's car. It parked right next to my car on the far side of the men's truck and it sat there, large as life. 'Mom!' I screamed. 'Mom! It's me!'

That made the men pause and there we were, with me halfway into the truck, and what looked like my mom's car just sitting there. The car door opened and my mom stepped out. She held her cell phone in her hand, and was saying loudly, 'So, officer, you'll be here in two minutes you say?'

Just like that the men dropped me and I hit the ground hard, winding myself. My mom ran over to me and fell down on her knees and hugged me. It seemed like she'd missed me as much as I'd missed her, only we had both been too dumb to do anything about it. We sat there on the ground, rocking. She told me later she'd been driving home along a highway about 500 yards from the mall. She had had her windows up and the radio playing, but she said suddenly in her head she had heard a voice. It had said, 'Listen.' She had turned the radio off and opened a window, and then she had heard me calling for her. Somehow she had known where I was, and next thing she was saving me. I'll never know who spoke to her about me, but I'm told that Gabriel is the angel of communication, so maybe he set the whole thing up just to get me and Mom talking and making a new start together!

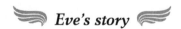 *Eve's story*

It was a beautiful Sunday morning, and I'd just finished my shift as a carer. I got on my moped and was soon on my way home. As I approached a roundabout there was a car waiting in the outside lane. I started round the roundabout when suddenly from the inside lane a car shot out. The car on my outside must have hidden me from the driver's view. There was no way it could not hit me. I closed my eyes and waited for the impact. I was sure this was the end. But... nothing! I opened my eyes and the car had stopped about three inches from my knee. I gathered myself together and drove my moped around the front of the car and headed home. I just kept repeating, 'Thank you, thank you,' to Spirit for saving me.

When I got home, still very shaken, I said to my husband, 'I should be dead, I need a stiff drink.' It wasn't until I had rested a while that it came to me that things had been very strange. Recalling what had happened, there had been no noise, no sound of car engines, not even a bird singing. No one got out of the cars and spoke to me, and I don't even recall the colours of the cars or the people driving. It was if the angels had stopped time in order to save me.

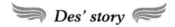

Des' story

Approximately eight years ago we had family visiting us in Ireland from the USA.

They stayed for three weeks in Derry, which is about 150 miles from Dublin. When the time came for them to head back to the USA, we needed three cars to ferry them back to Dublin Airport, because there were about 12 of them. As their flight was leaving Dublin that morning at 9 o'clock, we had to be on the road for about 3:30 a.m.

We were about 20 miles from Dublin and everything seemed to be on schedule. I was driving the middle car of our three-car convoy. I was very tired and I must have suddenly closed my eyes and dropped off to sleep. Almost instantly I was woken up by the sound of a loud thud on the windscreen. My eyes flew open to see a bird caught in my screen wipers. I slammed on the brakes and just about managed to slow my car down, regain control and pull in at the side of the road.

The third car in our group immediately pulled up behind me and, when the driver reached us, he said that he'd really thought we were all goners, as my car had been travelling diagonally along the road at speed straight towards a clump of trees. Had it not been for that bird we would have been, at the very least, seriously injured, as I'd been driving at about 60 mph. I realized then that the four passengers in my car had been dozing, too.

In all the years I've been driving and all the years since that incident I don't think I've had a bird fly across my windscreen, let alone hit it and become entangled in my wipers. Also, this happened about 5:00 a.m. when you wouldn't expect birds to be flying around anyway.

This is a full and honest account of an incident that happened to me, and I believe my guardian angel was there that night.

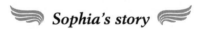 *Sophia's story*

The little boy was totally immersed in his game. He crawled about, moving his small plastic figures around in the dust of the front garden of a terraced house as I passed by, and I wouldn't have even noticed him except for his cry of 'Skywalker! You will die!' There it was again, a reference to the word 'sky'. What on Earth was going on?

It had started when I woke up in the morning to my radio alarm playing the song 'Sky' by Sonique. I noticed because it was an unusual sort of choice for my local radio station, but I'd thought no more about it. I went down to the Tube and that's when I started to get a weird feeling that something was going on. Nearly all the hoardings had the word 'sky' in them. Ocean Sky Jets, Sky Insurance, Sky Bingo. It was crazy. I walked along starting to wonder if I should take some notice of all these coincidences. I started to think I was some sort of Chicken Little and the sky was going to fall on me!

When I came to a poster that didn't mention the word I sighed with relief – for a moment, anyway. Then I saw that the poster had a corner that wasn't stuck down properly, revealing several layers of old posters underneath. My curiosity got the better of me and I pulled the corners back. Sure enough, a couple of layers down, there was an old advert for the film Vanilla Sky. I was getting a little freaked out by then.

My train came and I got on. I didn't know what else to do. It started again. The ads on the tube train all had the same theme. The posters right opposite me were for Stars in the Sky Dating Agency and SkyTours. My head started to buzz and I felt fuzzy and faint. Something was going on. I was getting some sort of warning or message, but what was the point if I couldn't understand it? I scanned my fellow passengers. I think everyone who travels on the Tube does that nowadays. I don't know exactly what we think we're going to see. A man in a hoodie with the word 'bomb' on his rucksack or something! Everyone looked normal – well, as normal as a random selection of commuters all crammed unnaturally together like sardines, trying not to invade each other's personal space as much as possible, could look. But anyway, I thought, what would the word 'sky' have to do with a terrorist on a tube train? I got to my station without incident, rode up the escalator, numbly passing an ad for Sky TV, and then walked through some residential streets towards the office where I worked.

That was when I heard the boy playing in his tiny front garden. I really didn't know what I was supposed to do. So I walked on, puzzling over it. As I waited to cross the street, standing on a narrow pavement, I glanced across the road, almost already knowing what I'd see. There was a huge hoarding advertising a film called Look to the Sky. Suddenly something clicked in my brain and, without thinking any more, I turned and sprinted from my place on the kerb as quickly as I could. Instantly there was a terrifyingly loud crashing sound, and sharp particles snapped into me, peppering the back of my neck with tiny nicks. I stopped and for a moment I was frozen to the spot, unable to turn around, feeling my head for injuries, but finding only red dust particles. Eventually as silence fell I turned round. There on the pavement where I'd been standing, and scattered all over the road I'd been about to cross, were the remains of a large Victorian chimney pot. I looked up and saw, three storeys above me, the snapped off remains of the stack. Apart from the tiny nicks, I was unharmed. If I hadn't moved fast the pot would have hit me on the head, and I'm pretty sure I would have been lying there dead right then. More red dust floated in front of me on the air and I stared at the swirling shapes incredulously as the cloud seemed to form the shape of two outstretched wings.

Is it possible that my guardian angel knew exactly where I'd be standing and at exactly what time? Did my angel know that the chimney pot, which must have been loose and tottering in the wind for days, was going to fall on that spot at exactly the time I was going to be standing there? Were there an usual amount of repetitions of the word 'sky' around that day, put there by my angel, or had my subconscious been programmed while I slept to be especially receptive to that word so that I'd get the message? I don't honestly know, but I do know that I missed death by inches that day, and it was because of the 'message' that I avoided it.

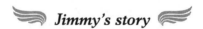

Jimmy's story

It doesn't matter which country this happened in – in fact, strangely, I'm still not allowed to give away too much information after all these years. I was in the US Army at the time and had been sent to fight a war, like so many other young men of the time. I didn't like it, I hadn't chosen it, but I had to do it. The worst part was leaving my mom. She would be alone, as my dad had died some years previously, and she still missed him. I lived just a few doors down from her and checked in with her every day. She wasn't clingy, she was too thoughtful for that, but she would miss me and she was scared for me.

So there I was, in a hot place, sweating, part from the humidity and part from the fear. I'd been cut off from my comrades and spent hours crawling along trying to find my way back to my side of the fence. I was very scared that I was too far behind enemy lines. Eventually, exhausted, I crept into some cover and went to sleep. It was dark – and I mean really dark. No lights, no moon and no stars. At some point the clouds must have cleared because when I woke up I could see a little, enough to freeze my bones. Coming right at me was a troop of enemy soldiers, guns drawn. They couldn't possibly fail to see me because they were cutting a trail right at me. I didn't dare move, because that would make them hear me. I didn't know whether to cock my gun or stay lying down and make myself as small as possible. I heard a noise behind me and for a second the fear intensified – were they coming from that way, too? But no, behind me was just a glowing light. The moon, maybe?

I looked back and saw that the soldiers were literally feet away. I raised my gun. They would virtually tread on me at any second. But then something, I still don't know what, started to materialize around me, and in a few seconds I could see that it was a ring of figures. My gun fell from nerveless fingers. I'm not going to say they were beings with wings, but I do think they were angels. They made a solid ring around me, their backs to me. I couldn't see their faces, but in the light they cast with their soft glow, I could see the enemy soldiers' faces, and I know they couldn't see the figures, or me. Incredibly, as if the beings were a tree or a wall, the soldiers just detoured around me and moved off deeper into the trees and undergrowth.

By the time my breathing had calmed down the ring of figures had faded, and within seconds they were gone. I don't know if they were there to save me – or to stop me from shooting someone I wasn't supposed to shoot. Either way, the memory has lived with me for all these years and I'm never going to forget it.

One last thing. When I got home my mom asked me if I'd almost been killed one night. She said she'd seen me in a dream, hiding from men with guns. The dream had scared her so much and seemed so real that when she woke up she got down on her knees and prayed for my guardian angel to watch over me. I think her prayers were answered.

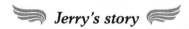 *Jerry's story*

I was driving up from Sedona to Flagstaff, Arizona. People know this is a very heavily wooded road with many steep and twisty hairpin bends. It was dark and I was driving too fast, but I was young and foolish and I liked taking dares. I'd just reached the top of the final rise and, a little drunk on my own invincibility (or so I felt), I speeded up some more. Suddenly, right in my headlights was a huge deer. I thought it would run away, but it just stood there. I slammed my foot on the brake as hard as I could, but it was no good. I was going to slam into the animal or skid out of control. The deer was going to get whacked up onto the hood and come through the windscreen, probably smashing into my head. I thought I was dead.

Then suddenly a golden light appeared between us, like a big golden orb. I hit it and it splattered harmlessly away like a bursting bubble, making a spray of rainbows that glittered as they splashed off the hood of my car and dissolved away to nothing. Miraculously, the impact stopped my car about three feet from the animal. The deer stared through the windscreen at me, right into my eyes, as if to say, 'You have been warned,' then it went leaping away. I never told anyone – who would have believed me? But I believe my guardian angel saved both me and the deer, that day, and I got the message. Since then I drive really carefully – never faster than my angels can fly, as they say.

I also stopped going hunting, because I figure if a deer can bring me a warning from an angel, then I have no right to be shooting them.

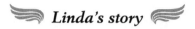

Linda's story

I confess I am a very bad driver. After the car door was pulled off by accident when I was pregnant, I thought, 'That could have been my belly!' I had been out of the car when I saw it starting to roll backwards. Without thinking, I had jumped in to stop it. The car door had hit a stone pillar and been ripped off seconds after my belly had been in the same place! I turned my driving over to God as I prayed, 'You know I'm a terrible driver. Please take care of me and my unborn child, because I don't seem to be doing a very good job!' My daughter was born soon after and I forgot about the prayer until the following incidents happened.

The first time, I was tired and driving home when I nodded off. The next thing I knew, an invisible hand grabbed the steering wheel and turned it to the right. This woke me up and I saw a truck coming at me in the opposite lane. My car was now safely in the correct lane, however. While I had been asleep it had been gliding over the double yellow lines into oncoming traffic. My guardian angel had saved my life by turning the wheel! I thanked him and was now very much awake for the rest of my drive home.

The next incident happened early one morning as I was driving to work. The narrow country road I was on came down a steep hill and merged into a state highway. I stopped at the stop sign and was just about to pull out after looking, when a man's very deep voice shouted, 'Watch out!' I slammed on the brakes and turned around to see who on Earth had said that. I assumed some criminal had slipped into my car when I wasn't looking. There was no one there, but when I spun my head around to the front, there was a car in my blind spot that sped past me just after I had hit the brakes. I know I would have hit that car if not for my guardian angel's advance notice.

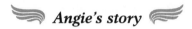 *Angie's story*

I went on holiday to Greece when I was in my twenties, and decided to stay on afterwards with my friend and work there for the summer. This friend turned out not to be a good choice and caused me all sorts of trouble, including a horrible experience involving a sexual assault. Then my boyfriend at the time came over to Greece and ended our relationship. I had no money to get home... you get the picture... I realized that this place was not right for me. Sure, I could have rung home and got someone to buy me a ticket, but I felt compelled to move on to the next island.

This was a completely different place to the mainland and mostly non-commercial. There were a lot of artists around there and Greek families with holiday homes. I discovered my ex-boyfriend working in a moped hire place, and for short while we got back together, so I thought that was why I'd felt the need to go to this island. However, after a while things got nasty and I ended up sitting in the village square crying my eyes out and spending my last drachma on waffles and chocolate sauce!

I was feeling so alone and desolate and then I heard a voice saying, 'Don't worry, I am sending you help.' I really thought I must have imagined it, but was comforted by it anyway, and then I saw two gorgeous young Greek men approaching me. They said, 'Here she is... our angel.' I thought, how bizarre, but also my 'gaydar' went off overtime around them, so I felt no sexual threat from them.

I told them about my situation and they invited me to stay with them. I know it sounds illogical to trust strangers like that but I really just knew they wouldn't harm me. We became great friends and they soon admitted that they were in a relationship together and that one of their fathers had found out and tried to beat it out of him. This was their last summer before going to do National Service, and of course they really wanted to be together, and being very spiritual people, they had prayed to their angels for someone to help them. They saw me straight away – with my white blonde hair, crying into my waffle, and they just knew I'd been sent to help.

We hatched a plan where I pretended to be the girlfriend of one of them and this kept the father off their back, as he was happy to think that his red-blooded son had just gone through a strange phase and was now 'normal'. We had a fantastic summer and I kept in touch with them both for many years.

I feel that angels sent those guys into my path to renew my faith in people, especially men, as they were both so kind and protective, showing me how men could be. Their presence helped me to stop the pattern of inviting not-so-nice men into my life, so that things worked out better for me in the future. Soon after that I met my now husband, and we've been happily married for 16 years.

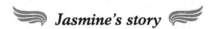

Jasmine's story

I'm of a faith in which I'm not allowed to believe in what I choose and I thought that angels wouldn't protect me because of this. I was so afraid all the time, but not after what happened.

One day I was going up a steep flight of stone stairs near my home and I didn't notice that someone had spilled cooking oil on them. My foot slipped and I fell over backwards. My head hit one step and I tumbled over and over, unable to stop. At one point my body took flight and I knew that when I landed at the bottom of the steps I would be knocked out and almost certainly would have broken some bones.

But, suddenly, a pair of arms snatched me out of the air. They were so real that I assumed a man had been standing on the steps and had caught me as I flew past him. I clung to the strong body and he placed me on the ground. I was dizzy but I looked up to thank him, embarrassed at having been held so close by a strange man. There was no one there. No one on the steps, no one on the street below and nowhere the man could have gone. Apart from a few bruises and a sore head I was completely unhurt.

I just know it was an angel who saved me and that I am protected, even if my beliefs have to remain a secret.

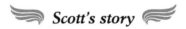 *Scott's story*

We were on a trip in a rental car in the middle of nowhere. It was snowing and we were on an isolated stretch of the Glenwood Canyon in Colorado late in the evening. Suddenly, some rocks fell down the mountainside and blocked our path, sending our car into a ditch. We also had a flat tyre from the impact. I had a terrible sinking feeling as, not only did we have to get the car of the ditch, but the trunk was full, which would make it difficult to get out the tools and the spare tyre. The highway emergency phone wasn't working, so we couldn't send for help.

It was getting darker and it was really unlikely that anyone would come by, but I didn't panic because I always send angels ahead when I travel. So I wasn't totally surprised when, out of nowhere, several young people suddenly appeared. Within minutes the trunk was unpacked, the tyre was changed and they'd called the rental company on a mobile phone to arrange a replacement car at the next town, as our car now sported a temporary tyre.

It all happened so fast and was too 'convenient'. Not just that, but the young people who had saved us just disappeared into the night as mysteriously as they had come.

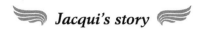 *Jacqui's story*

One winter, my first as a driver, I had my first trip out in snow. I skidded badly and had no idea what to do. I'd been told of course, but at that moment I just couldn't remember. The car slid from one bank to the other and I thought it would tip right over. *Somebody help me!* I pleaded.

Suddenly, I heard a voice speaking as clear as a bell. It said, 'Steer into the skid.' As soon as I did so, the car came back under control. Obviously, I wasn't alone in the car! I'm certain my guardian angel heard my thoughts and said just what I needed to hear.

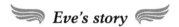 *Eve's story*

I was on my way home from the funeral of a dear friend, the brother of my best friend, who herself had only passed away three weeks before. You can imagine how upset I was – it was heartbreaking. I was invited back to the family's house, but just could not face all that again.

I know I should have walked around the gardens to get my head straight before riding my moped home, but I just wanted to go, so I headed off. Tears were streaming down my face – my best friend was gone, and now her brother too. I felt so low.

As I indicated to pull out from the slip road onto the main road, a car behind me flashed to let me out. He was indicating to take the flyover to the left of me. As he passed me he looked at me and gave me the thumbs-up sign. At that moment the love he sent hit me in the chest like a bullet. I was so overwhelmed with love I just had to smile and once again thank my angels.

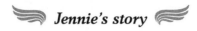 *Jennie's story*

My twins, Sam and Holly, had to go into intensive care when they were born. They gradually got stronger, but then we were told that Holly's tummy was blue and that the next 48 hours were crucial. I was terrified of losing her, and of course Sam needed me just as much. It was devastating.

That night we learned that a woman called Jenny Smedley had put a message out saying that angels had told her the letters C S H meant something urgent to someone, that the children were ill, but we were not to worry as everything would be fine, and that their Great Grandma Sonia was looking after them! Suddenly the future seemed bright. I went to visit Holly, and the nurse looking after her was called Sonia! Back at home I lit a candle, and although there was no wind in my bedroom, the flame went crazy.

Over the next few weeks Holly became stronger and eventually came home, although after three days she stricken with meningitis. Again Jenny told me that she would be fine, and she was!

Sam and Holly are now really well and thriving, and it's all thanks to the angels and their Great Nan Sonia.

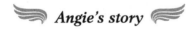 *Angie's story*

Once I was getting into my car in the dark and an urgent voice told me, 'Quick, lock your door!' so I did. Almost immediately a man approached my car and tried the door handle. He was angry the door was locked, and he shouted a lot of abuse before putting his head in to his hands and crouching on the ground. We locked eyes and I remember willing this man to seek help. As I drove off he put his hand up in a friendly way and I took that to mean he had understood. I felt this was meant to happen to show this man that people have compassion and to give him the courage to seek help.

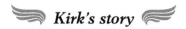 *Kirk's story*

I was walking home late one night, a little tipsy, I admit. I had to cross a wide road junction made up of several different carriageways and road directions. I crossed where I could and continued along an exit lane where people weren't really supposed to walk. I found myself walking along a very narrow pavement, only about 18 inches wide, against the oncoming traffic. To my right was a high curving wall, which held the bank back. I could have turned back – should have, but you know how it is, you just tend to think you can't be bothered and carry on.

I didn't think the drink had affected my balance too much, but suddenly I felt myself tipping sideways into the road. I just knew my days – minutes – were numbered at that point, because the traffic was non-stop, fast and literally inches away.

Suddenly someone shoved me backwards so hard that I swayed back out of danger and came up hard against the retaining wall of the road. There was no one else there, though.

Once I'd recovered from what I'm sure was angelic intervention, I walked carefully sideways along the path, clinging to the wall as if I was 100 feet up in the air. I might not have been given a second chance!

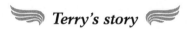 *Terry's story*

This happened one Friday evening after I'd got drunk with a group of friends. I was pretty 'out of it', sort of knowing what was going on but not really having any common sense about anything. I felt invincible, I guess, a bit like Superman. In those days I did tend to go too far. I ended up at the train station waiting to get a train the couple of miles home. No one else was waiting on my platform, so after a while I thought I'd just walk home along the tracks and not bother waiting for a train. The tracks went right behind my house, so I knew I couldn't get lost, and that was the only worry I had. The thought of a train coming along never crossed my mind.

I jumped down and immediately some girls on the other platform started screaming at me to get back up. I turned and was immediately blinded by the headlights of an oncoming train. Then it was me who screamed. My legs weren't working too well and there was no way I could get to safety in time.

Right then a man landed beside me on the tracks. I had no idea where he'd come from because there hadn't been anyone else on my platform seconds before. Suddenly, everything went into slow motion and there was near silence, like when your ears have popped and everything sounds fuzzy and far away. I could still see the train coming, but it had slowed down and I felt that I was walking through quicksand.

Then the man grabbed me and I felt myself rising up. Suddenly all the noise and movement roared back into the station and I found myself swaying on the platform as the non-stop train shot past inches away from me.

There was no sign of the man and I felt like crying. He had to have been hit. He'd jumped down to save me and he'd been killed. I felt sick as I watched the train fly by, unable to snatch my eyes away, waiting for the inevitable sight of the blood and gore, and knowing that my life had been saved but also ruined by that reckless stranger's courageous act. How would I live with the guilt?

My breath was sobbing in my throat as the train cleared the station. And then I couldn't believe it – there was nothing there! The clean rails sparkled in the station lights with not a bloodstain in sight. The girls were still standing on the other platform, staring at me in disbelief. I ran for the bridge. I had to ask them what they'd seen. But by then their train had pulled in and by the time my drunk and shocked legs had carried me over the bridge it was too late – they'd gone.

There was only one explanation as far as I was concerned: I had been saved by my guardian angel. I stopped getting drunk after that day, and maybe, just maybe, that was what it was all about.

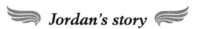 *Jordan's story*

When we were visiting the USA we were unfortunate enough to get caught up in a store robbery. We couldn't believe it when we talked about it afterwards. There we were, thousands of miles away from home on holiday, and we really were in the wrong place at the wrong time.

Three men wearing rubber masks rushed into the store and grabbed my dad, shoving him onto the floor. I was terrified and tried to go to him, but they made me lie down too. The next thing I knew there were sirens going off. I was even more scared by then because of course American cops have guns and I thought we'd get caught in the crossfire.

It didn't quite happen that way. One of the gunmen pulled me to my feet and I knew I was going to be used as a hostage. He stood me up against the wall and yelled to the cops that he'd kill me if they didn't let him go. Of course, they wouldn't do it, and I almost passed out when he pointed the gun at me and I could see the hammer rising up, just as I'd seen on TV, only this was real and I was about to be shot. I could hear my dad yelling, but my whole world had shrunk to the gun barrel. I thought I could see the bullet coming out – and then it did. I was dead, no question.

Then, suddenly, I felt a pressure building around me. It pushed me against the wall. At first I thought I'd been shot, but I hadn't been. The pressure got harder and I felt squashed, crushed. There was a pop and the man with the gun was lying on the floor, bleeding. He wasn't dead, just wounded in the neck.

The police told me later that the bullet had ricocheted from something behind me and a chance in a million meant that it had hit the man. I don't believe that for a second, and neither does my dad, who says I was surrounded by white light when the gun went off and it was so bright he couldn't keep looking at it. We both know that, for whatever reason, I had angels around me.

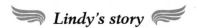

Lindy's story

I know I have my guardian angel around me all the time, and he has been looking after me to the point where I can become quite carelessly complacent while driving. One day I was driving along a familiar route home and I had to make a left turn across an intersecting road. People who are not familiar with the suburb where I grew up don't realize that there are two roads intersecting right before a T-junction, and on many occasions I have seen near-misses between vehicles.

As I was driving, I was singing along to the radio, not paying any attention to the road and going quite fast to boot. Suddenly, I heard a voice say 'Stop!' and I immediately braked. I was just going around the blind corner and, as I did, there in front of me and about to cross my path was a car driven by a learner driver. She stopped also and for a moment we sat there looking at each other, then I waved her on because she had right of way. I got goose bumps and thanked my angel, because if he hadn't told me to stop I would have T-boned this car.

I have had many instances where I have been driving and heard a voice tell me to slow down, change lanes, stop, etc., and if I hadn't listened I would have been in an accident. I even got told by a clairvoyant some years back that I should pay more attention while driving because my angel was getting sick of looking out for me and one day he would have had enough! That was an eye-opener for me.

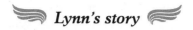 *Lynn's story*

I was 16 at the time, and I was going out with a guy who was in the RAAF (Royal Australian Air Force). His best mate was also a 'raffy', and lived down the road from my house. My boyfriend came from an RAAF base in Sydney, and would travel up a lot to hang out with his best mate, who was stationed here in the Newcastle area. In fact, that's how I met my boyfriend in the first place.

Gary was my boyfriend's name (I later married him, but lost him in an accident three years after we were married and when I was eight months pregnant with our son). Dave was his best mate's name. Dave had a girlfriend by the name of Robyn, who came from a town up the coast. It was Easter time, and the Sydney Royal Easter Show was on, so Dave, Gary and I were going to go up to Robyn's town to go on a coach trip with her from there to the Sydney Show.

My mum was a bit worried about it, but she eventually agreed to me going. Finally, we were all set, so we left from my home and went to a petrol station in my suburb to fill up with fuel for the trip to Robyn's, which was about an hour and a half away.

I was sitting in the back waiting for the boys to come back to the car and I was feeling a bit weird. I was known to have these feelings and as I sat there I was saying to myself, 'It's all OK. We have money, we have food, we have fuel. It's all fine, we will be fine,' then I went to put on my seatbelt to be ready to leave. But as I went to put it on, a voice – a male voice – inside my head, said, 'Don't put it on,' which was very strange because we have the use of seatbelts drummed into us. But when you hear something like that, someone talking to you inside your head, you can't help but obey!

I felt uneasy then, and it felt so weird to have heard a voice in my head. Anyway, the boys came back, I kept my seatbelt off, which felt a bit wrong, and off we went. Everything was going along normally, but

I was feeling anxious and just wanted to get there and be safe, as the strange feeling I'd been having was getting stronger.

We were going through a place called Raymond Terrace, and just outside that, where the freeway restarted, was an area called the 'mad miles'. It was called that because once everyone got out of Raymond Terrace the highway opened up and everyone used to just put their foot down and go, go, go! As it was Easter, the traffic was incredibly heavy coming down towards Newcastle. We were going north, but the southbound traffic was bumper to bumper, very, very heavy though still moving at a decent pace. I smoked at the time and, as I was nervous, I took a cigarette out and was about to light it when I just had this incredibly strong feeling not to do so. I didn't hear a voice this time, but I might as well have, because the force that was stopping me wasn't me. I put the cigarette away and was getting really scared, as there were a lot of trucks going in the opposite direction and every time one went past I'd cringe.

I was stressed. Then, all of a sudden, Gary yelled to Dave and pointed to the front of Dave's car. All he got out was, 'Watch out for the …!'

Then, all I knew was that there was a huge crunch, a flip and a twist, and we ended up spinning down the road on the roof of the car, upside down. People who've almost died sometimes say they saw their life pass before their eyes. Well, I really did, and it was incredible! As I was tumbling around in the back of the car, seatbelt-less, I could see my life pass before my eyes, from when I was a baby all the way to where I was then. It was like looking at negatives from a camera; each frame has a different picture, with all those holes top and bottom so it can be held in the camera. It was just like that, and each frame showed a different part of my life, all running very smoothly past my eyes. I know it sounds weird, but that was what I saw. Very interesting, really!

The car finally came to a stop. Gary was able to get out of the car, and I could hear him, sounding very stressed, trying to get the people who'd gathered around to put their cigarettes out, because there was a whole tank-load of petrol streaming out everywhere. Dave and I were stuck in the car, and Dave was pretty badly injured. I was squeezed into this tiny squashed space in the back, and couldn't get out. Luckily I hadn't lit that cigarette. One shudders to think what would have happened if I had.

It turned out that a young 16-year-old who'd only had his bike licence for two weeks had been riding a brand new 650CC Yamaha and was coming down from much further up the coast, the opposite way to us. He'd been travelling with a friend who was way, way behind him, going at a much more sensible speed. The reckless Yamaha rider had been car-hopping all the way down, taking risks, his friend said. He'd then come out from behind a big semi-trailer (hence my fear of them on the way) and crashed right into the front of our car, on the driver's side, which pushed us, then flipped us over and sent us spinning down the road. The roof of the car was so damaged and squashed that it had moved over to the right. My Gary had burned one of his fingers because he had been trying to hold the roof up so hard that one of his fingers pressed onto the road, not the roof. If I'd had my seatbelt on I would have died. Instead of being tossed away, I would have collided with the road and my head would have been dragged along it as we skidded! But as I didn't have the belt on, I'd been thrown into the middle of the backseat, where I'd been relatively safe. (But only because I'd stopped myself from lighting the cigarette that would have ignited the petrol.)

The 16-year-old was, sadly, dead, and his mate was devastated. He told us then about the car-hopping, risk-taking and crazy driving.

We later took pictures of the car at the wrecker's, and our friends also came to look at it. The car had been completely opened up by the bike and truck like a tin can, and it was so squashed and broken, no one could believe any of us had got out alive. There was no way for us to have survived in that car, but somehow we did with the grace of God and huge help from our darling angels and guides. I like to think it was the Archangel Michael who spoke to me that night. I would really love to know for sure.'

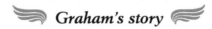 *Graham's story*

I'd enjoyed a lovely day out in the country with the family and the dog, and we were driving home along the main road to Norwich. We were all feeling relaxed and happy and were bowling along in the car at roughly 60 miles an hour, none of us expecting any problems to crop up. But suddenly, as the car approached a blind bend, I heard a voice saying, 'Slow down!'

I felt a need to obey right away and it's a good job I did, because just round the bend there was a young girl standing in the middle of the road holding a pushbike. Because I'd slowed down I was able to stop in plenty of time and go round her, but if I hadn't listened to the voice in my head I would have definitely run her down and possibly killed her, which just goes to show that one must always listen to one's angels.

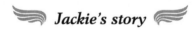 *Jackie's story*

We were driving home late one night. My hubby, Stewart, was driving our Volvo estate, because I couldn't stand the bright oncoming headlights and tended to drive like a frightened rabbit in the dark, clinging to the edge of the road, which I could barely see. The radio was playing country music songs and in hindsight maybe heavy metal would have helped us more! I tried and tried to stay awake but I kept drifting. Every time I prised my eyes open Stewart looked wide awake and happy, so eventually I gave in and fell asleep.

I don't know how long I slept along the A303, but suddenly a voice literally screamed in my ear, 'Wake up!' My eyes shot open to see

Stewart slumped in his seat, head back, and the car heading straight for a concrete bridge support on the wrong side of the road.

It was my turn to scream then. Stewart woke up, grabbed the wheel and the car just cleared the pillar! It was doubly lucky that there had been no other vehicles to crash into us as we'd veered right across to the wrong side of the road.

Chapter 7

ANGELS WHO HELP US TO HEAL ANIMALS

One of the most interesting things about animal healing is that there's no place for the placebo effect. This is especially relevant in distance healing, when the healer and the animal don't make direct contact. If direct contact is made then a sceptic might easily say that the healer is just a very good person with animals, and that the animals might just be responding very strongly to their presence. I'm quite aware that this isn't so. The truth is rather that people who are very charismatic to animals often use this natural ability to get close to them and be trusted enough, so that a spiritual exchange between them might take place. The placebo effect in essence means that if you tell someone that a certain pill or action is going to improve things for them, it will often have that effect. It works very well when people are given a pill that they think contains a powerful drug that still works even though the pill is made up of nothing but sugar. Of course, with animals what you see is what you get, and the animal cannot be 'told' that the treatment it receives will help it. In distant healing there is no expectation at all on the part of the animal. Unlike a human patient it can't be told to expect healing at a certain time, so whatever happens must therefore be a genuine result of the treatment.

Anyone can connect with their pet. You know your pet already and all you need to do now in order to communicate is to get to know him even better. Take time to observe his behaviour in the garden, his reaction to other animals and people. Learn to be a body-language detective, and mirror the little movements and expressions that your pet uses. Watch how he places his body instead of using words when he wants something and learn this hidden language. Sit quietly with your pet, just connecting in a mental way, not physically nor emotionally. 'Think' a message to your pet, whether it be to send them somewhere or bring them closer to you. For instance, if they're a retriever dog, try sending them an image of a certain toy and see if you can get them to fetch it. Also ask your pet to 'telegraph' to you an image of what they want, whether it's 'walkies', some food or to play. Their reaction to whatever you choose to respond with will soon tell you if you 'heard' them correctly. If you can progress and establish a strong mental rapport like this, it can come in very useful should your pet ever go missing or become ill with an idiopathic illness (symptoms for which no cause can be identified).

Thank goodness there are animal healers like those featured here – who recognize that animals have souls and angels – and possess the compassion to help them. If only the perpetrators of cruelty realized that they stand no chance of their own angels helping them in life while they are committing acts of barbarism against animals, the angels' best-loved children. I recently watched a video on the internet of a cat in Turkey that was filmed trying to resuscitate his partner who had been killed by a car. The cat tried to revive her for two hours, kneading her chest and abdomen with his feet and touching his nose to her nose. Anyone who could watch that and not believe that cats, and indeed all animals, have souls, defies reason.

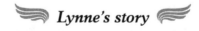 **Lynne's story**

Mabel is a beautiful five-year-old British Blue cat. Anita, her owner, bought her when the cat was three years old, after she'd had two litters of kittens. She was as small as a kitten herself when Anita went to see her. The breeder said she was selling Mabel because she couldn't keep any more cats in the house.

When Mabel arrived at her new home she used the litter tray several times – at the time Anita thought this was due to the stress of moving to a new home. However, the next day there was blood in the tray, and this ominous sign continued on a daily basis. Then there were times when she didn't use the tray at all. She also bolted her food and then very often vomited.

Anita took Mabel to the vet. He agreed that the symptoms could be due to stress and gave advice on diet. However, after a month with no improvement and, in fact, deterioration, Anita returned to the vet. He diagnosed colitis and thought that Mabel had had this condition for a long time. He suggested this could have been caused by an overgrowth of bacteria in her gut or a food intolerance. Mabel's diet was addressed again and she was given antibiotics over nine months. This initially helped, but gradually the symptoms returned. At this stage, Anita called me to ask if I might help Mabel. Anita had recently lost her husband and the situation was causing her additional stress, too.

When I arrived at the house I took off my coat and sat down on the settee. Mabel came into the room, jumped onto the settee and lay down on my coat. This meant I was easily able to give her 'hands-on healing', which she accepted happily, and in fact she dozed off. Although I'm often asked to give healing just to an animal, I like to give healing to the owner as well, if they are agreeable. They have a partnership and their energies are closely connected and so I gave Anita healing, too.

As a healer my intention is to be a healing channel for the natural universal healing energy, and send out love to the animal unconditionally for its higher good, without any expectations of the outcome. A cure cannot be promised, but I believe no limitations should be set either. The animal will receive the healing needed at that time.

Healing can sometimes be successful after one treatment, depending on the condition. As Mabel's condition was chronic, I gave her healing every month. The length of time I spent healing Mabel lessened as she improved. (Animals will dictate the length of time needed for healing by getting up, moving around or becoming restless after previously being in a relaxed state. There are times when they may not need any healing at a particular time.)

I continued to visit once a month over the next year, giving healing to Mabel, who continued to improve. Mabel has now put on weight, is eating well and is not bolting her food. Her toilet habits are now impeccable with no sign of blood. I still have continued to give Anita healing each time I visit, which I do because healing is beneficial for the maintenance of good health.

Mabel is now symptom-free and she and Anita are enjoying a happy and healthy partnership.

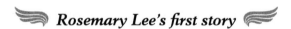 *Rosemary Lee's first story*

Arielle was a lovely whippet dog that had a severe mitral valve prolapse. In the sonogram you could see the prolapsed valve and the blood pouring back through the valve. The prognosis was bad. She was being treated with homeopathy, but her owner wasn't convinced she was having the right treatment. She contacted me after Arielle had had a particularly bad night. Her breathing was up around 60 breaths a minute (for dogs, 10 to 30 breaths is normal). She was on Lasix, a diuretic, to clear the fluid out of her lungs, but it didn't seem to be working very well. She had lost her appetite and she was underweight. Her owner was very worried about her.

This was the communication from her owner after the first distant-healing:

'I just wanted to tell you that Arielle is doing much better. She has both her energy and her appetite back. I took Arielle and Lily (my other whippet) to the park yesterday and Arielle actually ran and romped! She hasn't done that in several weeks. She seems really happy and perky – the spark in her eyes is back. Her breathing is settling into the 20s (per minute). At one time her breathing was in the 50s, now it's in the 20s most of the time, which is within normal range. Thank you, thank you, thank you for the healings and advice.'

Then there was a further update:

'This is good news! Arielle is doing very well. She has gained 1lb 4oz! Her appetite is very good and 28lbs 4oz is a normal, good weight for a whippet. Her breathing is much better. I took Arielle and her sister Lily for hikes on Saturday and Sunday, and as always, I let Arielle set the pace, which was normal! Usually when we go for walks it is extremely slow, and I have to tell myself, 'This is a walking meditation,' so I don't mind the slowness. But she was keeping up a good pace this weekend. There are a couple of uphill segments on our hike, and she didn't seem to need time to recover (although I made us stop, just in case). She seemed super happy and perky. Thank you ever so much for your help with Arielle; she really is doing well. I am very grateful.'

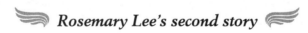

Rosemary Lee's second story

Rosy's owner wrote to say that their dog had been diagnosed with mass cell tumours throughout her body and had been given approximately one week to live. They asked that I perform a healing session for her as soon as possible. Rosy was a rescue dog, and is approximately seven years old. She was in pain and was extremely uncomfortable. This was her third bout of tumours – she'd undergone two operations at different times and her owners really didn't want to put her through another round of surgery. They had had some brief success with homeopathy but thought it was probably too late for it to help much. She now had three major tumours on her left back hip. The day they contacted me they'd been to the vet's and Rosy's X-rays showed that the tumours had spread to her lymph glands and were causing various blockages around her colon as well as pressing on her bladder. Blood work showed infection.

This was their response after healing had taken place:

'Thank you for your session yesterday. Rosy is on Tramadol, given to us by the vet on Saturday to ease her pain, so it's hard to tell if she is in less pain due to the pills or from your session. I will say this though, she seemed to rally a bit yesterday. But last night was not so good – her breathing was shallow and we were pretty sure the end was near.

Now, this morning it's a different story. She seems to be more alert. She ate, with my help, eliminated in the yard, and has been lying in her favourite spot all morning. We wanted to ask you if you would be able to do another session on her today.'

Of course I did another healing on Rosy, and this was the result:

'Rosy is doing so much better today. She seems to be more alert, less bloated, even walks around (a little). These last couple of days she wouldn't even do that. Her breathing does not seem to be as shallow. Rosemary, it's a good day for her.'

Next update:

'Let me tell you about Rosy today. I took her to our traditional vet on Thursday morning for a follow-up. The vet said that our goal now was to just keep her comfortable. For the last two mornings Rosy and I have gone for a little walk in front of the house. Yesterday morning I

took Rosy there and she began walking the route we take to the park.
She trotted on ahead of me, sniffing and peeing here and there. She was
doing so well that I let her continue to the park, as it's not too far. She
sniffed some more, greeted a dog that was in its backyard, then home
we went.

This morning was pretty much a replay of yesterday. She is not the
sick dog I thought I was going to lose last weekend. We have a room
for the dogs and they have their own beds; last night was the first night
Rosy wanted to sleep in her bed and not in the bed we made for her in
our room. I am cautious with her, try to not overdo things, and at the
same time give her some of her life pleasures. You are a good woman,
Rosemary, blessings to you and all that you have, all that you are.'

Last update:

'Good morning Rosemary. Rosy is doing wonderfully. We have gone
for our full walks these past two days. The walks are about a mile. Her
energy level keeps improving, and her body functions appear to be back
to normal. She is happy once again, wagging her tail and being excited
about her walks, and her ears perk up when we pass other dogs in their
yards. She's alert and follows me from room to room, and sleeps in her
own bed.

The tumours on her leg appear to have shrunk in size, and she is not
licking at them or seeming to be as bothered by them. Her coat is the
best I have seen it for a long time. We are so grateful to have our Rosy
back. A few of my friends came by the house to see her when she was
so sick, to say good-bye, now they come by and are amazed by her. She
got her toenails cut today and just two weeks ago I did not think we
would be doing any more grooming for her. Thank you for your work.
She is our miracle pet.'

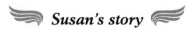

Susan's story

In August 2007, Briony found my distance-healing website and contacted me in the hope that I could be of help to her cat, Willow, whose liver was failing, as the vet was not giving her much hope. I checked in intuitively and determined which of the distance-healing processes I use would be of help to Willow, and let Briony know. I explained that although I never know what will be the final results of the distance-healing work I do, I have seen a lot of miracles. Briony lives in the United Kingdom, and I am in the United States. Briony agreed to have me send Willow healing. The following is Willow's story taken from Briony's own communications.

The first feedback:

> *'Thought I'd share the really good news about Willow! She had all her blood tests and her repeat liver scan yesterday. Her bilirubin level (the stuff that made her go yellow!) should be 12. Last week hers was 50 and it has now gone down to 20. With the other two blood tests they did, one is back within its normal range and the other is just outside it, but has also dropped back significantly since last week. Even better than that, though, is that her liver scan shows that her liver has gone back to its original size and with no obvious problems. I can't tell you how thrilled my husband and I are about this! Providing she doesn't relapse for some reason, we only have to go back to the vet in two weeks' time for a check-up.*

Then the update:

> It's official! The cat's a miracle! *Just thought I'd let you know the latest on my cat, Willow. This week we were back at the vet for her normal annual check-up and booster shot. We saw the vet who had seen her when she first got sick, and he couldn't believe the change in her. She has put 5 lb back on and is a 100-percent healthy old mog*

again! The vet said he has only seen a couple of cases where a cat has made a full recovery after being so ill, and that initially it looked as though Willow had liver cancer, which would have killed her in four to six weeks. In fact Willow has even started to chase our dog Holly! Take care and a final big thank you!'

I contacted Briony again in May, 2010 to get an update on Willow so I could share her distance-healing story. I asked her also to describe what the distance-healing process was like at her end. Again, in Briony's words:

'How great to hear from you! Well, I'm very pleased to report that Willow, Holly and Ruda are all doing great. Willow is now 12 years old and is still the madam of the house and in good health. She has managed to fool both me and the vets for two years running by showing all the symptoms of having a thyroid problem, but her blood tests come back normal. Willow has an unusually large thyroid for a cat anyway, so that tends to complicate matters! She still manages to astound the vets whenever she goes in, as they look at her history, see her liver failure problem and then can't believe that she is still alive, let alone as well as she is! I just smile to myself and quietly send my thanks to you every time that happens.

As to how the healing went at my end when you sent it; I've been trying to think how best to describe it. After I asked you to go ahead and send healing to Willow, there was no amazing, sudden 'light bulb' moment as to when she received it. I think I would best describe it as a very gentle, but immediate, improvement to her health. That first day she started to pick up and just kept going from strength to strength. As I said before, it was to the complete amazement of the vets, as they said they had expected her to pass away within six weeks of diagnosis. As you can see from the photo I've attached, she has certainly regained all the weight she lost when she was ill, plus a bit extra for emergency use!'

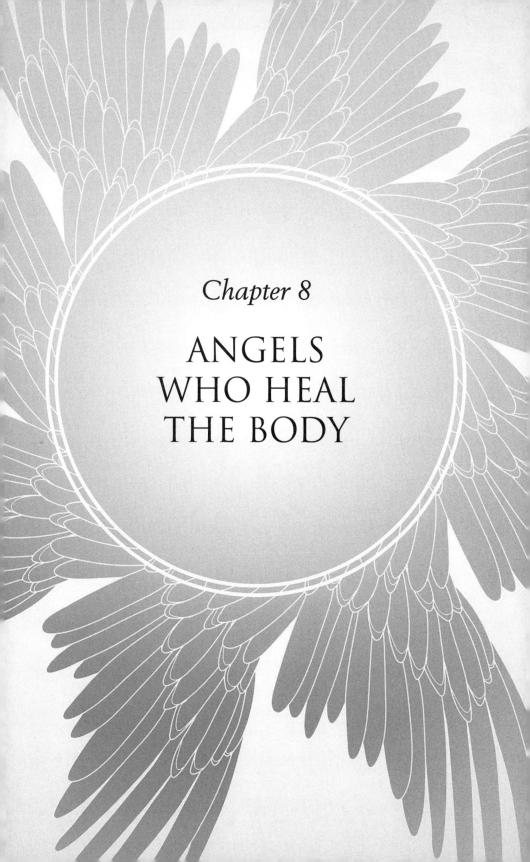

Chapter 8

ANGELS WHO HEAL THE BODY

We humans are incredibly strong beings. We humans are incredibly frail beings. Which of these do you believe? The right answer is both. There are those among us who have channelled the ability to heal ourselves. It is said that we can all do this, but some of us of the weaker kind need the help of angels to heal ourselves. After all, is it *we* who, in the end, manipulate our own cells and thereby create healing, but we have such little self-confidence and such a small connection between soul and body that those of us who can do this without angelic help are very few.

After reading these stories, next time you're under the weather with a cough or cold, do try and connect with your angel and ask, not to *be* healed but to *be able to heal yourself.*

You never know, you might just perform a miracle!

If you need more help, there are many healing modalities that use angelic energy. Just do an internet search for 'angel healing' and you'll be as amazed as I was at how many there are. There certainly is something for everyone.

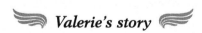 *Valerie's story*

I haven't always been particularly religious or spiritual. If anything I'd label myself a 'rebel Christian'. I rebelled against going to church. It didn't mean I didn't believe in God or his existence, it just meant that

I didn't want the words rammed down my throat by an undeserving pastor. I'd heard of people working with angels or spirit guides, but I'd never really paid much attention, as I didn't think this related to me.

One day, I was particularly tired. I had been working late into the night and attending several networking events. I was also feeling pressured, due to very tight work deadlines. Early next morning at about 4 a.m., I woke up and couldn't get back off to sleep. Rather than getting up and looking for something to do, I stayed in bed and waited for the sleepiness to return. Not long after waking I felt a sudden nudge on the left-hand side of my bed. I sensed that I was no longer alone and, although my eyes were still closed, I could 'see' different forms as they floated towards me. Strangely, I felt no fear. I very quickly realized that they were spirits or angels. I didn't want to scare them away by showing that I was fully awake, so I lay still with my eyes closed and waited to 'see' what they would do. To my utmost surprise, they laid their hands on me. First it was one pair, then another and another. I couldn't see or smell them, only sense and feel their interaction with me. I believe there were three or four present.

It was only when their hands started to move over me that I realized I was receiving a full-body massage. Strong feelings of calm washed over me, as well as a tingling sensation where our energies mingled. In my mind's eye I could see their movements, as if I was watching a film. I was being massaged by invisible hands and I knew intuitively that this was to regenerate my very tired and slightly aching body.

The massage seemed to me to last for about three minutes, although it may have been a lot longer. The angels were female, of slim build, and at least one of them had wings. They all wore garments like long dresses, with long sleeves. The material was strong, heavy and light in colour. I know this because one of the angels was massaging my head and forehead, and her sleeve brushed over my nose. I was so thankful that I'd been awake to see them and to receive this wonderful gift.

I wanted these beings to visit my dad and relieve his pain, as he suffers with tinnitus. I wanted him to receive the relief they could offer with their special massage. I contacted him and asked if he'd noticed anything unusual of late – a dream, anything. He said he hadn't. I was a little disappointed, but I have never given up hope that they will visit him one day.

I still wonder if the angels knew that I was awake when they visited me. Either way, they blessed me with a divine massage. I'm eternally grateful and hope to encounter them all together again in the very near future.

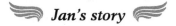

Jan's story

I was 17 years old and living in a basement flat beneath an antique shop in Northam Road, Southampton. At the time I had a number of part-time jobs locally and I used to help out in the shop selling antiques as well. I had a bed-sitting room and a kitchen that led to a small, enclosed yard that in turn backed onto a railway embankment. The apartment was tiny but all I needed at the time. It suited me fine even though I often used it as a bit of a storeroom, too.

On this particular evening it was very, very cold, almost frosty. I tried to light the coal fire and then remembered I needed to go to the corner shop. I went up the internal stairs and through the antique shop because the bin men were coming in the morning and there was loads of rubbish piled up outside the front door of the flat.

When I came back I had a quick chat with the shop owner before he locked up. I went through the back room and down the stairs to my flat.

The fire still hadn't taken hold, so I started poking it. I was wearing the coat I had just bought the day before. It was a very beautiful and unusual coat – it was patterned with cream and navy blue diamonds in a Mary Quant style, and knitted from thick pure wool.

There was still not much sign of life in the fire. All I got was a few fine sparks that floated up into the air. As I was rattling the poker, I looked to the side and I saw some big cans that I didn't recognize. While still poking the fire I reached over, picked one up and shook it, thinking, *What's this?* It had no cap on and contained cellulose thinners. I had no idea where it had come from.

Poking the fire had caused sparks to float up into the air and shaking the can of thinners now created fumes all around me. The sparks caught the fumes and I saw the air ignite. Then the flames shot back into the can and it went off like a bomb. My hand took most of the blast and my fingers were blown back. I was aware of the pain for only a moment and then I was completely on fire. As it had exploded, the bottom of the can had blown out and sprayed the cellulose thinners everywhere. The whole place just ignited in a massive great whirl of fire all around me. Luckily, I had been holding the can to one side. If I'd been holding it in front of me it would have gone off in my face.

Although my wool coat didn't go up in flames, my stockings melted and my legs were badly burned. I patted myself as best I could, trying to stop myself from burning, and I knew I had to get out. I couldn't go out of the front door because of the rubbish and the back door led to the railway line and a 16-foot drop, so the only way out of the flat was through the shop. I went through the door that led to the stairs and it slammed shut behind me. I was out of the room but I was still on fire. I just collapsed at the foot of the stairs.

As I lay there I had an automatic astral projection. I felt as though I was in a fast car. I was accelerating extremely quickly and I could feel my astral body moving away from my physical body. It wasn't the tunnel experience that many people describe, it was like a vortex. I was being sucked up into a tornado of energy. I could hear wonderful sounds and unusual 'singing', and see amazing colours. I had a wonderful sensation of being set free. It felt lovely.

Then, as I was halfway up the stairs, I looked down and saw my body smouldering away and I thought I was dead. But it was cool. It felt really good. I could feel the vortex of energy moving around me and hear a whistling sound and I felt as though I was being comforted and wrapped in cotton wool.

I noticed a silvery blue translucent wave of energy pulsating and flowing from me to my body lying on the floor and realized I was still connected to the physical body. *That doesn't seem right*, I thought. *I am here and I can think, yet my body is down there on the floor.* I understood then that I couldn't be dead and I had to get back.

Suddenly, there was an incredibly high-pitched whistling sound and a whole host of angelic beings just appeared. There was no individual angel or being – just a multitude of vibrations and sensations all moving in and out of one another, all merging, with every colour you can imagine, translucent, rather like oil on water, not still but continuously moving. Then the shapes started forming into huge beings. The whole area was filling up with amazing energy. It was all around my physical body and I could feel myself merging with it. It seemed that the angels had come to take me home.

In my awareness it was as though they said to me, 'We have come. We will assist you.' I can't remember all the words now, but I have never forgotten the last thing that they said: 'We will always remain with you.' With that, I felt as though my spiritual body had been absorbed completely into them like a sponge. I was completely with them and I felt enormous.

It was an experience of absolute bliss and pure love. I had merged into the amazing energy and I felt so safe. Yet something didn't feel right – I knew I was still linked to my physical body.

As I looked down at myself, I saw my body rising up off the ground. *This can't be happening*, I thought. *How can I move?* I had no essence; there was nothing inside my body because I was outside it; yet I saw it floating up as if it was being levitated. The angelic energy had lifted it from the ground.

Then I saw it coming up the stairs towards me. There was a whooshing sound and the angelic energy started moving away like a white cloud, leaving me there. I felt absolutely enormous and wonderful. I felt so full of love and I didn't want to go back inside my body. *No. I prefer this, it's lovely*, I thought.

But then, as I came back to with my physical body, there was an incredible sensation. Remember when you were a child and blew through a straw into a drink and made hundreds of bubbles? It felt as though that was happening inside me, as if all my molecules were changing.

The next thing I knew, I was in my physical body again. I could see my legs were swelling up, blood was everywhere and my long hair was singed, but I felt no pain at all.

I don't remember walking up the rest of the stairs, but I do remember going through into the shop and looking at the front door. It was a plate-glass door and it was locked, but it was the only way out for me. I had to go through it.

I have no memory of smashing that door or doing anything to it. I just remember going through it and landing on my feet. It was as if I was in a dream state. The police later commented that the size of the hole in the door and the way the glass was broken didn't make sense. If something had been thrown through it, it would have shattered in a different way and if I had gone through the glass then I should have been badly cut, but there were no cuts on me. It was as if the hole had been made for me to leap through.

As my feet hit the ground, I suddenly came back to the reality around me. I heard a car screech and somebody shouting, 'Oh my God!' I still had smoke coming off me.

All I knew was that I had to get across that road and to the people in the taxi rank opposite. I was in total shock and it felt as though I was walking on sponge. There was a man polishing headlamps with some chrome cleaner. I just remember saying, 'Help.'

He gasped and ran over to me, wrapping a big cloth all round my hand because my fingers were hanging off. He sat me down and the next thing I remember was the paramedics coming. They sat me in the ambulance and took me away. It was all such a haze.

Eventually, I came out of a semi-conscious state like a deep sleep and started to focus. I was in a special room in hospital. I had no clothes on and a cage over me with a blanket on top. My legs were open and raw. They had swelled up to two or three times their normal size. My hand was supported on a little table. I went to move, but I couldn't because I had drips in my arms. It was a terrible experience.

A policeman came and he was very nice. 'What are you doing causing a scene like this?' he said to me. 'They are going to take you to Odstock hospital. You're going to be all right. You're going to a special place. I've got your parents here with me.'

During all the months I was recovering in hospital my father only came once to visit me and my mother came twice. But I had other visitors to look after me. My angels came to me many times. At night the energies would come and tap me on my head – a lovely feeling. I'd wake up immediately, so alert. I know they weren't talking to me in the normal way, but I'd hear strange words inside my head, saying, 'You're going to be just fine. We'll be with you. We will never leave you. We are part of you. You are part of us.' I went on to make an extraordinary recovery.

Chanelle's story

I had recently had an accident and had been feeling sad because of it. I had fractured my front tooth quite badly and broken the tooth next to it. Part of the fractured tooth has since been removed, but the gum area has been a little swollen – although apparently this is normal. I am a student so I was also worried about the treatment and the mounting costs. Balancing university work, the upset of the accident itself and the resulting costs did get me upset sometimes, so I decided to really focus upon calling upon God and my angels to help me speed up the healing process, as I needed the gums and the whole mouth area affected to heal sufficiently so that the treatment could continue without them having to do anything drastic – I'll spare you the gruesome details!

I felt that it was working, as I hadn't been experiencing the amount of pain I'd thought I would, and that would normally be expected. Also, at one point during the treatment the anaesthetic had not worked properly or had worn off a bit, so I felt some pain, but something told me just to breathe slowly and relax. I did this and the pain went away.

One night I had the following experience, which I can't exactly explain. I was praying to God and the angels to heal my gums and the affected mouth and teeth areas, as well as to continue guiding me through the situation and giving me strength. I also gave them thanks for their assistance thus far.

In the middle of the night I had the sensation that my head was being lifted off my pillow up to the bedroom ceiling. It was kind of misty and seemed as if I was looking in on myself. I felt someone putting my tooth back in, having taken it out, which caused a twinge of pain but then nothing. My gum area behind the worst affected tooth also felt a bit puffy.

I woke up and felt fine. Then I remembered the experience and thought maybe it was God and the angels beginning the healing process. I thanked them, and asked them to give me a sign.

I eventually fell back to sleep clutching my clear quartz and rose quartz crystals – I had had these in my hand all night. I then had a dream in which I had a visit from the Archangel Michael. He gave me various messages, mostly concerning my father, who I do not speak to due to incidents in my childhood. One of these incidents had been on my mind a lot since my accident, and I had been asking if it was time for me to speak to my father about what had happened so I could get some closure there. I also felt that healing had begun on my tooth again during the dream state.

I had never had this type of experience before. I do receive visions from time to time but never anything like this.

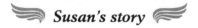 *Susan's story*

About six years ago I was due to have three operations over a period of two years, and I felt quite anxious about this. The first was to have reconstruction work on both of my feet. As I was lying on the operating table being given a general anaesthetic, I became aware of a comforting, sweet-smelling perfume around me – I even mentioned it to the nurse who was attending me.

During the second operation the following year, when I had my thyroid removed, I experienced the same sweet smell of flowery but indeterminable perfume.

Six weeks later I was due to have a total hip replacement. During the night before the operation, I awoke to find a glowing golden figure standing over my legs. It was an outline of the body and head of a being about seven feet tall, who seemed to be made out of solid, glowing fire. It was like looking into the sun, but it didn't hurt my eyes. The being didn't say anything, but radiated an intense power. I became frightened, so I closed my eyes and recited the Lord's Prayer, and then went back to sleep surprisingly easily.

I stayed asleep until the morning and when I woke up, all my worries about the operation had gone. I had complete faith that Spirit and the angels had taken away my fear, and that I would no longer be aware of their comforting presence through the sweet smell of perfume. I felt that all would be well.

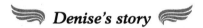 *Denise's story*

About two years ago I had to go into hospital for a hysterectomy. After the operation I woke up during the night to find a nurse beside my bed asking if I was all right. Now this nurse had a distinctive hairstyle, which, despite the darkness, seemed totally different from any I'd seen worn by my nurses before, so I was puzzled. However, I felt very comforted by her presence. I never saw her face, just her silhouette.

The next morning when the usual nurse came into the ward I assumed it must have been her and thanked her for checking on me. But she didn't know what I was talking about as she had been elsewhere in the hospital at the time I'd had this visit during the night. Even now I can still remember very clearly the mysterious visitor and the lovely feeling I got from her.

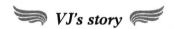 *VJ's story*

In 1987, I was 32 years old and diagnosed with breast cancer. My surgeon said a total mastectomy was my only option. The tumour was large and he had seen women with smaller tumours who had died.

I went to a bookstore looking for information and overheard a woman telling the clerk that she wanted to work with cancer patients on visualization. I told her that I wasn't sure if I was going to survive this cancer or not, and she said she would support me whatever happened.

Two days before my surgery she was guiding me through a visualization in which the intent was for the best possible surgical outcome, when I had a vision of my guardian angel sitting next to me. I was told that I would not die from this and I did not have to have such radical surgery. I was shown a more limited procedure.

The next day in the pre-op with my surgeon, I 'negotiated' over what he could and could not do. He told me that what I was asking was impossible, but I stood firm against his medical objections.

The upshot is that he performed a new type of surgery – a quadectomy – in which he removed a quarter of my breast (I'm in medical books).

When the bandages were removed, my breast looked exactly as shown by my guardian angel in the vision and, 25 years later, I'm *still* alive!

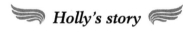 ## Holly's story

When I was a teenager I had a bad accident. I'd become really, really angry about something and I smashed my fist into a shed window. The glass shattered and sliced into my arm. There was such a lot of blood suddenly. It turned out the glass had severed my main artery in my wrist as well as three tendons, and I lost over 50 per cent of my blood before they could stop it.

I had to have emergency micro-surgery and I died twice during the operation. During this time I could see my body lying on the bed, with doctors running around me. I heard two of the nurses suggesting that I'd done it on purpose to self-harm, but that wasn't the case. I seemed to be looking down on myself and I could even see the blood transfusion bags hooked up to my feet, and I wondered how I could see that if I was lying down. But the weirdest part was that my sister Belinda was there, holding my hand and saying, 'You're not going anywhere!' over and over while squeezing my hand. When I finally came to, my family was in the hospital room but I couldn't see Belinda, so I asked, 'Where's Bel? She was there holding my hand during the surgery.'

My older sister Narelle said, 'No. Bel isn't here yet. She stayed at home, keeping Dad up to date.' My dad was in Alice Springs, although of course as soon as he heard what had happened, he'd jumped into the car and driven to Adelaide, arriving at my bedside within 14 hours. When I told Bel what I'd seen while I was dead, she said, 'I was at home praying and saying, 'You're not going anywhere.'

Even today we still speak of how Bel was there with me. This experience taught me a valuable lesson about the power of prayer and made me who I am today.

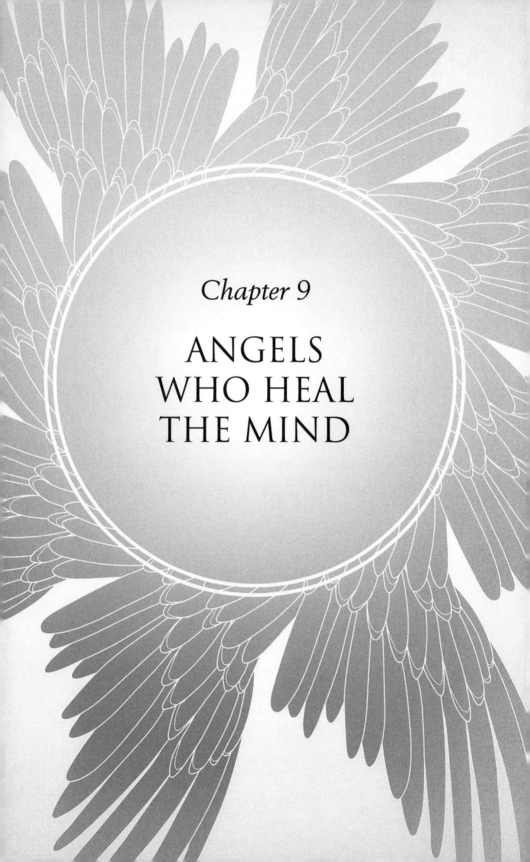

Chapter 9

ANGELS WHO HEAL THE MIND

One of the scourges of the modern world is our human propensity to become addicted to various behaviours and stimulants. Many of us know that a healthy diet works wonders for our body, but fewer realize that it can also work wonders with our energy. It's important to look at ourselves holistically, because while the body, unlike the soul, is mortal and therefore may appear less important, it is, during each life, the envelope for the soul and as such needs to be as pure as possible.

When people overindulge in anything they ingest or put their body through physically, they're polluting their body – their soul's carrier. There are always reasons for this misuse, and I believe these reasons are often related to past-life experiences. For instance, someone who was once stabbed to death will often overeat because subconsciously they think a layer of fat will protect them 'next time'. Or, if they were responsible for others who died from malnutrition in a past life, they will starve themselves to assuage the unnecessary guilt they feel. Of course, if in either case they have their past healed by having past-life regression, these reasons will disappear, a healthy life will follow and their energy will become clean, allowing connection to angels.

Smoking won't help a connection to angels, either. Anything you take into your body that is unnatural and bad for it will damage your ability to communicate with angels. If you're trying to give up smoking, please continue to do so, bearing all this in mind!

Being promiscuous is a recognized dangerous way of being, what with all the health implications in our current time, but, like drink and drugs, hopping around from bed to bed, whether you're male or female, mixes up the emotions and therefore interferes with your energy. Loving sex between two people can enhance spirituality, because love creates positive energy like no other state of mind, whereas sex alone with no love is merely a carnal act. Actual promiscuity, where the sex is performed with many varied partners, is an addiction as real as alcoholism or drug abuse. When people are promiscuous because they're desperately seeking love, they're only setting themselves up for more disappointment and a gradual and inevitable downward spiral.

Then, of course, there are those poor souls driven almost out of their minds by loving the wrong person. Any form of addiction must by its very nature take away from other aspects of the self, including one's spirituality. So if they are asked for help, angels will step in to help someone unfortunate enough to become 'hooked' whether through stupidity, innocence, upbringing, peer influence or the cruel intervention of another person, such as in cases of abuse.

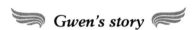

Gwen's story

It all happened so easily. I started out 15 years ago, just having a laugh with cannabis, and moved on from there, so imperceptibly that I didn't realize what was going on. I was ashamed of myself because my parents had made a lot of sacrifices to put me through university, and I'd done really well, but before I knew it I was stealing money to pay for more and more drugs. I don't need to elaborate.

Anyone who's been hooked on drugs knows this painful story. I was at rock bottom, or so I thought. I'd run out of money. I'd been thrown out of my digs because I couldn't pay the rent and was squatting in a place that once I'd never have thought of even going into, let alone living in. It was reaching the point when suicide seemed like the only option, and then one day something extraordinary happened.

I was hunting around the backs of shops looking for stuff to steal or food past its sell-by date that I could eat, and I saw a sack full of stuff outside an Oxfam shop. Someone had obviously left it as a charitable donation – well, I was the best charity I could think of, so I took it. Unfortunately someone had beaten me to it, and there wasn't anything of much use in there, but there was the torn-off cover of a book. It had a drawing on it of a beautiful, lit-up being, with wings. Of course as a kid I'd heard about angels in school, and seen Christmas cards and decorations featuring angels, but I'd never believed they were real and never thought about one in relationship to myself. Nevertheless, there was something about the light in this drawing. It made me want to keep it, so I stuffed it into my pocket.

That night, by the light of a burned-down tea-light candle I got the picture out. That was the night I was expecting to die. I didn't have anything to take, and withdrawal was starting to make me shaky. I thought I might as well die. I was sure my family wouldn't miss me as I'd been nothing but trouble for the past three years, so I thought dying was a good idea. But as I sat and looked at the picture something clicked in my mind and I thought there just might be someone after all that I could call on for help.

I went into a peaceful sleep and when I woke up the next day I was determined to escape from my self-imposed cage. That day I started to turn my life around, and my inspiration was the picture. I knew somehow, in my heart, that the angel in the picture would love me no matter what and would help me. During the next few painful months I used to look at the picture whenever things got too tough.

It was six months later that I started to get angel messages all over the place: from posters, TV ads, car number plates, you name it. And every one of them pointed to one place – 'home'. I was so scared. I thought that if my family rejected me, as I thought they would (and I didn't blame them), it would push me back onto the drugs. But I took my courage in both hands and called my mum. She cried. I cried. I'm not sure if she believed me at that point when I said I was clean, but she invited me to visit her. I did and I've never looked back. When my mum realized that I really had changed, she talked to all the family and they agreed to accept me back. I'm not going to let them down again.

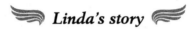 *Linda's story*

On the day that I did my *shanka prakshalana* (yogic cleansing) I definitely felt a presence as I had asked my angels and guides to be with me, and I had dedicated that day to ridding my life of alcohol. That was three and a half years ago and, thanks to their help, I haven't wanted or had a drink of alcohol since.

I asked my angels to help me communicate with my son, Kim, to help him find a way. He would abuse me via e-mail and phone calls, and our relationship was disastrous. Prior to that I'd been asking my angels to help him directly, but there hadn't been any real change as a result.

After reading *Angel Whispers* I asked my angels to talk to Kim's angels instead, and to help him find his way. Lo and behold, what a change! He has become a new person! Kim was in Denmark at the time. He was doing a show and staying with his father. When he returned home to Australia to stay once again at our place, there was a real change in him. He apologized for how he'd been treating me and not once did he abuse me right up until he left for Queensland a month later.

Since then, his phone calls to me have been just to say hello (not asking for money or complaining) and to tell me that he is well and happy. The fact that I can have a decent conversation with him now is just amazing.

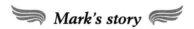 *Mark's story*

My son's mother left me in 2001 when she was six months pregnant with my second child. I had become very depressed as my first child had drowned five years earlier and I knew our break-up looked permanent. I was also deeply sad because I knew my new child would not be sleeping under my roof and would live far away from me.

I had little choice but to become more spiritual or I would cease to exist. I gave up booze and drugs, and prayed daily. I did this faithfully for the entire following year as well as changing many other character traits and trying to live by God's Will.

For two months I had been praying at bedtime, asking the Lord the same question, pausing and listening in vain for His answer. I would not force it as I was trying to be a better person, so I simply went to sleep and waited for Him to tell me.

One night I was sitting in bed reading and the answer to my daily question entered my head out of the blue. I knew at that very second it was the true answer as it was accompanied by a bright light reminding me of a cartoon depicting a light-bulb moment... I'd finally got the answer. It felt right and made total sense and I was so sure that God gave this to me that I stopped and thanked him and I also told him that I was now a total believer. Immediately after this I saw a face flash in front of me, which made me look around my bedroom like I was crazy. I could not see anything but then I heard a voice. It didn't speak out loud but was more like a voice in my head. I was sure it was an angel. The voice said 'Mark, you must take care of yourself now because in three to four years from now you will need to look after your kids.'

I shed many tears after this experience, not only because of what I had heard but because I felt it came directly from the Lord. Till today I do not doubt this happened and that angels are real. I thanked

God for His answer and told him again that I completely believed in Him. Only then did two angels enter my bedroom – they were my late grandparents.

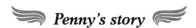 *Penny's story*

People said I'd joined a cult, and in hindsight maybe they were right. I found myself under the spell of a woman I'll call 'Jane'. When you're desperate for a spiritual experience and really need to have something to cling to, it's easy to be drawn in by someone who appears full of confidence and is very charismatic and forceful.

Jane would insist on meeting with everyone in her group, at first once a week and then it gradually came down to once a day. She'd split with her husband, doing very well out of it, and had a lovely house into which I was welcomed as if a family member. There were about 15 of us at this time and we all hung on Jane's every word. She'd told us that red wine would enhance and change our brainwaves, making them receptive to spirit. I didn't understand the scientific stuff she spouted, but it all sounded very plausible and, let's face it, I wanted to be convinced.

During our gatherings – and by then several of us lived in the house all the time – we felt like a big family. We had support and love, and an opportunity we couldn't walk away from. We revelled in belonging. Each evening we'd drink the red wine and, sure enough, after a while things would start to 'happen'. It ended up where we all totally believed we were having nightly conversations with aliens. I can still hear those weird voices in my head if I try. Looking back, I feel there was an element of group hypnosis about it. It's the only way to explain it.

Then one day when I was out alone, which was unusual, I met Clive. It was an instant attraction for both of us and I was so happy to have finally met someone wonderful. I couldn't wait to introduce him to Jane, my friend and mentor, but her reaction dismayed me. She was furious and, because he didn't want to join our group, she forbade me from bringing him to the house. She even tried to stop me seeing him altogether.

One evening I committed the ultimate sin and went out with Clive, missing the meeting. I snuck back at about 2 a.m., realizing how ridiculous it was that here I was at 45, acting like a naughty teenager. I crept into the lounge area where the meetings were, and discovered a horrifying sight. They were all drunk, plain and simple drunk. There wasn't anything mystical going on. They were all talking gobbledegook, and it wasn't in any way the smooth, spiritual connection with other beings I'd thought it had been. Jane alone was sober, and she sat there with a smug smile on her face that made me feel sick. It was like she was soaking up their energy. I honestly believe she was feeding on them in some way.

Needless to say I left there that night and moved in with Clive. I'm scared to go back there now. Since I left I've found real, gentle, angel communication is possible, and I do it all with a clear head!

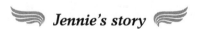

Jennie's story

I was a sex addict. No other word for it. I had my chances at a stable relationship, but every time it could have happened I'd mess it up, run away, whatever you want to call it. It wasn't till I was 30 that I felt a real need to change my life, but I couldn't do it. Eventually someone suggested I go for past-life therapy, and I found out that I'd been abused by a man for 40 years in a previous life! No wonder I didn't/couldn't bring myself to trust any one man in this life. I think I was also punishing myself, because, like most battered wives, I guess, I felt that I had to be to blame in some way.

Anyhow, after that I found Jenny's book, *Angel Whispers*, and I haven't looked back since. Three months ago I met a great guy called James, and I really think we have a chance together. I actually want to settle down!

Gypsy Maggie Rose's story

The early 1970s were a difficult time for me when my ex-husband came out of the closet, or rather, I told him it was OK to be who he was. That didn't make it any easier, mind you. I had three little ones, and right in the middle of this I lost my brother, whom I loved more than anyone else on Earth. At night I'd just lie in bed and cry for hours. I had never even gone shopping alone before, my husband had controlled everything. But when I was alone in my bed a presence would enfold me within gentle arms, and just hold me until I slept. This helped me let go of all the pain, and slowly I learned to stand on my own feet. Sometimes I still feel those gentle arms.

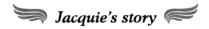

Jacquie's story

When I was going through a divorce, I couldn't believe how I started to see angels everywhere – everything from seeing the shape of an angel in the string from the window blinds lying on the floor, to a truck driving by with a life-sized angel in it. These signs made me feel I would be totally fine.

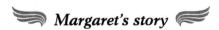

Margaret's story

A few months before I split from my husband, I was always getting stuck in traffic jams in the same exact spot. It was next to a building called The Angel Centre, and I found that they did angel readings and spiritual healing. I booked an appointment with a woman called

Claire. As she was reading angel cards for me, she stopped and said, 'Are you in an abusive relationship?' I told her I was, and she said that I had to leave. I left my husband, and Claire and I became friends. My confidence grew, and when Claire said she was starting an awareness class, I joined, and now help other people. I thank my angels for sending me to Claire.

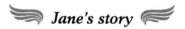

Jane's story

I didn't realise that my husband was an abuser until it was too late. His aunty had tried to warn me at the wedding, but I'd somehow become mesmerized by this man and I couldn't seem to do anything about it. When I told him I was pregnant, his reaction was that I had to 'get rid of it'. I thought that if my baby had to die, then I should, too, so I took a bottle of pills. I was alone in the house and I hadn't told anyone what I was going to do, but an ambulance and the police turned up, and together they saved my life. I will never know who called the police that night. I believe it came from my guardian angel. I had a beautiful baby boy, and we're well away from my now ex-husband.

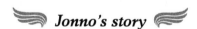

Jonno's story

One night about two years ago, I was feeling so low that I decided to kill myself. There didn't seem to be anyone who needed or cared about me and I felt so alone. My parents had recently died and my wife had left me, taking our children with her. My house was mortgaged up to the hilt and I was likely to lose it. I hated my job and it didn't pay well. It was no wonder then that I felt I had nothing to live for.

I didn't want to involve anyone else in my suicide so I was going to drive my car into a bridge, before it could be repossessed. I set off to do just that, but on the way there something magical happened. I'm a fellow who drank a lot and I was, I confess, also a bit macho. I didn't have a spiritual bone in my body, but when I saw a light glowing at the side of the road, I simply had to pull over and investigate. It was just hovering there with no apparent source that I could see. It was blue and reflected off the sandy ground at the side of the road. It was really eerie. I got out and walked over to the light. I still couldn't see any reason for it, and it crossed my mind that maybe it was my easy way out. Maybe if I walked into it, I'd just get absorbed, really quickly. So, taking a deep breath I walked right into the light and then, as if someone flicked a switch, it went out. It was pretty dark and also preternaturally quiet, and everything felt muffled. There was not a sound: no traffic noise from the distant freeway, nothing.

Then I heard it – a pathetic, whimpering noise. I still couldn't see much, only from the side-wash of my headlights, so I felt along the ground that was almost hot to touch and came across something fluffy. It was a hairy little body. As I picked it up something warm and wet licked my hands. I took it back to the light, which revealed a scruffy little dog. It had obviously been hit, was covered in blood, scared and in pain, but it didn't bite.

To cut a long story short, once I took this little thing to the vet I then took responsibility for him, and he turned into my best pal. I couldn't think of leaving him. The weird thing was, I chose that road for its remoteness and I can't understand how this little dog got out there, or how he was struck by a car, because I never saw another vehicle in the ten miles I drove first one way and then the other, up and down it.

Things are slowly getting better for me and my little pal.

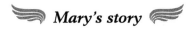

Mary's story

I was an alcoholic, and one day I came to, after a blackout. When an alcoholic comes out of a blackout they're no longer drunk but quite sober, so they're quite frightened and ashamed, not knowing where they've been or who they have spent the last few hours with. Suddenly, with no preparation or expectation, I had a vision. It was like some curtains opened for a few minutes and I was able to peer beyond them to see what needed to be changed in my life.

There were enormous bright lights illuminating everything everywhere, a calm and warm atmosphere in which everything felt safe and angels were flying all about. I was bestowed with new knowledge about how I would have to change and I understood completely. It was as if the angels imparted this knowledge to me. There was an immense presence of love and healing in the air.

This scenario only lasted a few minutes because I understood and accepted the message right away, and then just basked in the love. After the moments of clarity had accomplished their purpose, the curtain closed. I went to bed, slept well, and upon rising, I started to follow the instructions. I have continued to lead my life according to the angels' advice and never looked back. I changed because of their visit and became a far better person.

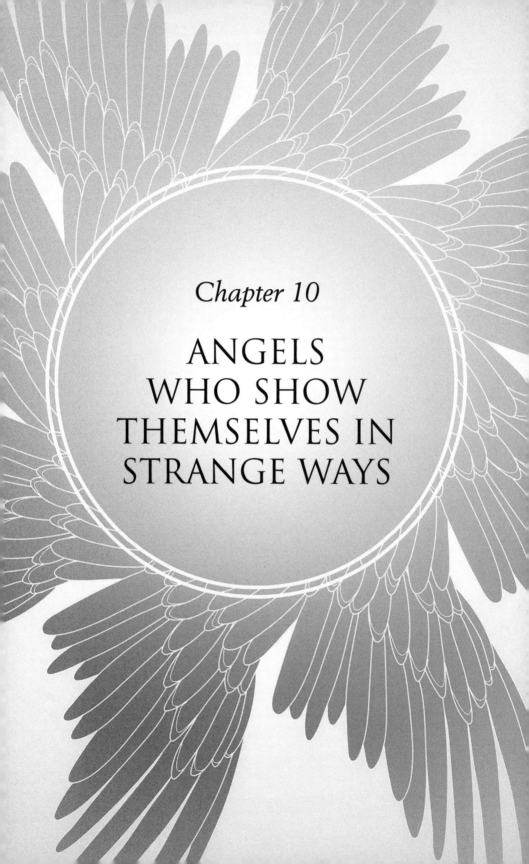

Chapter 10

ANGELS WHO SHOW THEMSELVES IN STRANGE WAYS

Angels show themselves in many and varied ways. I've written this chapter to show you some of the more unusual signs they can use. In truth, anything that happens repetitively and makes you sit up and take notice – whether you want to or not – is likely to be a sign. Angels aren't averse to using technology either. In other words they'll work with what they're given.

Computers can be vehicles for their signs. I myself connect to angels through my computer. This is how I create my digital angel paintings. Given a pencil or a brush and paper I am unable to create any paintings worthy of the name, but if I sit here where I am now, writing this, I can connect to my angels and have my hands guided by them. It really is magical! They will also use cameras, for instance, to allow you to capture orbs. Some orbs, of course, are created by natural phenomena, but that doesn't mean angels aren't asking you to accept the orbs as a sign. If something unusual happens, don't say, 'It can't be.' Instead, ask 'What if it is?'

People who know someone who has interacted with angels often want to ask them what angels look like. I've always said that they can appear to you either just as you expect them to look or just as they need to look. Sometimes they will even appear as animals, birds or insects, which is why you'll find quite a lot of stories involve animals. This is because angels know that most of us will be less afraid and more willing to accept help from, say, a dog or a cat than from a glorious, fiery angel appearing suddenly before them.

Also there is the symbolism of animals. Butterflies, for instance, are often used because to most people they immediately signify rebirth and metamorphosis, and are readily accepted. One of the most dramatic incidents I've had of this was when I was doing a telephone reading with the mother of the late British reality TV star, Jade Goody. I was telling her that Jade was showing me a beautiful lemon-coloured butterfly and that the beats of its wings were Jade's breath telling her mum she was still around. Jade's mum gasped and told me a yellow butterfly had been following her everywhere for weeks. She then gasped again, because she said the curtain of the room she was sitting in had lifted as if buffeted by a breeze and yet there was no window open.

With children, of course, angels will often appear as fairies, unicorns or cuddly teddy bears, or even as an invisible (to you) friend, so never discount what your child tells you. Anything is possible.

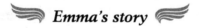

Emma's story

My first experience was with Archangel Raphael. At the time I needed healing from stress relating to college and family life in general, and I had no one to turn to. As a kid I had always had a huge belief in angels and other realms, and that belief carried on through to adulthood. Around four to five years ago was when the experiences started, and at that time I was 16 years of age. I hadn't been meditating for long so I thought why not give contacting angels a go and see what happens? Honestly, I wasn't really expecting anything to happen, but how wrong I was.

I closed my eyes and simply called out to Archangel Raphael. I started explaining my situation and about two minutes later, I felt some fingers gently brush against my forehead. It kind of felt like a cool breeze; this caught my attention and I immediately opened my eyes. No windows were open and nothing was there physically that could have caused the breeze. To this day I still believe it was Raphael showing me in his own way that he had heard my request for help.

As time went on, Raphael was the only Archangel I talked to for at least a month or two, and he told me many wonderful things. He told me about being an incarnated angel and gave me information and images about my past life as a nurse in Bulgaria in the 1700s. I used to let my rational mind make me believe this was all in my imagination and I went through a phase where I thought I had totally lost my mind, but I soon got over this when I had all the details confirmed by another angel reader. I knew then that this wasn't my imagination, it was all real.

When I turned 17 years old, I wanted to expand my contact with angels and was excited to meet the other archangels. The second angel to come to me was Archangel Michael, who is the angel who has helped me the most. He has become a very dear friend to me. I used to look at pictures of Archangel Michael on Google, and many images showed him with a sword. This sometimes made me feel reluctant to talk to him and I wondered about his personality. Was he like Raphael? But when I first talked to Michael I found him to be very sweet, with a very strong fatherly quality to him, but he can also be amusing and never fails to make me laugh and cheer me up.

Michael has helped me with so much, especially with cutting cords from people, situations and feelings that haven't been serving my highest good or have been pulling me down. Michael has told me many times that he 'has my back', which he always says with a grin on his face.

Between the ages of 17 and 19, I only felt the angels' energy – I had not yet begun to see them. This happened when I reached 20 years old. Then, my connection with the Archangels was improving daily and I was having angel experiences every day. It happens so often now it's got to a point where it's perfectly normal for me to hear an angel say something to me or to feel their energy, and I enjoy their company.

At the age of 20 I was still meditating and I started working with my chakras, especially my third eye chakra, as I wanted to see my angels as well as hear and feel them. But this wasn't an easy task for me as I had major problems visualizing and would constantly get frustrated by this. At these times I would hear Michael laughing slightly at my reaction, and telling me to have patience and that I'd get the hang of it eventually. Since I had no choice, I did finally succeed in visualizing my chakras and at that point I was rather surprised how fast my third eye opened – much quicker than my other chakras. I continued to visualize for a total of four weeks, and then I started to see things and became very 'jumpy', as this was something I was not yet used to.

The first time, I saw a wing fluttering at the corner of my left eye while I was watching television one afternoon. The ability to see things started in my peripheral vision, but that day the wing I saw was clear and I could make out what it was. I could see the movement and colour, but it would still vanish as soon as I looked straight at it. However, it always returned when I looked away again.

As the weeks went by I saw angel flashes or angel sparkles – whatever you call them yourself – and the first was from Archangel Gabriel. It was a beautiful golden light that suddenly flashed brightly and then just vanished. Since then I've seen Gabriel do this many times, even outside of my home, in unlikely places like the back seat of my car.

One thing that I hadn't taken into account was that because I had opened my third eye chakra and activated my psychic sight, I would now be able to see other things besides the angels themselves, and that wasn't always pleasant or enjoyable. I would see shadows or, as some people call them, shadow people, and other random spirits walking around. I remember being in my parents' living room and turning around and seeing the spirit of an elderly gentleman just staring at me, and then he vanished. Again this is something Archangel Michael helped me with, and made me feel safe and calm about.

Once I was used to seeing and also hearing angels and spirits talk to me, I wanted to meet my guardian angel and learn as much as possible about him or her. I was surprised how quickly my guardian angel responded. I found out his name is Trevor, and he's very beautiful. I always see him with shoulder-length blond hair, which he has in plaits at one side of his head. He has blue eyes and sometimes appears wearing casual clothes, such as a jeans and a white T-shirt. He also had a love heart tattoo on his right shoulder. Even though he's not as talkative as Michael, Raphael and the other archangels, I know he's still there when I need him.

By the end of 2009 I could see the angels normally and no longer just in my peripheral vision. I would see them walking around and interacting with me as a physical person would be doing. I no longer have to meditate to see them and it's something I enjoy. They continue to show themselves to me that way. I used to ask Michael many times why it didn't happen sooner, but Michael would respond that I hadn't been ready then and that first I had had to get over my fear.

Many people ask me what the angels look like, and this is a question I can't really answer – I always explain that the angels will appear to you in a way that makes you feel comfortable, and will show themselves to each individual differently. But to me, personally, all the archangels seem very tall – much taller than an average human male. Michael and Raphael appear to me at least 7 to 8 feet tall. They don't always show their wings, but they can change their appearance whenever they like.

My favourite way of interacting with the angels when I'm with family and friends is through signs – physical signs such as feathers, clouds and sometimes, on odd occasions, vehicles. One cloud experience I had with the Archangel Gabriel was when I was in the car coming home from college and on the way to the supermarket. I asked one of the angels for a sign of their presence, and when my mum and I parked at the supermarket I had an urge to look up – and guess what I saw? A huge cloud in the shape of Gabriel holding his horn!

My favourite feather experience was with the Archangel Michael, but it had a funny twist to it. I was with my grandparents on a busy day in Sheffield and, because I'm sensitive to emotions and energies, I was feeling sick and had a headache. I asked Michael to send me a feather as a sign of his presence, but I forgot to be specific about the form I wanted this sign to take. My grandad sat down on a bench and behind him was a huge advertisement, featuring a hand holding a giant white feather.

On rare occasions the angels have shown me signs using the radio. This happened one day when I went to see the doctor. I hadn't been feeling that great and my mum had booked me an appointment. In the waiting room there was a small radio in the corner. Usually I showed no interest in it but for some reason I listened that day and before the doctor called me, a particular subject came up on the talk show. And guess what this was? You're right: archangels!

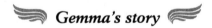 *Gemma's story*

I was on a train going to Manchester once, and I asked the archangel, 'Michael, can you show me a sign?' Minutes later we went past a warehouse with big black letters on the side that read... yup, you guessed it: SIGN. Later, I was looking through the business phone directory and I said, 'Michael, I need a job. Please guide me about what job to look for, by giving me a sign.' I flicked through the directory and the page fell open right on 'sign makers'. He's so funny! I love having a joke with him.

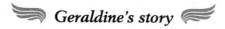 *Geraldine's story*

I was feeling quite sad one day as a good friend and I had fallen out. I wanted to see her, I wanted to talk to her, but you know how it is, you're afraid of rejection. So I sat among the daisies on my back lawn and gazed at the sky for inspiration.

I found myself watching the clouds and becoming fascinated with how white and fluffy and sort of 3D they were, floating up there like ships. Then I started noticing that one of them was shaped like a hippo. I smiled at this. I felt better. Next I saw one like a crocodile. Then a giraffe followed by a wolf. When, finally, a cloud just like an angel with wings appeared, I knew I was getting an angel message.

Seeing the clouds in the shape of animals inspired me. I lived only about five miles from Bristol Zoo, so I thought, why not go and see the real thing? I got in the car and went there. When I got to the wolf enclosure, there was Clara, my friend, just sitting watching the wolves. Needless to say our quarrel was forgotten, and when I told her about how the clouds had led me there, we both laughed and shared a hug.

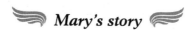 *Mary's story*

When I was around seven years old I saw something I've never really been able to explain. It was about 6 a.m. early one spring morning, and I got out of bed and sat on the window seat looking out of my bedroom window. The sky was a pure blue with no clouds at all. I could see the area of grass at the front of the house and I suddenly noticed something that looked like a small light, flitting around out there. It was bright and round and about the size of a walnut. It glowed at the edges and had a lemon-coloured halo around it. It seemed to be moving in a deliberate way and everywhere it passed it left a circle in the grass, which looked at if it was made of frost, although it was much too warm for that.

The light really did seem intelligent. It moved with a real sense of purpose. My first thought was that it was a fairy, and I was full of childish wonder. Apart from that I just accepted it, like it was my secret, and special, but nothing to get too excited about. I watched it for some while before my mum called me, and in an instant I forgot all about it and ran to get my breakfast.

Nowadays, though, I do remember it and wonder what it could have been. Perhaps it was an angel come to help me and give me strength. I was to need it, because the next few years were very traumatic for me – I lost my mum and then, two years later, my dad. I think perhaps that angel – if it was an angel – wanted me to know I would never be entirely alone, and it showed itself in a form I would perceive as a fairy, so that I'd accept it without a fuss. What I do know is that it was definitely real.

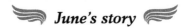

June's story

It was June 2010 and I'd arranged to meet a male friend I'd known for a long time. As we came to the end of the afternoon we agreed it would be best, for various, difficult reasons, if we no longer kept in contact, although it made us very sad. So with heavy hearts and a few tears we said our final goodbyes.

The weeks that followed were heart-wrenching because I missed my friend so much, and I cast around for little ways to connect without breaking any promises. I asked a female friend if she would go to see a clairvoyant with me to see if she could come up with anything, and we made an appointment for late August.

On the day of the appointment it was very sunny so I waited outside for my friend to pick me up. While I was waiting I closed my eyes and with every ounce of strength I had in me, I asked the angels whether my male friend missed and thought about me as much as I missed and thought about him. I asked them to send me a brightly coloured bird, such as a parrot, as a sign. I opened my eyes and looked up at the sky and smiled to myself – was I expecting to see a parrot fly by?

At that point my female friend drove up and we set off on our journey. We'd been driving for about 35 minutes when we pulled off the motorway, where we hit very slow-moving traffic. I looked at the car in front and turned to my friend, asking, 'What's that in the car in front of us?' Just as I said that the driver in front opened his window and perched a very brightly coloured, live parrot on the wing mirror. My friend laughed at this very rare sight, while I thanked the angels very quietly from the bottom of my heart.

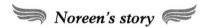

Noreen's story

I was really worried because I had to ask my boss for a pay rise – otherwise I was going to lose my rented flat. I'd never been one to blow my own trumpet or stand my ground in the past but I was determined that this time would be different.

On the way to work I saw a shield drawn in chalk on the pavement, so I stopped to have a good look at it. It was very impressive and I had to admire it. That drawing had a big impact on me, but I didn't really know why. It was very colourful and had a kind of 3D quality, so I wondered who could have been skilful enough to do it and why. The shield was quite ornate and yet I couldn't really make sense of the characters depicted on it. Were they some kind of birds?

When I met with my boss later that morning, I had the image of the shield still in my mind. He started talking as if to pre-empt what I was going to ask – I felt he already knew what it was, and was going to say no without even hearing me out – so I just started talking, too. For once I was articulate and strong and able to point out all the extras I'd done and how he'd be in trouble without me. Bizarrely my boss put up no fight at all and getting my pay rise was easier than I'd ever dreamed possible.

On my way out the door that night I was looking forward to seeing the shield again to have a better look at it, as I really felt it had helped me somehow. But when I reached the place where it had been, it was completely gone. It hadn't rained all day and yet there wasn't even a smear of chalk left. It was as if it had been absorbed into me or had been there especially for me to see.

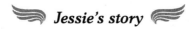 *Jessie's story*

I loved my sister in-law very much. Out of my whole family, including those of my own blood, she was the one who really understood me and gave me most support. When she died a couple of years ago, I was very sad. About two weeks after she had passed over I was sitting on my bed feeling very down and crying, when something made me look up – and there she was sitting on the end of the sofa as if it were perfectly normal for her to be there. Despite my amazement, I managed to notice that although she'd died of a wasting disease and had weighed very little at the end, she now appeared looking very beautiful and as she'd been before she got ill. I was still astounded to see her there so I asked her, 'How can you be here?'

She replied, 'You didn't think I wouldn't be back to keep an eye on you, did you?'

She smiled, and then started to fade away – her smile was the last part of her to vanish, just like the Cheshire Cat in *Alice in Wonderland*! I felt so much better than I had for ages, and although I'd always thought that seeing a spirit would make me scared, it just wasn't like that at all. It was as if she'd popped in to say hello, just like she used to, and she wasn't really dead. It was wonderful.

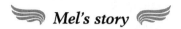

Mel's story

A few years ago, my brother-in-law got word that his brother had been missing for several days. Of course, my brother-in-law and his family were very upset. I went over to visit him and keep him company for a while. Just half a mile into the drive home I saw a figure standing in the middle of the street. It was a tall, transparent male figure. He pointed firmly in the direction of my brother-in-law's home. I was shocked because it happened so very quickly. I braked instinctively but it was too late, and I drove my car straight through him. I looked anxiously in my rear-view mirror because I thought I'd hit the figure and he would be lying in the street, but there was no one there.

As startled as I was, I somehow knew that seeing the figure meant that my brother-in-law's brother had died, and sure enough he had. When I shared the story of the figure with my brother-in-law and his wife, they were equally stunned. Until this day, I'm utterly amazed how angels can appear out of nowhere and deliver messages very quickly when a loved one has passed away.

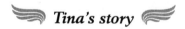

Tina's story

I've always believed in angels since I was a child, and even saw an angel appear in my room one night while in Costa Rica. I'd just finished an energy treatment in a cabaña in the jungle and was so tired that I nodded off to sleep.

In the middle of the night I woke up and saw a beautiful man in a white robe floating at the head of my bed. I shook my head and stared again to see if he was real and he was still there. He had dark hair, a porcelain face and was wearing layers of white robes.

I started to scream as I realized something paranormal was happening, yet he stayed there hovering above my head. Why is it we sometimes freak out when something beautiful happens? I woke my husband who said, 'You've been working hours as a medium. Tell him you're not available right now.' I realized right away that this was not someone needing my help – this was the gift of seeing into the angelic realm. I calmed down, knowing this gorgeous man was a protector – an angel – and that I could sleep safely, knowing that someone was watching over me.

I was a news reporter and anchor for many years and so sometimes I saw both the worst and the best of humanity. In the course of that career I covered one too many plane crashes. I always say a prayer to my angels before I get on a flight because I refuse to allow my fear to limit my life.

A friend who is a psychic alerted me to the fact that Saint Cupertino is the patron saint of flying and so I carry a card with his image on whenever I take a flight. One night when I was heading back to Arizona from Hawaii, we had an unscheduled stop-over in Los Angeles. We were told that we all would be put on the next flight out to Tucson, which was four hours later. But I had a feeling that we weren't going home that night.

As we were standing in line to board, an elegant man in uniform walked up and said he would not be flying tonight. He was too tired to fly us all to Tucson and his conscience would not allow him to take our lives in his hands when he was this exhausted. The people in the line were stunned. Some started complaining about what an inconvenience this was to them. But I started jumping for joy. I told the crowd, 'Really... you are only worried about your schedule. This man may have just saved your life. I always pray that if I am not supposed to get on a flight, I don't and this is an answer to that prayer. You will be alive tomorrow, so be glad.' I then turned to the pilot who was still trying to calm the passengers and said, 'Thank you – I know angels do exist.'

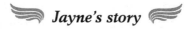
Jayne's story

I've believed in angels for many years and although I have many books about them I always feel when I read them that I also have some personal knowledge of angels, just through my own intuition. I've introduced my beliefs to many of my friends when they've been at a low point in their lives. Some just laugh, but many now share my faith in the existence of angels. It's a pure joy when I feel my angels with me and I've called upon them many times when I've needed guidance.

Last year my husband was diagnosed with leukaemia and when he was in isolation in hospital for seven months before he finally had a bone marrow transplant, I used to speak to him every night on the phone. I'd always finish our conversation with 'I'm asking the angels to watch over you', and then before I went to sleep I'd call them in again to remind them, particularly on the occasions when he was suffering the horrid after-effects of chemotherapy.

One day, when I was feeling terribly unhappy about the situation, I took my dog for a long walk across the fields. My husband was having one of his bad days and I began to have a few doubts about whether the angels really were answering my prayers.

For some unknown reason I turned and looked behind me on the pathway, and two figures appeared and walked on either side of me. It was at that moment that I realized they were dressed identically in blue cloaks and had greying hair. They didn't look how I would have envisaged angels to look, but I felt sure they were angels. The strangest thing was that I realized they were twins and then I knew intuitively that they had come to assure me they were looking after my wonderful husband.

That night I had a vision of one twin sitting at the head of my husband's hospital bed and the other at the foot. They had covered him with the two blue cloaks I had seen them wearing. This vision went on for weeks, every night, and I took great comfort from it.

Several months later, as my husband began to respond to treatment, I realized I had stopped having the vision. The angels had gone. I think they had done what I had asked of them and that's why it was time for them to leave. I felt a bit sad that I wouldn't see them again, but they had given me hope and reassurance and I will never ever forget that.

My husband continues to recover and I still converse with angels every day. If only people would reach out more and invite them into their lives in times of need, then perhaps the world would be a better place.

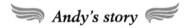 *Andy's story*

I do three night shifts a week and one morning I arrived home a little after 6 a.m. I had breakfast and went to bed. Two hours later I woke to find that my cat, Tilly, was sitting on my chest, quite literally poking me in the eye. I was rather cross at first, but then I quickly discovered that the entire flat was full of gas. It seems that I must have nudged a gas tap on the cooker to the 'on' position during breakfast, but hadn't lit it.

A couple of things occurred to me later. I had an old central heating boiler then with a pilot light burning merrily away. The next few minutes could have seen an explosion that could have killed all the people in the entire block, as well as Tilly and me. She herself obviously didn't know this (but perhaps the angel that took up temporary residence in her did) and she could have just said to herself, 'I don't like this smell. I'm out of here!' and legged it through the cat flap. But (thank you, Universe), she didn't.

 *Mary-Ellen's story*

My granddaddy and I grew very close in his latter years. I no longer had parents by then, and I was happy that Granddaddy approved of my soon-to-be husband, Josh. He became more like a dad than a grandparent.

It was in the build-up to our wedding that Granddaddy became very ill, quite suddenly, with pancreatic cancer. He was given only weeks to live and it was a terrible shock. I felt that I was going to have no family left. He died the day before the wedding, and both Josh and I were there to say goodbye. It was very sad. My granddaddy made my fiancé promise he'd always be there for me, and he did.

The wedding took place in November in Canada, so it was pretty cold. There was snow on the ground. In the middle of the ceremony a large blue butterfly appeared above us where we stood, and then it landed on my left hand. Incredibly it stayed there while Josh placed the wedding band on my finger, and none of us made any attempt to move it. As the words ending the ceremony were spoken the butterfly took off and circled above us. It accompanied us to sign the register, too. Everyone saw it. There shouldn't have been any butterflies around at that time. As we and the congregation started filing out for photos, the butterfly flew over us. I was getting a bit upset, as I felt drawn to it, and I figured there was no way it would survive outside in the cold. Even if it stayed in the church there was nothing for it to live on, so it seemed doomed. The photos done, I was looking up watching it, wondering where it would go, when suddenly it just faded away. I swear – it didn't fly off, it just vanished. I couldn't believe it.

Later I wondered if my angel could have used the butterfly to let me know that Granddaddy was still close and watching over me. All I can say is that ever since then, whenever I ask for help, a blue butterfly will appear. Sometimes it's a real, live one, and sometimes it takes the form of a window hanging or an ornament in a store window, or even a logo on some packaging, but it's always there, somewhere.

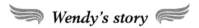 *Wendy's story*

My best friend Lesley lost her father four years ago. She was very close to him and she misses him very much. He was a sheep farmer who kept many collies over the years, and they were all much loved. Just recently, Lesley has been having a very hard time at work and is completely exhausted. When she got her rota for work on Saturday she was very upset to see she had yet another week of gruelling shifts, and she felt like she was at the end of her tether. On Saturday night, she asked her dad what to do. She asked him to send her some help.

The next morning (Father's Day), she got out of bed late and noticed a collie sitting on her driveway. She went out and the dog came over to her and brushed himself against her legs affectionately. He was a well-cared-for dog and had a collar with a phone number on, so she went into the house and called the owner. While she did this, the dog sat at her feet and laid his head on her lap, as if they were old friends.

When Lesley's husband and her own dog returned from their walk, her husband said the dog had been there since the early hours when he'd gone out, just sitting on the driveway as if he were waiting for someone. Lesley's dog, Nipper, and the collie were totally at home with each other, and Nipper never seemed to think it odd to have this strange dog in his house.

Lesley was sure the dog had been sent by her dad. She felt better for having him around and, on the Monday, feeling much stronger, she went into work and sorted out her rotas once and for all.

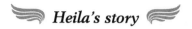 *Heila's story*

I bought Rosie, my horse, from a dealer when she was about 12 years old. She was on the thin side and had a bad cold, but we soon got her restored to fitness. She was such a beautiful girl: a cob/Connemara cross, 14.1 hands high, with a teardrop-shaped birthmark on her hindquarters. I loved her so much. She really looked after me and I trusted her 100 per cent. We used to go out together with no saddle or bridle, just bareback with a rope halter. When she cantered, if she felt I was unsafe, she would slow right down till I got my balance again. We truly bonded and loved each other. If she wanted anything she used to tell me by nudging me with her head, and she used to draw me into her chest and cuddle me.

When Rosie was about 19, she developed cancer of the intestines. It was very quick, and within a week I knew it was her time. It was the most heartbreaking decision I have ever had to make, but the day I called the vet, before he arrived, she kept nudging me as if to say, 'Come on, you know what you have to do.'

At that time I worked in a New Age shop, and there were mediums and psychics who used to work there, too. I am very psychic too and within a month I knew my Rosie hadn't left me, not really. I could see her and smell her and I could feel her with me when I was out walking my dogs. I told one of the mediums and she said, 'Next time you feel her around you, ask her if she'll allow you to step into her spirit.' I did that, and oh what a wonderful experience it was! I immediately felt the bond again, which I'd thought was gone. It made me cry tears of joy.

It's now been about six years since Rosie passed away, but to this day she's still around me when I need her.

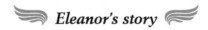

Eleanor's story

After losing our last dog, Coco, who by then was fifteen and a half years old, and had been our very first long-haired mini dachshund, my hubby and I were quite lonely and sad. We'd gone from having three mini dachshunds to losing all three in three years and the house was, of course, very empty.

It had been a few months since Coco had passed and my hubby and I were in the basement doing some chores. We started talking about how much we missed Coco and how much we really loved her. When we both fell silent for a minute, we heard a strange noise coming from upstairs. There was the sound of a small ball being dropped then bouncing three or four times (kind of like the sound of a ping-pong ball).

We looked at each other in puzzlement. I'd certainly never heard that noise before, and I'd spent many hours in that basement. I went dashing upstairs to the area the sound had come from. Of course, I could find nothing and I also realized that the floor is carpeted so we couldn't possibly have heard a normal ball bouncing up there, but the sound had been unmistakable. Suddenly I knew the answer and said to my husband, 'You realize that was Coco, letting us know she was still with us in spirit?'

I spoke with my daughter Alicia about it later, and she reminded me that when Coco had been a young dog she had loved to play with a small rubber ball, which my daughter would bounce for Coco to try and catch. I'd forgotten all about that.

I also realized after talking to someone who had had to put their old dog to sleep and had wondered what to do with the ashes, that I still had all three dogs' ashes together in a desk, right about where the bouncing-ball noise had come from. Upon further research I learned that the ping-pong ball bouncing is a paranormal phenomenon others have experienced, too. I have goose bumps thinking about it and feel such a blessing to have had that experience. Thanks Coco, for being our dog.

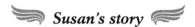 *Susan's story*

We got Dillan when he was eight months old. My son rang me from Exmouth and asked me if I wanted a black Labrador pup. Of course I said yes, as I had recently lost my old girl who'd lived to be 17. I also had a small Jack Russell terrier, who was still lively, and I thought we still had room for another dog, as they are our lives.

When Dillan came to us he was thin as a greyhound and frightened of everything and very aggressive towards dogs and people because he hadn't been socialized, but we loved him. It took us two years of hard work to bring out the qualities that made him so special. We took him on holidays and everywhere with us. When our Jack Russell grew really old (he was an incredible 21, in fact), we got a new terrier pup called Cindy. She loved Dillan with all her heart, and seemed to think he was her pup, even though he was so big and she was so small! He had a really good life. Cindy cleaned him every morning: his ears, teeth and eyes. My God, she loved every inch of him.

When he started to become poorly, we took him to our vet and she diagnosed diabetes. I cried a lot, but even though I was scared stiff of needles, I injected him every day, and he was OK. But then he started to have a job getting up because his back legs were giving out. He was strong – we knew that because he had got over a stroke and he had had his spleen removed – and still he battled on.

One evening I went to work and had only been gone ten minutes when my phone rang. It was my husband telling me that Dillan's legs had gone again and this time we knew what we had to do. It was the hardest thing ever, as he was fine from the waist up, but our vets were brilliant. Our best friend had gone and the house was empty. We were devastated. It will be four years next March, and it still hurts, but Cindy grieved for him even more than we did.

We fostered several Labs, but Cindy didn't accept any until Gus came along. He was another black Lab from Lab Rescue. He looked like Dillan and is very respectful towards her. She loves him, although he's scared stiff of her. He's really naughty on the lead, although perfect in every other way. When we were on holiday I kept saying I was going to swap him for a black poodle as a joke. Cindy was running around chasing him, but she doesn't play with other dogs (she's a proper lady), only plays with her doggy mates who live nearby.

One day we went to Cockington, near Torquay, and a black poodle there made a beeline for Cindy, although there were hundreds of other dogs around. Her tail was wagging like mad. I let her off and they ran around together like old friends. It was amazing how she just seemed to accept this poodle instantly.

Then I really got the shivers and goose bumps because the owner came along and called the poodle by his name: Dillan! You could have knocked us over with a feather.

'I'm sorry, what did you call him?' I asked.

'Dillan', she replied.

I then asked how old the dog was, and she told me he was three and a half.

This was almost exactly the length of time since we'd lost Dillan. I don't believe in lots of things, but I believe that this was our Dillan and that Cindy knew it.

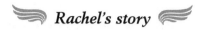 *Rachel's story*

This story is one that happened to my mother when my older brother was a baby (before I was born). The year was 1976 and my mom and dad lived in Cumberland, Maryland. My brother was a small baby. My dad taught art classes at the nearby college in Frostburg, and my mother was a stay-at-home mom. They would often attend small parties with some of my father's colleagues that would last late into the night. My mom was not much of a party type, but she would sometimes go along and bring my brother with her to these get-togethers.

One of these nights, my mom decided to leave and walk home. My father did not want to leave yet, so he stayed behind. My mother started out up the long street, which was on a steep hill, pushing my brother in a stroller. It was late and the town was quiet, with few cars passing by. A few minutes into the walk, she passed a man on the opposite side of the street. As she glanced over at him, she realized the man was exposing himself to her. Gripped with fear, she walked faster, scared for her infant son and herself. She was now too far from the party to turn back but still a way from the house.

With chills, she realized that the creeper had crossed the road and was following her. He began to shout things at her. She upped her walking speed, but the man still followed.

Then out of nowhere, two large dogs appeared from between the rows of houses. They walked next to her, somewhat playfully nipping at each other. They never asked for her attention, just walked next to her, circling around her as she pushed my brother. From that point, and for at least the next 15 minutes, she walked with the dogs forming almost what seemed like a circle of protection around her and her baby.

The creep persisted in trailing her for several minutes, and shouted a few times, 'Those your dogs, miss? Those your dogs?' but eventually he fell back and walked away. Even in his seemingly drunk state, he knew not to mess with someone who was flanked by two big dogs!

As she turned the last corner to get home, the dogs walked off the other way, fully present and then, just like that, they weren't there. They'd appeared and stayed with her the entire time she needed them, and then faded off like mist when she got to the safety of her own street. She has always thought of them as guardian angels for her and my baby brother, and I believe they were!

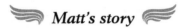 *Matt's story*

We live in the country, right out in the middle of nowhere, and are quite used to all the wild animals around us, and their behaviour. But recently we started to notice that the crows that had set up a nest in our chimney for the summer were acting really strange. They would sit on my car bonnet and peck at the windscreen – really hard, too – so that you can still see the chips on the glass! I'd wake up every morning to really loud pecking noises and open my bedroom window to scare them off. They were doing this for about a week and I could think of nothing to stop them. They started to do the same thing to the landing window and we thought that maybe it was because in between the double-glazing was a silver strip around the outside of the window and I heard somewhere they liked shiny things.

We tried everything, from covering the windows with mustard to hopefully put them off, to placing a big stuffed toy cat in the window to act as a scarecrow. But nothing worked. We didn't know what to do and in the end we thought we just had to live with it.

Our big German shepherd dog then began to act a little oddly and would look at our fireplace and tilt his head to one side as if he had heard something stuck in the chimney. My mum came to me saying she thought a bird was trapped in the chimney, so we went to investigate. With a torch we looked up the chimney as far as we could, and lo and behold we saw not one but two little baby crows that had fallen from the nest nearly into the fireplace.

It took me a while to reach up the chimney as far as I could (it's a really small fireplace with not much room to reach up) and manage to catch the baby crows, one at a time. We checked over them carefully and it looked like they had been there for days. They were really scraggy, covered in soot and so skinny and worn out they couldn't even cry for their mum.

We gave them some bread and water and sat with them for a while until they regained some energy, and after a couple of hours one of them started to call for its mum. She would circle us overhead, keeping a keen eye on her young, so we left them both outside on our garden table for her to come to them. One of the babies had obviously learned to fly, and after a while we saw it take off and fly over our house and away. The other one, however, was in a bad state – it was so weak and helpless it couldn't do anything but call out for its mum with its small voice. We left the baby in our outside chicken run with shelter from a wooden box filled with straw and some food and water; that way, if the mum wanted to come to the baby, she could. As we were caring for her young she and the dad would circle us overhead and sit in the trees watching, and I believe without a doubt that they knew what we were doing.

Sadly the weak baby had died by the next morning so we put it under a nearby tree so its mum could find it. After reading your book *Pets Have Souls Too*, I put two and two together and realized that the parents pecking at our windows every day were trying to tell us about the plight of their young.

I've heard that animals do not have the concept skills we have and if you were, for example, to drop a ball on a table, a dog would look for it on the floor as it doesn't understand the concept of higher surfaces, but I totally disagree. And I now know that the parent crows knew exactly what had happened to their young and that they were inside our house!

A friend of mine recently lost his dear wife, and one of my best friends, to cancer. He was distraught and really wanted a sign from his wife that she still existed, somewhere. One day he was sitting on the bed she'd died in, gazing at the little hand-bell that was on the top of the covers. He'd given it to his wife in her last few days, when she was weak, so that she could ring it if she needed anything. He sat staring at the bell and willing his wife to please, please ring it, to prove to him that she was still around. Nothing happened for the longest time, and he was starting to despair.

His wife had absolutely adored their cat, and had had a very close relationship with her. My friend heard the cat padding up the stairs at that point and really didn't want it to come into the room and disturb the moment. But the cat came in, paused for a second, and then jumped onto the bed. Then she batted at the bell, just once, quite hard, enough to make it tinkle, and promptly left the room and went back downstairs. It seems obvious and appropriate to me that, because she was not able to ring the bell herself, my friend asked her cat to do it for her.

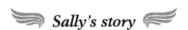

Sally's story

I always say that there is a reason for everything, so when my beloved cat, Christa, was run over and killed, I tried to tell myself that there was a reason for that, too. Christa was crossing a road that she'd crossed safely hundreds of times, but this time she was hit. We never knew who did it because we didn't find her for several hours. Christa and I were very close and she always used to come when I called her. She used to lie across my shoulders while I walked around our garden.

Two months after she died I was driving home. I was nearing a rather nasty crossroads, not far from where Christa had been killed. Naturally I always thought of her whenever I passed that place, and this day it was the same. As I neared the fatal spot, I could make out a small shape in the road. I braked frantically, and as I got nearer I could see that it was a cat crouching there. It was the same colour as Christa, but I told myself there are thousands of tortoiseshell cats around. It couldn't be her! The car wasn't slowing quickly enough and I started to panic, as the cat didn't look like it was going to move. I couldn't bear the thought that I was going to kill another cat, right where Christa had died. 'No!' I screamed, 'Move!'

The cat stood up. Shivers ran over my body as I could see that it was Christa! 'Christa!' I cried. She didn't move and the car slid irresistibly towards her, turning sideways as it went. It was like one of those nightmares: the car seemed to moving in slow motion, but no matter how hard I braked it wasn't going to stop in time. *Why didn't she move?* I wondered. The cat's face stared at me over the bonnet of the car, and even though I knew it wasn't possible, there is no doubt it was Christa looking back at me. The car loomed over her and there was a sickening thump, followed by a bump as a tyre went over her.

Finally the car slewed to a stop, sideways across the road. At that very second there was an ear-splitting hooting and a roaring sound, as an oil tanker shot across the crossroads without even slowing down. It was in my right of way, and if I hadn't stopped where I had, the tanker would have ploughed into my car. I found out later that the tanker had failed to stop because of a hydraulic brake failure.

I stood looking after the tanker for a moment, and then thought of the cat that had saved my life. I rushed along the car to the back and looked. There was nothing: no blood, no fur, no torn body. There was no sign of a cat anywhere.

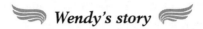 Wendy's story

When Scampi was 12 days old, his Persian mother, Jessica, disappeared and she was never found. Scampi and his four sibling kittens were left alone and hungry in a basket on the top shelf of a remote shed on our farm. Only the kittens' pitiful mewing alerted me to the problem when just by luck I was passing the shed one day. All five kittens had crawled out of the basket, searching for food, and fallen over six feet down onto a cold concrete floor.

One had already died, and the other four were cold and hungry, so I quickly stuffed them beneath my sweater against my skin to keep them warm. Then I drove the one and a half miles home. There I filled a hot-water bottle and wrapped them up with it to get them warm, and prepared a jar of powdered cat milk, feeding each one with a small syringe.

I continued to do this for the next three weeks, getting up every two hours to feed them. I'd put them in an empty fish tank with the light left on to keep them warm, and I kept the hot-water bottle underneath them at all times. I had to wipe their bottoms and keep them clean, even bathing them on occasion to keep them smelling nice. And, so that I never woke the rest of the household by setting an alarm and getting up so frequently, I'd drink a huge glass of water at the end of each kitten feed so that before the two hours were up I'd need to go to the bathroom and I'd know it was time to get up and feed the kittens.

Even the night I had to take my son to the airport, I took the kittens with me so that they never missed a feed, and eventually they grew to be able to eat solid food and use a litter tray. There was Chooch-Chee, a long-haired tabby female; Chip, a silver tabby male; Jessica, also a silver tabby; and Scampi, a long-haired, blue-grey male – the rascal of the bunch. I still gave them a bottle of milk each day, but Scampi was never prepared to wait his turn. He'd run up my leg, right up to my shoulder, snuggle beneath my chin and down to my lap, and shove aside whichever cat I was feeding at the time.

As they grew I knew I could never part with Scampi, but one night he became ill. I had no idea what had happened to him, and then discovered my young son had been playing with him and had dropped him. I was frantic. Scampi appeared lifeless. I'd just been attuned for Reiki first degree, and I called upon the help of the angels, and before my very eyes I saw Scampi bathed in emerald light. Seconds later he started to purr. Another minute and he was up and running again, as if nothing untoward had ever happened. I was delighted!

I sold his brother and sisters, and Scampi stayed with us. He became such a handsome cat. Beautiful, long, flowing dark grey-blue fur and amber eyes, he was stunning! We taught him – or he taught himself – to play fetch, chasing balls of screwed-up paper and bringing them back in his mouth and dropping them at our feet. He would play this game till he was puffed out. He followed us everywhere, got on well with our old cat Smokey (now 17) and, whenever we were gardening, there he'd be watching, taking an interest and we'd tell him what we were doing and why.

He was almost a year old when tragedy struck. He'd been watching my husband repair our son's bicycle tyre, and so the pair of them and Scampi were on the roadside when a car came speeding towards them. My husband thought Scampi was in the garden when the car thundered past, but he was still on the roadside and he'd decided at that moment to run across the road to the garden. The car hit him head-on. Scampi somersaulted three times, six feet in the air. My husband knew he had to be dead before he hit the ground. He shouted for me and I came running, scooping Scampi off the road, and I lay him on the lawn in the garden. I could see his soul was long gone, only his body twitched. I held him and spoke to him till he was still, then I sat a while talking to his soul, because I was sure it was nearby. I told his soul to look for the light and go towards it. We buried Scampi in the garden that day, August 1st 2007 and cried our tears.

That night I stood outside in the dark and I called him, as I used to do. A cat ran from the grave up the drive and out onto the road. I knew it was him. That night I felt him walking along the bed on top of me, coming up to my face, and I reached out a hand to stroke him, knowing I wouldn't really be able to. I felt him settle at my feet to sleep, though he and Smokey had never slept in the house, having their own shed in the garden to sleep in, where I'd lock them in at night.

On 1 November, All Saints Day, I went to get Smokey up for her breakfast. In the box in the shed where she lay curled, I saw Scampi lying there beside her. I couldn't believe my eyes. I turned away and looked back and he was still there. I spoke his name and told him I loved him and when I looked away and then back again he had gone.

Scampi had so short a life, yet he enriched ours with his. His memory lives on, and though he is missed, we know he is still with us, unseen. But on one day a year I know I'll see him again, so I look forward to 1 November so much.

Gemma's story

My cat, Kitkat, is like a guardian angel to my daughter. We got Kitkat as a kitten, when my daughter was just a baby, and she hasn't left her side since. If Kitkat sees Hannah doing something dangerous like trying to touch the fire or the cooker, or if Hannah falls over, Kitkat will meow and meow until Hannah stops what she is doing or until I or my partner come and help. If Hannah cries, Kitkat will jump up next to her and lick her like she's one of her babies, until she stops crying. She doesn't act like a cat at all – for instance if my hamsters escape, she'll pick them up very gently and bring them to me or my partner and she doesn't hurt them. It's as if she knows they're family and shouldn't be out, and she watches until I put them back in their cage where they should be.

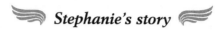 *Stephanie's story*

In July 2007 my brother gave a springer spaniel pup to my daughters Sarah and Ciara. The excitement of choosing a name began, and we finally decided on Sparkle – she's lived up to it ever since. From the moment she arrived she was full of fun and has brought us a huge amount of pleasure. When I meditated she would whine outside the door until allowed in to join me and through this we bonded very closely.

I became ill the following year, and Sparkle would lie on me and follow me about in a very protective way. She's very intuitive and took every opportunity to comfort me. With my daughters in school and my husband at work, this canine company, I believe, helped me through a tough time with the unconditional loving way she cared for me. I believe she was sent to help us all through this. We've since also rescued a husky-mix pup from an animal rescue centre and called her Crystal. Both dogs are highly intuitive and sensitive to our energies. We're so lucky and blessed to have them.

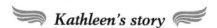 *Kathleen's story*

Alfie was a lovely ginger-and-white fluff ball when we got him as a kitten and he grew into a very beautiful boy. He had a fox-like tail and a beautiful mane on his chest, which made him look like a lion. He was a nervous but very affectionate wee thing. He loved to chase pigeons around the garden, although he never once caught one. We all loved him so dearly, he really was part of the family. When we went out he would wait at the top of the stairs for us to return home.

Although sometimes he'd be asleep, the moment the door opened, he'd jump down onto the floor with a thud to come and greet us.

Alfie only ever got sick once – this was two months before he passed away at just three years old. He had picked up a virus, which we got treated straight away and within 24 hours he was right as rain. Luckily, my daughter came home for two days from university as, unbeknown to us, this would be the last time she would see dear Alfie. We were sitting watching TV when he suddenly jumped up and sat looking around the room, staring up at the ceiling like something was there and then seeming rather frightened. Jokingly my youngest made a comment, 'He must have seen a ghost!' The next day my daughter gave her usual cuddles and said her goodbyes, which always held my husband up as he sat waiting in the car.

The following day Alfie woke me up as he would always do, standing on two legs, meowing at me at the side of my pillow, like he was talking to me. I got up and let him out. It was a beautiful summer's morning. I sat watching him pacing up and down, chasing butterflies and pigeons. He'd sit under his favourite rose bush, waiting. I watched him launch himself and scratch the fence as he tried with all his efforts to catch that elusive pigeon.

I went upstairs and got ready, and my husband brought Alfie in and fed him, and then my son and husband got into the car and waited for me to come down. Suddenly, I noticed Alfie coming up the stairs, but not in his usual manner. He looked frightened and he turned to come to me and suddenly rolled over. I ran over to him, realizing something wasn't right. I thought he was having a fit or had been stung, as he loved to catch bees. Just as I was about to go down the stairs to get help, I heard him take a breath (unknown to me, it was his last breath). I remember touching his cheek, just under his eye, and telling him how much I loved him. I ran downstairs and my husband came up to see what had happened. We were afraid to touch Alfie in case he was fitting. Deep down, I knew he'd passed but I refused to accept it. My husband picked him up and just gave me that look – Alfie'd gone and I went to pieces.

We took Alfie's body to the vet, who confirmed it was more than likely a heart attack. We said our goodbyes and I told him how much we loved him, and to go into the light where the family would be waiting for him. It broke our hearts. Over that first week when I was sitting alone, twice I could have sworn he was at my side meowing. I thought I'd imagined it the first time, but the second time I heard the distinctive sound he'd make when he yawned.

A few weeks later we were packing to go off to Cornwall. My son started yelling at us to come outside. A pigeon had been sitting under the windowsill. Then it walked into our hallway and into the kitchen, and turned around and walked into the lounge, whereupon my husband let it out the patio door. I think that it was Alfie's way of letting us know he was there, because he loved pigeons so much.

Recently I was at the garden centre and the Christmas decorations were all going up. There was a sale area with a Christmas cat bauble and a wind-up musical merry-go-round. I wound it up and I was amazed when it played, 'You are my sunshine,' because that was the song I sang to Alfie the day his ashes came home.

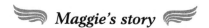

Maggie's story

Smudge was a canary. He used to live with his mate Sam, until Sam had a stroke and despite the vet's best efforts his condition worsened, so with tears in my eyes I had to have the bird put to sleep. I'd heard of the Rainbow Bridge, where our pets go until it's our turn to go to the other side, but had no idea how fast the transition was.

Within days Smudge was reacting to an unseen presence, getting agitated and staring at the ceiling. To investigate this further I took a digital picture, and there in the photo was a faint orb over the cage. I believe Sam visits regularly to see how Smudge is getting on and, as a psychic person, I just sense him in the room, sometimes briefly.

One day, when I was taking more pictures, the flash wouldn't go off, even though I had just replaced the batteries. There was a blue light in the room that was almost ultra-violet in colour, which canaries and budgies can see, hence I believe Smudge was finally able to see Sam. After that Smudge was content, and the camera resumed normal operation.

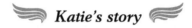

Katie's story

My dad was a great joker. He was always teasing us kids and playing tricks on us. Sometimes it was like he was the kid and we were the parent, but I wouldn't have wanted him to be any different. He was the best dad ever. But things change and Dad changed, too, when he was 48 years old.

Since he'd been a kid Dad had been obsessed with homing pigeons. He loved those birds so much. He had become an expert on breeding them and was very proud of each and every one.

He took us children into the aviary every night and talked to us about them, showing us each bird and telling us all about its history, how he'd bred it and what races it had won. He explained all the different colours and strains and how he'd learned to breed the best. He hated to sell any of his birds, although sometimes the aviary got too full and he'd have to, but he always checked up on the birds' new home and was very fussy about where they went. The only days he wasn't there for us were the days his birds were racing. Once they'd been released, Dad would start scanning the skies with his binoculars, waiting for the first speck to appear. His greatest nightmare was sparrowhawks. Sometimes when his pigeons were out he'd be up at dawn, watching and praying that he wouldn't see the classic sneaky approach of a hawk coming after his birds.

I wished everyone had a dad like mine, but then, like I said, when Dad was 48, tragedy struck him. His pigeons developed salmonella. One of them must have picked it up during a trip out, because Dad's birds were kept as squeaky clean as we were. He was heartbroken and tried everything to stop it, but one by one his precious birds died. Dad blamed himself, but no one could have cared for them better than he did, and we kept telling him that. Finally, Dad was left nursing his favourite and last hen, Cleo. That wasn't her real, fancy name, but that was what Dad called her. When she died I thought Dad would never stop crying. I know there are people who'd say it was only a bird, but not to Dad – she was so much more. He'd spent the best part of his life carefully selecting and breeding strains of birds to create the ultimate racing pigeon, and Cleo was 'it'. When she died I guess he thought his happiness had died, too. She was a very beautiful specimen, even to me, being a quite rare mosaic colour. This colour is as it sounds – made up of many different colours mixed together – and the result is unique and very pretty.

Dad went downhill after that very quickly, and it seemed that his kind and happy nature had another side to it – the reverse of the coin. Within six months he was diagnosed with lung cancer, and two months after that, we lost him. I think he got cancer out of grief, and he never really tried to fight it. It was as if he wanted to leave. We were all devastated, of course, but we felt we'd lost Dad the day Cleo died, and that maybe he was happier now. A few months passed and we'd fought our way through our own severe grief to a place where we could start to remember Dad the way he'd been before he lost all his pigeons.

One day I was sitting in the garden. Dad had torn down the aviary, swearing he'd never want to use it again, and in a fit of trying to forget through hard work he'd built a summer house where it had stood. I was sitting in that summer house thinking of Dad and wondering, as we all do when we lose a loved one, where he was and whether he was OK. Just at that moment I heard the classic rustling sound of a pigeon's wings as it came in to roost. Then I could hear its soft cooing. It was a wild one of course, or so I thought. The bird fluttered to the ground and walked around to the front of the summer house. It was a mosaic! I stared and stared at it, too scared to move and frighten it away, because I swear it was Cleo. Her markings were unique, and this bird was definitely a well-bred racer, I knew enough to recognize that fact. But, if that was the case, it should have had a ring on its leg. All top-quality racing pigeons have an identifying leg ring, giving a unique serial number for that pigeon. But this bird had none. I stared harder, and as if it knew what I was doing, the bird opened its wings and walked round in a circle, letting me see all its body markings. I would bet a thousand pounds that that bird was Cleo, Dad's Cleo, and yet she was dead.

I watched her for about five minutes, still sure that if I went to get Mum, she'd fly off. She kept winking at me. Pigeons do that a bit, but this wink was slow, as if it had meaning. Eventually I got up and very carefully leaned down to pick her up, but she wasn't having it and flew up onto the roof. I ran and got Mum, but of course when we came back out there was no sign of Cleo.

Whatever anyone ever says to me, and however silly it sounds, I believe that this bird was sent by my dad. After all, pigeons were used in the war to send messages from resistance fighters in France back to England, so what better way for my dad to send us a message from the other side than by his beloved pigeon? It has a certain poetry to it, doesn't it?

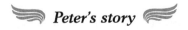

Peter's story

When I was a kid my nan and granddad had a grey parrot, which was (of course) called Polly. She was an African Grey and, as I know now, they are the best talkers. I was a little intimidated by Polly as a kid, because I thought she had a huge scary beak and beady eyes. I was always sure she was going to bite me, but she never did. She was very good at impersonating, too, so I never knew if it was Grandad, Nan, my parents or Polly calling to me. Whenever someone like the milkman knocked at the door, Polly would shout, 'Who is it?' in Nan's voice. The person would naturally call back, 'It's the milkman!' Polly would repeat, 'Who is it?' and, if the caller was new, he would assume that some old deaf lady was calling out to him and keep answering louder and louder until someone put him out of his misery. It used to make me laugh, but I still regarded Polly with some mistrust.

Anyway, some years later we lost both Nan and Grandad within weeks of each other. They were in their eighties and, it seemed, didn't want to live without each other. It was very sad, and my dad was devastated. The next thing I knew, Polly was installed in our house. Of course, parrots live a very long time and so we had to look after her. She was soon yelling out, 'Who is it?' to all our callers, and she'd keep visitors entertained for hours by impersonating them. She'd start off by saying something in their voice, they'd laugh, she'd copy their laugh, and before you knew it everyone was crying with laughter. I realized then that Polly wasn't so bad after all.

One evening we were sitting in the living room. Polly's cage was covered with her night-time blanket. We had to do that or she'd spend all evening impersonating everyone on the TV! Mum and Dad were talking about Dad's parents, and how much they were missed, when Polly suddenly started talking in Grandad's voice. We all looked at each other in amazement. First, she never talked with the blanket over her cage, and second, she had rarely spoken in Grandad's voice since he'd died. Then we were even more shocked, because Polly was saying stuff we'd never heard before. It went something like this.

'We're OK. We're happy. Look after Polly and have a good life.'

Dad ran over and snatched the cover off the cage, startling poor Polly, who looked totally innocent. We'll never know for sure to this day if Grandad somehow used Polly to give us a message, but I think he did. She never spoke in his voice again.

They say that parrots are as intelligent as dogs and cats, so it's surprising we don't hear more stories about them. Perhaps that's because birds that have escaped life in a cage don't want to hang around! Peter's story above reminded me of another anecdote I was told recently by my friend, Rosemarie Davies. A friend of hers used to have a parrot that was allowed a lot freedom and was very attached to its owner, whom it used to call 'Mummy'. When this lady died it was in the times when coffins were left open in the parlour, so that family members could pay their respects and say goodbye. The parrot was also allowed to be there to say goodbye, and when the coffin lid was shut, the bird said, 'Mummy gone to sleep.' Birds such as parrots and budgies are said to be mimics unable to make rational statements formed by their own intelligence. But how then could this bird have understood and voiced the concept of someone 'going to sleep' or dying, unless it was sentient?

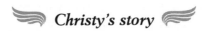 Christy's story

I live pretty much out in the 'boonies', and have to drive down a long, winding dirt road to get home. It's worth it, though, when you get there, because the place is so peaceful. Colorado is one of the most beautiful places (if not *the* most beautiful place) in the world, in my opinion. My brother Pete and I inherited the house and land from our parents, and we lived there (not always in perfect harmony, but always with love) for the next eight years after they died. Pete used to joke and say I'd never find a husband, and he'd never find a wife, stuck out in the backwoods, but I never cared. I loved the place and never wanted to leave it. We had just one neighbour and that was fine, too. Their daughter was Megan, my best friend, and we used to go to work in the city together every day.

Pete used to say I should get a dog. He started worrying about the times when I was alone at the house, sometimes all night if he was off partying. Much as I loved animals, however, I preferred to leave them wild, and besides it wouldn't be fair to a dog to leave it alone all day when we were both at work. Pete used to counter with the fact that he sometimes did night shifts and so the dog wouldn't always be left on its own, but I managed to talk him out of it. Every time we went to a mall where there was a pet store, though, he'd 'ooh' and 'ah' over the pups in the window, trying to emotionally blackmail me into taking one home. I was getting used to the idea that one of these days he'd actually turn up with one and I'd have no choice in the matter.

I wish now I'd given in to him – well, in a way I do – because I lost my dear brother a year ago. He was killed in a freeway accident. I was in a state of shock for weeks, and because Pete's work hours had been so irregular, it was too easy to keep expecting him to walk back through the door. Eventually, with Megan's help, I adjusted to life without him and was able to go back to my job after a lot of sick leave.

One day, a few weeks later, Megan and I were driving back up the dirt track when we saw a dog standing at the side of the road. He looked like an English pointer and we couldn't imagine what he was doing out there. Megan wanted to stop, but although the dog looked calm and placid enough, I'd once stopped to help another lost dog and it had attacked me, forcing me to jump back in my car and high-tail it. Besides, I told Megan, it didn't look lost or upset. It was just standing there, gazing solemnly at us as we drove by.

I figured it was out with some walkers or something and was just waiting for them to catch up. But the next day it was still there, or there again, I'm not sure which. Yet, I still wouldn't stop the car – I think I was being stubborn. I hadn't let Pete get me a dog, so I wasn't going to have this one. However, when it appeared again or was still there on the third day, it was too much for me. I let Megan pull over and get out of the car. I was still too scared of being bitten. She walked cautiously over to the dog, cooing softly at him. He wagged his tail and then, to my surprise, he walked around her and stared at me, where I still sat in the car.

'He wants you to get out,' said Megan.

'No way,' I said, 'Don't be crazy.'

Megan reached out and took hold of the dog's collar. 'He's wearing a tag.'

Well of course he was. You wouldn't get a pure-bred dog like that wandering around without a tag.

'Is there a number?' I asked, pulling out my cell phone.

There was no answer. 'Megan. Is there a number?' I repeated.

I looked at her, and she was looking back at me, a stunned look on her face, 'You have to see this.'

Sighing with frustration, I finally got out of the car and walked over. Megan was holding up the tag for me to see. The dog huffed amiably at me as I bent down to read the tag. There was no number, no address, just one single word, PETE.

I blinked. The dog was called Pete!

A tingling sensation travelled up from my toes to my nose and I knew I had to take this dog home. I grasped his collar and led him over to the car. 'In,' I said. He jumped in, clambered into the back and sat on the seat, looking straight ahead through the windscreen, as if to say, 'Well, come on then. Let's go home.'

Thinking he was a valuable dog that someone would be missing, we called around, but no one ever claimed him. Pete lives with me to this day, and by now I don't know how I ever got by without him. I'm not saying Pete was my brother reincarnated, because obviously the dog must have been born before Pete died. I'm not saying anything. I'm just telling you what happened.

I wanted to include here an amazing story I've just read about a dog with an angelic message. It is about a retired headmaster called John Lawes. Mr Lawes used to walk their dog regularly (unfortunately the source neglected to name the dog or its breed, which is sadly indicative of many people's attitude to the importance of pets!).

Apparently one evening Mr Lawes' wife noticed the dog behaving strangely; it kept sitting and staring at her husband in what she described as 'a quizzical fashion'. It was so unusual that she asked her husband if anything odd had happened. Mr Lawes then confessed that during their walk that day he'd got his feet entangled in the dog's lead and had fallen quite heavily. He said he'd banged his head, but only on a soft piece of ground and that he was fine.

Mrs Lawes retired to bed and it was only later that she heard a shout from her husband. She hurried downstairs to find him collapsed on the floor. Knowing that he'd had a fall, she immediately called an ambulance. Sadly it was to no avail, as Mr Lawes had suffered a terminal brain haemorrhage and he died. Mrs Lawes was left to puzzle over the fact that their dog had tried to tell them something was wrong despite the outward appearance of normality.

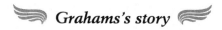

Grahams's story

When my girlfriend Anna died, it was a terrible shock, despite the fact that she'd been terminally ill for months. I'd met her at a fairground and had been instantly captivated by her free spirit and her love for every living thing. It seemed so tragic that she should die so young. She was just 28. We'd had plans. We were going to get married, have a house with a picket fence, two dogs, a cat and four kids. It was hard for me to give up on that vision.

But four years later I met Tracie, and my life started over again. Within two years, we'd bought our first home together and started planning for the future. There was just one problem. I'd never told Tracie about Anna. Somehow I thought she might be upset that I'd once loved someone else and had been going to marry that person. I worried that Tracie might feel second best, although of course she wasn't.

In the end, however, my conscience wouldn't let me be, and I decided to tell her. So, one June day when we were sitting on the tiny front porch, the air very still, I knew this was the right time. It was very quiet. There was no one about but us. As I'd feared, Tracie took it badly and started with all kinds of questions. Who did I love best? Did I still yearn for Anna? Who would I have chosen if she was still alive? I fumbled with answers, wanting to be honest and not wanting to say the wrong thing, which I inevitably did, and Tracie started crying. I felt helpless and she sagged against me, sobbing. She wasn't mad at me, and maybe it would have been better if she had been, she was just hurt and scared, as if I'd taken her security away.

Suddenly, down from the blue sky, a fluttering cloud started to descend. At first I didn't understand what it was, then I saw it was a crowd of bright blue butterflies. They came down to us and started to land on both Tracie and me. At first I was too scared to move in case they flew off, but they showed no sign of it, just sitting there, their wings slowly opening and closing. Most of them were on Tracie and I gently turned her head so she could see. She sat up, startled, and still they stayed on her. We were transfixed and as we counted them we discovered there were 28 of them, the age Anna had been when she died.

I felt these butterflies were an omen, a signal that Tracie and I were perfect together and she shouldn't worry any more. I had loved Anna, but now I loved Tracie and that was that. They stayed with us for about 10 minutes and then took off as one, spiralling up into the sky and finally vanishing.

I had a thought – something I'd once read and pointed out to Anna when she was still alive. I got on the internet and then called Tracie indoors. On the screen was a photo of some bright blue butterflies – the same ones that had landed on us. And their name? … Anna's Blue.

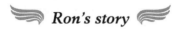 *Ron's story*

A few years ago, international healer Bill Harrison and I were treating a man called Bob, who had a brain tumour. Bob would visit Bill on a Monday, then come and see me at home a couple of times a week to take advantage of my Usui Reiki treatment. Bob and I became friends, and his wife would drop him off then pop off to work, and Bob would sit and chat with me for a couple of hours.

Sadly, Bob's condition deteriorated after a time, and he ended up in hospital, where I went to visit him. During my talks with Bob, one of the things we discussed was our fears, and I told him about my fear of birds, especially large black ones.

A few days later I was woken up at 4 a.m. because there was a banging noise coming from the lounge. I got up and went to investigate. When I went into the room there was a huge black crow attacking my patio window with its beak and claws. I couldn't believe it. I tried to scare the bird away, but it kept coming back. Later that day I found out that Bob had passed away at the same time the crow had attacked my window.

The following morning I was woken again at 4 a.m. by the same thing. I decided to cover the window with a plastic sheet, just in case the crow could see his reflection and was attacking that. It didn't work, and the crow attacked the plastic sheet just as violently as he had the glass.

During the day the crow would sit on the telegraph pole outside the house and watch every move I made, and then attack the window early every morning. On the day of Bob's funeral the crow stopped and disappeared, but on the first anniversary of Bob's passing he started again. This time I walked outside and said, 'I know you're here, mate, now please go away and stop attacking my window!' To this day the crow has never come back.

There was an amazing animal healer and communicator called Sue Smith, whom I was lucky enough to have had on my chat show many times. Her messages were of such importance to her that Sue would struggle to the studio even while in the throes of a bad lupus attack, and would have to partially cover her face, such was the state of her illness. Among many other things, Sue had a special connection with crows and their collective souls, and she could bring through amazing messages and information from the animal kingdom. She rescued all animals and never turned any away from her small sanctuary, but she specialized in rescuing and rehabilitating members of the crow family.

Sue died a few years ago and her loss has been keenly felt. When she was dying, Sue's bedroom would be visited by wild crows if the windows were left open. Sue was buried in her garden, her most sacred place, but before she died she wrote her own eulogy, which was read out at a friend's house in the presence of all her friends and colleagues. At the end of the eulogy Sue promised to stay in communication with them all from the other side. She told them they would know it was a genuine message from her because they would hear either owls calling in the daytime or crows calling in the dark.

At the moment these words were read out, a flock of thousands of crows flew low overhead, doing low-level flypasts just above the heads of the people gathered there. They say the sky was dark with them. There was not a soul present who remained untouched by the sight, or wasn't convinced that Sue had used her crow friends to send them the strongest message of all – I am still here.

When I got sent this other story about Sue and crows, I felt I had to also include it here.

 *Rosemarie's story*

We chose Digby from an RSPCA overspill centre. He was the only one in a litter of tabby kittens with a white underside, and we thought that the little bit of white would be a help on the road on dark nights. Poor Digby had a lot of trials to endure, and as my husband Gwynne and I are healers, we often seem to have desperate animals come into our lives. During his life Digby suffered from bone-thinning (to the extent that the vet said he'd never seen its like before), a broken pelvis and a nasal polyp caused by a seed going up his nose. All of these things Digby endured with immense courage and fortitude. Finally, though, despite all our care, there came a problem that even our little trooper with the heart of a lion wasn't able to overcome.

It seems that a lot of cats who have had a fractured pelvis at some time during their lives end up with a paralysed bowel, and so it was with Digby. We got him over the problem once, but eventually he ended up at the vet's, a drip attached to his poor little paw. I really didn't want to lose him. By then our dear friend Sue had passed away, and later that day, when I went out of the back door, I was confronted by a large black crow standing on the step. It was regarding me solemnly, its head on one side. It wasn't at all afraid of me; it made eye contact with me and held it. I knew instinctively that Sue had sent the bird to warn me that Digby's time was up, and when the phone rang it was no surprise to find that the vet was calling to tell me that there was nothing more that could be done for Digby. Knowing that Sue had come to tell me through the crow, I was able to accept his passing better than I would have done otherwise.

We brought our brave boy home and buried him in his favourite spot in the garden. As we covered him over, four crows flew low over our heads, confirming to us that Sue had sent the one to our back door, and that she was ready to receive Digby into spirit with her.

It was a privilege to have shared the life of a beautiful, sentient being such as Digby. His grave has a stone circle around it with a picture of an angel inside, and there is a plaque that reads: 'Digby Davies. June 1999 – May 2008. BRAVE HEART' – for that is what he was.

When I learned of the work done by Genevieve Frederick, an incredible lady who is the Executive Director/Founder of an organization that feeds the pets of the homeless in the USA, I felt I had to include some stories about homeless people and their pets here.. If any pets can be said to embody angelic qualities, then it's some of those that her charity helps. These pets make life bearable for those who have nothing, and give them something to cling to in their desperate lives. They bring love to the unloved. Divine intervention certainly seems to play a role in these stories.

A *charity worker's story*

Last Saturday I forgot to bring the donated pet food inside from the van. Since I was tired and it was late, I left it until morning, and completely forgot about it until leaving for church Sunday morning. I didn't have time to unload it and left to pick up my two granddaughters. As we dashed off on the freeway I missed my turn, which meant two miles to the next exit. When we arrived at the intersection where we were going to turn around, the light was red. While I waited I glanced to my left, biding my time until the light turned green. There was a homeless man with two big Labradors by his side. I rolled my window down and asked if he needed food for the dogs. I heard a quick, 'Yes!' and I gave him several bags. When he told me he had a third dog that wasn't with him, I added another bag. Smiling, he said, 'God bless you!' and 'Thank you.' With tails wagging, the dogs walked eagerly around the bags, sniffing and hoping for a treat. The man never asked for a handout or anything for himself. This was a true need and I was grateful I'd left the dog food overnight in the van.

I gave the man information on where he could get more dog food from the homeless shelter and again he expressed his gratitude, still not asking anything for himself.

One never knows when the opportunity will come to serve the pets of the homeless. I don't feel this is a coincidence, rather that I was guided to someone who really needed help. Thanks for giving Dallas the opportunity to help those in similar circumstances.

 A formerly homeless person's story

Until quite recently I was homeless and living out of my car. My boyfriend and I had previously slept on the couch at various acquaintances' and relatives' houses when we could not afford a motel room.

But about six years ago I had walked into a house that belonged to the friend of a friend. The man who lived there was supposed to be taking care of our mutual friend's dog, but when I walked in the door I saw the dog was covered in cuts and gashes (many were still open and bleeding) and I asked what had happened to the dog. His reply was, 'I beat her with the weed-whacker.' He snickered to himself with amusement when he told me this, and he pointed to the corner of the room where I saw a weed-eater with blood and clumps of fur on it. So I immediately removed the dog from the situation. I did not have anywhere of my own to call home at that time, much less anywhere I could go with the dog. So from that night on I slept in the car with the dog while my boyfriend continued to sleep on the couch of whichever person's home we were staying at on any given night.

My dog and I lived in the car through winters and summers and everything in between for almost five years, because I did not have anywhere to go where I could take my dog, too. About a year ago, however, my parents asked me to move back into their house because they didn't like me sleeping out in my car. And they also agreed to let me keep my dog there, since they knew that if the dog was not allowed to come along, then I would not go either.

My dog has been such a loyal companion and I hope that good luck like mine will find the many homeless and their pets, too.

A second charity worker's story

In the pecking order of man and beast, there was no lower rung than the one shared by Randy Vargas and Foxy on the streets of Hoboken. He was 46 and homeless; regular work – like his fondly remembered machine-shop job – was long in the past.

Foxy was a member of dogdom's least-fashionable demographic, a ten-year-old brindled pitbull, compact as a pick-up truck, ears askew, two-tone face, white neck, the rest an arbitrary mix of light and dark. And yet in this city increasingly defined by creatures who drew the long straw — winners in real estate and on Wall Street, sleek goldens, pampered Yorkies, fashionable puggles and doodles — there was something transcendent in their bond.

Maybe in a world of opaque relationships, theirs was a lesson in charity like a parable from the Bible. He had rescued her back when she was homeless and abused, a scared runty thing living with homeless men who had no use for her. She in turn gave him purpose, companionship and love. Maybe it was how the relationship brought out the best in both. It brought Randy to life and into the world, as much a part of Hoboken street life as any young comer with his black Lab. And it made Foxy a creature of eternal sweetness, unfailingly friendly to people and animals, tail-wagging at the merest glance, a pitbull in name but not metaphor.

So if you spent any time in Hoboken the odds are pretty good you would have seen the two of them, sleeping in front of the Saints Peter and Paul Parish Center, visiting the Hoboken Animal Hospital, walking down the street – Foxy keeping perfect pace with Randy, dressed in winter in raffish layers of sweatshirts and T-shirts plucked from the St. Mary's Hospital Thrift Store.

A colleague remembered seeing Mr Vargas resting on a condo's shaded concrete steps on a sweltering August weekend day, flat on his back with Foxy in the same position one step below. 'It was the perfect image of man and dog,' she said, and added, 'This really was a dog with a deep soul.' Everyone who knew them said the same thing: Mr. Vargas cared for the dog better than for himself. If it was the dead of winter, the dog would get all the blankets, he'd get the sidewalk with nothing on it. If it was raining, he'd put the umbrella up for the dog before he'd put it up for himself.

But there's not much margin for error at the bottom rung. Once this winter Randy was arrested, accused of making threatening remarks to women. The case was dismissed, and friends say it should never have gone that far. Foxy had to be rescued from the pound in Newark, where she could have been euthanized, but they were reunited.

Then it all ended so fast, people still can't explain it. Aside from when she was on a dog run, Foxy had seldom been seen off the leash, but on the morning of 19 March in the park, there she was. She saw a dog she knew across Hudson Street, dashed across to say hello and was hit by a white pick-up, which stopped briefly and then sped off. Mr Vargas held the dog, blood spurting from her mouth, and waved at passing cars, but none stopped. So he carried her, all 60 pounds of her, as far as he could, feeling the broken bones in his hand. Then he put her down and ran to the Animal Hospital for help. But sadly it was too late.

People keep coming by the Animal Hospital every day, some fighting back tears, to leave donations – more than $900 so far. Some come from people who knew them, most from people who feel like they did. Alone they might have been invisible. Together, they were impossible to miss. In different ways, they're still around. Her picture is in some store windows, wearing a grey sweatshirt with a red T-shirt under it, gazing to the right like a sentry, a wondrous study in essence of dog with a touch of human thrown in.

Since the accident Mr. Vargas has had good days and bad ones, sometimes being up and around, sometimes, like the other day, looking groggy and defeated under his red comforter on the street. 'I feel,' he told a friend, 'like I have a hole in my soul.' At the Animal Hospital they're buying a pendant to hold some of Foxy's ashes, which he can wear around his neck. Friends check on him regularly, bring him food, speak of finally getting him a place to live. There's also talk of getting him a new dog when he's ready, which surely isn't now. 'It's like most relationships,' Mr Vargas says from under the red blanket. 'You have to wait for the right time.'

 ## A second formerly homeless person's story

Many years ago I lived on the streets. I had a pet hooded rat, my first one. His name was Benjamin. I am sure, looking back now, that what I fed him was not what a healthy rat needed to eat. But he never went hungry. He and I shared everything we found to eat. His home was a cardboard box and he lived in it happily. He never tried to run away, amazingly. When I slept in the parks or on the waterfront, Ben would curl up in my jacket. Sometimes in the middle of the night when it got extra spooky, just the feeling of Ben's little body pressed next to mine kept me sane.

When Ben got too old to continue living on the streets, the founder of the Mustard Seed (a home caring for the most vulnerable) took him in. He moved into a huge aquarium – it must have been a 50-gallon tank, or at least to my little eyes it seemed that big. It had every luxury a rat could want. After he went to live there the streets got a tad scarier. I still get tears in my eyes when I remember Ben; he was awesome.

ANGELS IN
THE NEWS

Brian, a three-year-old boy in the USA, got trapped under the automatic garage door at his home, and he'd been there for long enough that paramedics though him dead and didn't believe he could be revived. The door had closed right over his heart, stopping it. However Brian was successfully brought back to life and a while afterwards Brian said to his mother, 'Do you remember when I got stuck under the garage door? Well, it was so heavy and it hurt really bad. I called to you, but you couldn't hear me. I started to cry, but then it hurt too bad. And then the birdies came. The birdies made a whooshing sound and flew into the garage. They took care of me. One of the birdies came and got you. She came to tell you I got stuck under the door.'

In 2009 geologist Dr Morris Charles claimed that NASA lab workers found a carving of an angel in one of the rocks brought to Earth by *Apollo 11* astronauts in 1969. Dr. Charles was a NASA scientist for 23 years.

A CCTV camera in Cilandak Town Square in Jakarta, Indonesia took a remarkable film one night. It shows a winged being, made of light, land and then take off again.

In London there's a building called Topper's House. And one New Year's Eve four people decided to kill themselves by jumping from the roof of the building. Among them were the daughter of the Junior Minister of Education and a TV presenter called Martin Sharp. Believing themselves ready to die, they were just about to jump off the roof when all four heard a voice behind them, and they turned around to see who could be there. They described a man who reminded one of them of the film star, Matt Damon; however, this being was floating above the ground, and his figure was misty and insubstantial. The four people were filled with such a sense of joy in the being's company that they no longer felt like ending their lives, but instead wanted overwhelmingly to live to share the joy with other people.

Following a car crash Lisa and Anthony were trapped in their crushed cars. Both cars caught fire and both drivers were certain they were going to die. Anthony passed out from the smoke. A couple called Cheri and Cody stopped to help but couldn't pull Lisa from her car because it was too crushed. They cried for angels to help, and all three saw a pair of hands of light reach through the wreckage and grab Cody's hands where they clasped Lisa's, and suddenly both of them were outside the car. In the meantime another passer-by could see Anthony slumped in his car as it exploded. She prayed, and Anthony suddenly just floated free of the car.

A man called Bruce Van Natta was virtually cut in half by a massive PeterBuilt truck he was working on, when the jack holding it up gave way. His waist area was crushed to a depth of one inch by the 12,000lbs that fell on him. He was in terrible pain, his back broken and five major blood vessels severed as well as his intestines being totally crushed. His colleague pulled him out a little way at Bruce's insistence. Bruce then prayed for help, and the pain vanished completely. He floated up out of his body and looking down from the ceiling he could see his work colleague kneeling beside his shattered body. On either side of the body there were two glowing figures that were holding his body together. He believes they were angels and he was given the choice to return to his body or leave. He chose to stay and despite not being expected to live, he recovered, and even his intestines grew back, which is unheard of. Bruce Van Natta's story can be read in his book, *Saved by Angels*.

A woman called Rose found herself trapped in her car. She'd hit the barrier at the side of the freeway, her airbag had inflated and she was dazed. When she found herself safely outside the car and looked back, she couldn't believe she'd escaped injury-free. But then she saw a photo of her car taken by a photographer called Sharon from the fire department. In the photo a white, winged classic angel shape, made of mist, can be seen standing in front of the car. This shape even appears in the negative of the photo, so it's hard to believe it could be a fake.

After a terrible storm and tornado in Salem, Indiana, a little girl, appropriately called Angel, was found lying in a field surrounded by the bodies of her family. Angel mysteriously survived, while her whole family perished around her. She was found forty miles from home, and no one can explain how she lived, except to say that perhaps her namesakes, the other 'angels', must have saved her.

Brothers Gustav and Oliver, aged nine years old, had been left at home briefly while their mother ran an errand. But an electrical plug shorted out and started a fire. Instead of panicking, which would have been understandable, the boys felt they were protected somehow and they remembered being told that in a fire one must stay close to the floor. So Gustav and Oliver calmly crawled back and forth with buckets of water, with which they doused the flames until the fire was out.

RESOURCES

SITES OF INTEREST

www.flameofhealing.com

www.tinapowers.com

www.concettabertoldi.com/home

www.dianacooper.com

www.purplebuddha.co.uk

www.michellejones.me.uk

www.francesmunro.com

www.jackynewcomb.com

www.akija.com

www.sarielhealing.co.uk

www.julieangelguest.co.uk

www.elisewardle.co.uk

www.gypsymaggierose.com

www.rosereiki.com

www.rachelkeene.net

www.distancehealer.net

www.lulu.com/content/paperback-book/awoken-by-an-angel/870984

www.angelreader.net

www.petsofthehomeless.org

www.animaltranslations.com

www.healinganimals.org

www.animalthoughts.com

www.centaur-therapies.co.uk

www.animalscantalk2me.com

www.carolschultz.com

www.ukanimalhealer.co.uk

www.simonfirthseminars.com

www.animalenergy.com

www.june-elleni.com

This film claims to have captured an angel on tape. I'll leave it up to you to decide if it is real: http://tinyurl.com/ycftmu6d

ABOUT THE AUTHOR

Tony Smedley

Jenny Smedley DPLT has had a strong connection with angels since she was a small child. Her earliest memory comes from when she was just three years old: thinking she was being separated from her mum, she jumped from a moving train and was snatched to safety by a mysterious, unseen pair of arms.

Now based in beautiful Norfolk in the UK, Jenny is a qualified past-life regressionist, author, TV and radio presenter and guest, international columnist and spiritual consultant, specializing in angels and past lives. She lives with her husband, Tony, a spiritual healer, and her reincarnated 'springador' dog, KC.

Her current life was turned around by a vision from one of her past lives, in which she knew the man known today as Garth Brooks. Her angels then helped her to overcome a lifelong phobia of flying, enabling her to travel to the USA and meet Garth Brooks, so closing the circle.

For two years Jenny hosted her own spiritual chat show on Taunton TV, and has appeared on many TV and radio shows in the UK, USA, Ireland and Australia, including *The Big Breakfast*, *Kilroy*, *Jane Goldman Investigates* and *The Steve Wright Show*. She currently writes several monthly columns for, among others, *It's Fate* and *Soul & Spirit* magazines in the UK.

 author@globalnet.co.uk

 JennySmedleyAngelWhisperer

 @SmedleyJenny

 JennySmedley

www.jennysmedley.co.uk

HAY HOUSE
Look within

Join the conversation about latest products,
events, exclusive offers and more.

f Hay House UK

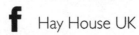 @HayHouseUK

 @hayhouseuk

 healyourlife.com

We'd love to hear from you!